The House of Ashes

The House of Ashes

Revised Edition

Oscar Pinkus

Union College Press
Schenectady, New York

The House of Ashes

Revised Edition

Copyright 1990 by Union College Press

First published in Israel as *Ud mutzal.*
Originally published in the U.S. in 1964.

Sequence of three photographs on pages 125 and 126 by courtesy of
Yad Vashem; photographs at the bottom of page 238 and 240 by
courtesy of Renée Glassner (Rivkah).

Second Printing

Library of Congress Catalog Card Number: 89-5220

ISBN 0 - 912756 - 23 - 3 (Clothbound)
ISBN 0 - 912712 - 24 - 1 (Paperback)

Printed in the United States of America on acid-free paper.

The House of Ashes

A page from my diary, on which this acount is based.

I was born and raised in Losice, a small town near the Bug River in Poland. The countryside, lush with wheat fields and forests, was inhabited by tough, pious, half-literate peasants. There were eight thousand people in Losice, eighty percent of them Jews, mostly craftsmen and shopkeepers. Jews had built Losice, and we had inhabited it for close to four hundred years. But the Poles, goaded by their patriots and the Church, considered us an affliction on the country. And so, despite their proximity, the two populations lived apart – the Poles in the villages and we in the towns.

Most of Losice lived at the edge of subsistence. So did our family. We ran a little store where we sold shoelaces, pencils, and bits of colored paper. Had my parents ever had to pay off their debts, they would have needed two such stores. They went on borrowing from the neighbor on the right to pay the neighbor on the left – and somehow we managed three meals a day. We lived on the top floor of my grandfather's house – a large, three-storey building facing the Square in the center of town. On the floor below lived two of my uncles: Erschel with a wife and child; Yankel with a wife and three children – Berko, Rivkah, and Itzek. Another uncle lived down the street in a house of his own. His son Herschek was my closest friend. He was the only boy in town to attend Gymnasium. He was adventurous, had great moral and physical courage, could walk on his hands, and was unbeatable in soccer and ping-pong.

Another friend, Mottel, was the opposite of Herschek: blond and reticent, he accepted the fate of small town life with almost religious resignation.

I had two sisters. Manya, good-looking and high-strung, was older than I. Soon after war broke out she married a man named Ignatz. My younger sister, Belcia, was still in grade school in 1939. Father was regarded the town intellectual because he could read and write, but, in fact, his interests ranged well beyond Losice's cultural definitions. An avid reader of history, literature, and political and religious commentaries, he knew Hebrew, Yiddish, Russian, Polish, and German. He wore a goatee and pince-nez and on photographs resembled Chekhov. A ridiculous businessman, he sat in the store reading newspapers and ignoring the customers. My mother, a simple woman with Mongolian cheekbones, was the one who earned a living for us. She tended the shop from morning to night, then shuffled home to cook supper and scrub floors. My father kept brushing up on Polish literature.

At various stages of my youth I had planned to be an artist, a surgeon, a physicist, a statesman, and, finally, a poet. But any of these required I attend Gymnasium, and there was none in Losice. Besides, Gymnasium cost money and we could not afford it. So, when grade school was over, I had become my own teacher, planning to pass the special state examinations given to autodidacts and in this manner complete my six years of high school. I was taking the first of these examinations in Miedzyrzec – the nearest town with a high-school – when the story begins.

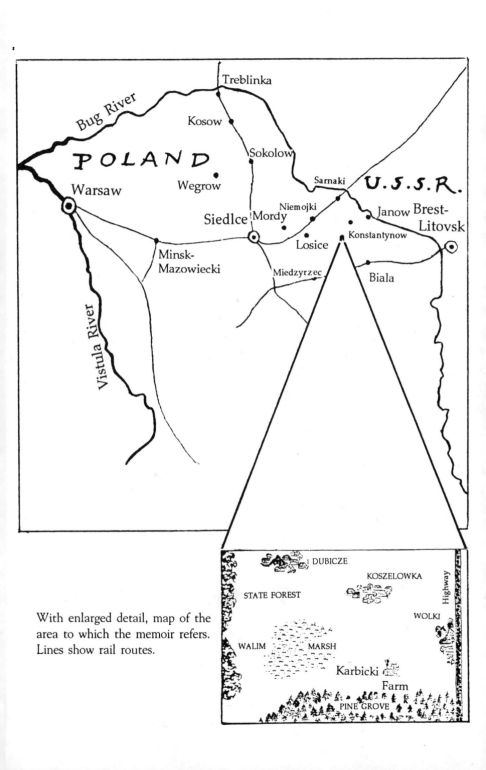

Bug River

Treblinka

Kosow

Sokolow

POLAND

Wegrow

Sarnaki

U.S.S.R.

Warsaw

Niemojki

Janow Brest-Litovsk

Siedlce Mordy

Minsk-Mazowiecki

Losice

Konstantynow

Miedzyrzec

Biala

Vistula River

With enlarged detail, map of the
area to which the memoir refers.
Lines show rail routes.

DUBICZE

KOSZELOWKA

Highway

STATE FOREST

WOLKI

WALIM

MARSH

Karbicki
Farm

PINE GROVE

Part One

The Sound of Hammers

1939 — 1942

September 1, 1939 was a Friday. At the break of dawn, the Germans invaded Poland, starting World War Two.

I had arrived in Miedzyrzec that very morning and went immediately to the Gymnasium to find its halls and playgrounds pervaded by that expectant emptiness of late summer vacation. We were a small group of boys, come to take the state exam given to self-taught students prior to the opening of the school year. Through the large vaulted windows of the examination room where we slouched over our papers, I could see red posters announcing martial law, mobilization orders, and numerous other proclamations. But these mattered less to me than the equilateral pentagon I had to construct in order to pass the geometry test. If anything, the distant threat intensified the hopes and prospects that came with a successful exam.

The grueling four hours over, I joined my friends outside, and together we walked down the familiar streets with their markets and stalls, watching the kayaks on the river and the crowds on the sidewalks. High overhead passed a squadron of unidentified planes. An hour later we heard that Biala, a town only fifteen miles away, had been bombed. It was a remote story with no more import to us than an air raid in Abyssinia or Spain. By nightfall, we watched the unfamiliar sights of blacked-out windows and dimmed headlights, and we bantered idly with the armed soldiers posted on all street corners. With the help of flashlights we made our way to the Olympia, a baroque coffee house featuring accordion music, where we sat late into the night arguing about every subject but war.

On Saturday afternoon I went to see Hinda, a girl with whom I corresponded. Her father, a former Austrian officer, sat in the little study among his books and the busts of Tolstoy and Tagore and listened to our chatter with sad, forebearing eyes. "We are not afraid of war," I remember saying. He only smiled bitterly, and continued to read the newspaper in which the Prime Minister, Slawoj-Skladowski, was boasting, "We shall win because Jozef Pilsudski has taught us how freedom is won and how it is defended." A most impressive sentence, I thought, in both its structure and its logic. While Hinda was showing me her latest books and we discussed the coming school year, more German bombers passed on their way to Biala. Troops marched through the town, and long lines of ambulances rolled toward the front. That night there were no more crowds on the streets, only the glare of Biala's fires against the dark sky.

By Sunday it was impossible to find transportation for the trip home; all buses and trains were reserved for the military. But there was always Nahum, a wispy old man who, for half a century, had travelled the Miedzyrzec-Losice route by horse and buggy. I located him in front of the tannery loading barrels of wax and foul smelling hides onto the wagon and we set off for home. Normally full of banter, Nahum was morose and did not even speak to his horse. As the moon, big and pale, rose above the forest, nothing but the horse's stomping and the squeak of the wheels in the deep sand could be heard. The old man, wrapped in a blanket, did not stir.

"A beautiful night, isn't it?" I said to him.

"So that's what's on your mind," he growled.

I wrapped myself with the other blanket, lay down, and watched the deepening night. It was late when we arrived in Losice, its roofs wet with silver from the setting moon.

The day I returned home England and France declared war on Germany and we thought the war now would end in a week or so. Instead we began to see the first signs of the German invasion: traffic through town grew daily as high officials evacuated their families eastward; cars flying the flags of foreign missions headed for Brest. The town's single gas station was soon emptied, and since the same was happening everywhere, many stalled cars were abandoned along the streets and highways. Streams of refugees flowed through the town, spreading news of merciless air raids and the brutality of the invaders. Orders came to dig air shelters and the whole populace reported for work. Public loudspeakers reported heavy fighting and urged the population to seek refuge in the eastern parts of the country.

By Saturday, September 9, the Germans had reached Sokolow, only thirty miles away. Distant explosions echoed in the brilliant summer air and the first enemy planes appeared over our town, circling lazily under a transparent sky. In the vibrant sunshine the planes glistened like sharp, tiny mirrors, filling the air with the slow melodic pull of their engines. We watched with fascination as they hung in the sky, motionless and alert. Anticipating an air attack, more and more people were escaping to the neighboring farms; my parents, together with my sisters, also left for Swiniarow, a village two miles away. I stayed in town, eager to see what war looked like.

In the afternoon my parents returned to stock some supplies. While they were out buying food, I sat at the window watching the refugees shuffle through town. Drowsy with the incessant stamping and the heat of the summer day, I must have just fallen asleep when I awoke with a start. In the streets people were crouching along fences and walls. I saw mother among them. She was waving frantically for me to come down. Then, against the sun, I saw the planes, snow-white and heading straight for the town. I raced down the stairs and headed for Herschek's house, which was near the edge of town, and thus safer than the center. When I got there he had already ducked into the garden. I hit the ground next to him. From somewhere the pulsation of the oncoming planes swelled until I saw them emerge over the house – three bombers flying tightly next to each other. As if pressed down by their weight, I squirmed into the dirt and crossed my arms over my head. When I thought that they had passed, I looked up. Just then one of the planes tipped and a shrill metallic whine split the air. The explosions followed immediately and a huge spray of fire leaped skyward, filling my eyes with smoke and dust.

We had cellars and even the slit trenches we had dug during the previous days, but no one trusted them. Unhinged by panic, people scattered in all directions like flapping chickens, we among them. We had barely reached the Polinov grove when the planes came in for a second bombing run. Huge clouds of smoke, dirt, and brick dust rose over the town. Seconds later came the flames. Losice was burning.

We were about a kilometer from the edge of town and we wondered whether the planes would spot us. We could not see much; we only felt the hot breeze of flames as it sailed over the fields. But soon, through the ash blowing in our direction, we heard the throb of engines. Some women next to me began to cry. A madman stood up and calmly, with raised head, started back toward town. The planes emerged from the wall of smoke like huge bats, diving as they circled the ponds. First the shrill whine of the falling bombs, then sheets of flame, jagged at the edges. We hugged the smoking earth, listening to the shrapnel ricochet off branches and tree trunks. Another wave of panic gripped us, and we started running into the open fields. There was a dull, dry rattle. "Down! They're shooting at us!" Herschek yelled. I remember staring at him in disbelief. Nearby, wounded men moaned while the machine guns continued firing.

Later the flames over the town turned scarlet. Although the planes were gone we continued to lie flat on our faces, afraid to return home. But the ground grew cold despite the hot wind, and the cold seeped into our bones. Slowly we rose to make our way back to the fires raging at the outskirts of town. There I found my parents, dazed but quite alive, and together we stumbled ahead amid burning houses, toppled fences, and tangled wires. Blistering gusts of air blew from the side streets and showers of sparks burst as gutted houses collapsed across the pavement. It was a long time before we reached our house. But there it stood, in the midst of flame and wreckage, intact – at least on the outside. Inside all was chaos: doors unhinged, a tablecloth fluttering through a broken window, and smoke drifting in and rolling under the beds.

We gathered a few necessities and, without bothering to lock the door, left to join the rest of the family on the farm. As we walked fires colored the sky in about a dozen places, some near, some far. Soon Swiniarow appeared, peaceful amidst its fields and gardens. Here lived Jozefowa, a farm woman we knew who had taken in our family that morning. When we arrived, my two sisters, upon seeing us alive, burst into tears. I threw the packs on the floor and drank the cold milk that Jozefowa gave us. There were too many people in the small house, and I went outside. The fires on the horizon were dimming, and the stars were returning to the sky. An old farmer sat down beside me, mumbling to himself, "Anti-Christ... Anti-Christ is coming...." I climbed into the loft of the barn, lay down in the hay, and immediately fell asleep.

The first streaks of dawn were barely visible when three enemy planes flew low over Swiniarow. They passed us to circle the highway, where the Polish army was retreating in disorder. When the bombers came, slow and heavy, flocks of crows lifted into the air and hung there till the planes left. Now and then small groups of Polish soldiers strayed into the village looking for food; at the sound of the planes, they hid under trees or in the barn. Not a soul was visible over the whole sun-baked countryside. Losice lay exposed in the valley, calm, chalk-white, seemingly indifferent to what had struck it.

Monday evening the men on Jozefowa's farm went to Losice for supplies to prepare for a long stay in the village. Losice was utterly deserted. All doors were open, exposing personal possessions, but nobody was tempted by it. Here and there corpses were still lying around, strangely poised and serene. Of all my relatives, grandfather alone – eighty years old – remained in town helping to bury the dead, a mitzvah by Judaic law. He told us the first bomb that fell hit and destroyed the town's synagogue. From our broken windows I could see the roofless and gutted hulk posing its questions at the sky and receiving no answer.

The bombs left about fifty people dead and a number of wounded who were given no treatment as, following the air-raid, the town remained without a clinic or doctor. There was on that Saturday a single soldier in Losice – a captain who had come to requisition bread for the troops expected to pass through Losice the following day – and cunningly the German bombers found him. As he stood hiding under a tree, a bomb came straight down the trunk, pulverizing him. On leaving town we saw a priest moving about the place with a basket on his arm, collecting parts of the man – a severed foot here, pieces of uniform there; his teeth the priest had to pry from the tree stump's bark. Fires again painted the sky a rusty glare on our way back to Swiniarow, but this time they were much nearer. Muffled thunder came from beyond the horizon. We turned our heads uneasily and hurried our steps.

Jozefowa's husband had been mobilized and the farm needed work, so the next morning I took the horse into the field to do some plowing. Except for the planes bombing the Bug bridges, there was an eerie quiet; the horse and I seemed the only live things in the entire landscape. Suddenly a single bomber, a Heinkel 111, appeared from the direction of the river. He headed straight for me, and as he approached he kept dropping lower and lower. There was nothing else around, just the bomber and I, and he was soon so low I could see the goggles of the gunner in the glass cockpit. I dropped the reins and crawled under the unhitched wagon, all the time staring straight at the German gunner in the cockpit. The hiding was foolish, but not the reaction; the Luftwaffe often strafed and killed civilians, including farmers in the field. For one single moment I could feel that the gunner up there hesitated between firing and not firing. Then, no more than a hundred meters overhead, the plane roared past me and returned to the Bug.

The boom of artillery we had heard the night before rumbled throughout the following morning with growing intensity. There were constant explosions along the railway line and near the bridge over the Bug. Early in the day a few troops of Polish cavalry were still galloping past our village but by noon nothing stirred anywhere.

Only that incessant thunder from the north that crept nearer and nearer. Suddenly it too ceased. A crushing silence now froze the sunny brilliance of the afternoon. A lonely machine gun opened fire somewhere and a house at the edge of Losice burst into flames. Then it was still again. Half an hour later a man on a bicycle arrived from the direction of town. "They have come," he told us. It was Tuesday, the twelfth day of the invasion.

On the morning of September 17, the Red Army entered Poland. Initially we thought they were coming to our rescue, but we soon learned that they were merely occupying a part of the country. The radio announced that the demarcation line between the Germans and the Soviets had been set at the Vistula. On the first day of Succoth, the Russians crossed the Bug and arrived in Losice. Stoic files of tobacco-brown uniforms, they stood pressed together in open trucks, many of the vehicles driving on solid rubber tires. On the square, a commissar mounted the podium and spoke about the New Order: about Culture, Socialism, and Happiness. A new mayor was appointed as well as a civilian militia. Red flags decked the town. Stores and offices reopened and we were told that school, too, would soon start. We went every day to watch the Russian soldiers and involved them in long discussions. They recited praise for the Soviet system and boasted that the Red Army could conquer Europe in forty hours. But above all they preferred to dance and sing, which they did with great gusto. As one of them played the accordion, the others vaulted about the street – preferably with girls, but if not, then with each other. Their music was both thrilling and pensive, evoking visions of the steppe, of the Volga, and of endless calamities.

Three days after the Russians arrived in Losice, we learned they were leaving. The demarcation line between the Germans and the USSR shifted from the Vistula to the Bug, and the Red Army, which had advanced as far as Warsaw, began to retire to the East.

The news that the Germans were to be our masters wrenched the town loose like an unhinged door. Soon the first lines of refugees were plodding down the Biala highway to make their way across the Bug. I expected that Herschek, too, would want to leave, for his Gymnasium was in Bialystok, on the Russian side. I soon saw him coming down the street, a rucksack on his shoulders, leading his bike as one would a precious racing horse. It seemed natural that everything should be difficult for him, for it had always been so. Now, too, close to graduation, he had to contend with a demarcation line drawn through the country's heart. He came over, tested the tires, and bounced the "old goat" against the cobblestones. "I am going to finish school," he said. "Are you coming?"

Herschek asked if I was going to stay or leave with him for the Soviet side. From the day England had joined in, I never doubted that the Germans were going to lose this war; so whatever awaited me here would end one day. The Soviet Union, once the turmoil was over, would, I knew, ring down its steel shutters and I would be trapped there. Though neither of us belonged to any political party, Herschek had great hopes for the Soviet system; I saw our sole salvation in Zionism. I shook my head that I was not coming and watched Herschek mount the bike and push off. With him, many others were leaving: on foot, in horse-drawn carts, in one way or another, they headed east behind the Russians. Mottel also left, as did most young people. Losice was soon a half empty town.

Alongside the refugees, military columns moved in long, patient streams toward the Bug. Troops bivouacked outside our town that night, cooking over campfires and shaving in the open. Several soldiers told me the Germans were already in Siedlce; a Jewish captain urged me to leave. Later, lying in bed, I heard the last Russian troops pass our town about midnight. Then, except for the rain splashing against the darkened windows, all was still again.

The next day, a Monday, was dull, full of clouds and wind and endless grayness. We pressed our faces against the steamed, cold windows and waited. Then, through the autumn wind, we heard the roar of engines, and the first German motorcycles crashed into town. In helmets and green rubber trenchcoats, gloves and boots gleaming black, the Germans halted in a semicircle around the square and stared at the town; then, with synchronized snorts from their motors, they raced down the Biala highway. After them came the main body of motorized troops, filling the square and overflowing into the side streets. The air was choked with fumes of synthetic gasoline and the staccato of military German. With those who timidly approached them the soldiers conversed exuberantly, offhandedly, asking for eggs and butter as if they were all professional grocers. In their vehicles beneath the mounted machine guns lay piles of looted goods. Then the infantry arrived, marching and singing a loud, jubilant *Heili-Heilu*; I stood and watched all day and all evening until the night effaced them and their song.

Over the weeks that followed, the town looked like a military camp. Though their rations were first rate and included chocolate, fruit, and wine, the soldiers were tireless in trying to get more food. They made the best possible impression: young, good-looking, clean. They were robust and cheerful, boasting about the Polish campaign, lauding the Führer, enjoying the easy victory, and wiping one palm over the other to signify how Warsaw was pulverized. They filled the town with shrill gibberish, laughter, and arrogance. They smelled of tobacco and perfume, as if they were returning not from a war but from a ball.

Proclamations signed by Brauchitsch, the army commander, were pasted on all walls. "On the order of the Führer, the German Army has occupied your country...." they began, going on to demand obedience and to warn against any resistance, and ending with: "For economic hyenas and Jewish exploiters there is no room in the New Europe." To implement this, there began immediately a systematic plunder of all Jewish stores. The owners were forced to open their shops and hundreds of soldiers pushed their way inside, stuffing bags and pockets with anything they found. Often, where there was not room enough for all "customers," a few soldiers threw the merchandise out on the street, and a mixed crowd of soldiers and peasants carried it off before it even touched the ground. After a few days the Kommandantur issued an order forbidding plunder, at the same time commanding a return to prewar prices for all commodities. The pilferage then assumed a different form; any purchase was paid for with no more than ten pfennigs and a sneer that the Almighty would make up the difference. In a week the goods were gone and the fun ended.

A certain way of life crystallized under our new masters. German troops kept coming and going; a hospital was organized where, to our surprise, the wounded of the early bombings received treatment; a Kommandantur was set up to act as a legal body; and each evening a military band played marches and Viennese waltzes to the applause of the mob. Off duty, the same musicians caused the wildest incidents. They liked to roll Torahs in mud, kick crucifixes out of windows, rob passers-by, and slap women in a sure, professional manner. The Germans' arrogance was disquieting, but their discipline exhilarating. With great ceremony, they installed and changed guard, clicking heels, goose-stepping, and presenting arms with magnificent flourishes. Even in small numbers, they moved in formation, accompanied by loud singing. Their speech was like the barking of dogs – snappy and shrill – and it did show their teeth.

ii

Soon the soldiers with their guns and cars and hospitals departed. They went west to another campaign, promising that, if Poland had held out for eighteen days, France would last only seventeen, and then be stripped to the bone. When they were gone we enjoyed a few evening strolls under a quiet sky while the town slumbered in its fall shadows. We even felt grateful to the *Wehrmacht* for having left us in peace.

Of course we knew it could not last, for in other parts of the country the Germans were on the rampage. Losice, only ten miles from the border, could gauge the intensity of the spreading terror by the swarms at the Bug as people tried to escape to the Russian side. One day we awoke to discover visitors, not soldiers this time but gendarmes in turquoise uniforms with brown patches on their cuffs and collars. The first snow had fallen that morning, and against its whiteness the Germans, tall and fit in helmets and jackboots, looked like Gothic statues. From behind closed shutters and drawn drapes we watched as they yelled themselves hoarse, then mounted their command cars and disappeared. This was our first glimpse of the *Schutzpolizei*, otherwise known as the *Schupo*.

They returned at noontime with a long line of horse-drawn carts packed with men, women, and children, a portion of the millions of Poles evicted from the western territories incorporated into the Reich. After disposing of the refugees, we thought they would leave, but instead they lingered on. Life quickly became unbearable. Beatings were routine. They sacked and plundered. They raided neighboring villages, and after each trip the notorious gray execution lists covered the walls. They incited displaced Poles to loot Jewish homes, then shot one of the looters. They promised both the Poles and us that they would be here a full year, during which time we would not have five minutes of peace – easily the grossest German understatement of the war.

One day they appeared with submachine guns over their shoulders, indiscriminately rounded up a dozen people – two bearded old men and some boys – and marched them off to the schoolhouse. Even though our house was far from that building, soon I could hear the men's screams. When, together with others, I ran toward the school, I saw a body hurtling down the front steps. It landed at the sentry's feet, trouserless, blood collecting in a thin puddle around the man's head. New screams erupted inside and another body landed in the gutter. The obscene sight of the men's pale posteriors and bleeding heads reversed us in the middle of our onrush and we began to back away, slowly at first, then at a run. On the square I saw Germans rounding up new victims – they were kicking doors open and pulling men out by their arms and legs.

When I reached home, without saying anything to anyone, I stuffed a few pieces of clothing into my knapsack and grabbed half a loaf of bread. Looking up I saw Father doing the same and Mother watching us both in utter silence. Father and I then left home without saying goodbye or intimating where we were going. There was no need; like thousands before us, we were escaping to the Russian side.

Through backyards and side streets we ducked our way out of town and, in the quickly gathering dusk, kept marching eastward.

Soon we stumbled upon the first peasants who, for a fee, were carting escapees to the river. We clambered onto one of the carts and, huddled amidst a dozen strangers, resumed our journey east.

It took five hours to reach the farmer's village, three miles from the Bug. We could not go farther because from there on the Germans were patrolling the roads. To reach the border we had to cut across open country in a wide seven-mile arc. A guide, we were told, would lead us to the border, where another guide would row us across the river. Altogether, twenty of us hoped to cross that night. In the relative safety of the farmer's hut, Father and I talked for the first time since we had left Mother and my sisters. The crossing would be difficult for a man of fifty-five, and the thought of abandoning our home troubled him. Father decided he would remain on this farm and I would continue alone; if the situation in Losice worsened, Father would follow with the rest of the family.

A guide in a huge sheepskin motioned to us, and we walked into the pitch-black night. Armed with walking sticks torn from the farmer's fence, we crossed a muddy trail and followed in single file across the plowed fields and into the woods. The village lights vanished and a fine drizzle began to fall. No one could see the person in front of him. We slipped in the mud, got up, and dragged on. At some point the girl in front of me stumbled and fell. She grabbed my leg, saying she could not get up. I unhitched her pack, put it on my knapsack, and helped her up. By the time we were ready to continue, the others, unaware of our halt, had disappeared. For nearly half an hour we went on alone uncertain whether even in the right direction. But evidently the group had noticed we were missing, for they were waiting for us at the edge of the forest.

We rested awhile looking down on the land that sloped gently toward the river. On the left, lights sparkled in the darkness – the lights of Drohiczyn, a town on the other side of the Bug – and it was strange to realize that for them there was no blackout, no war. As we neared the river a flare suddenly shot into the sky. We crouched as low as possible, watching the magnesium light trace a wide arc over the fields before it expired. Then we started to run. A second flare went up with a hiss just as we reached the first barns of the border village. We flattened ourselves against a wall, waited till the light died out, and dashed into the guide's house.

We did not cross the border that night. The weather cleared after midnight, the moon was bright, and the guide who was to row us across said he had seen Soviet patrols on the other side. We did not mind; it was dry and warm in the farmhouse, and the cold milk the guide's wife passed around was refreshing. Exhausted, we stretched out on the straw spread on the floor. Soon everyone was asleep except for the girl I could hear weeping in the corner. I, too, could not sleep, and so I lay and watched the moon splash across the floor and over the faces of the sleeping men. Beyond the window I could see the line of riverside willows and the cold surface of the Bug's waters. Intermittently, from the other side, came the sounds of cocks and of dogs barking, and they, together with the snoring of the other people, lulled me to sleep.

The following night we got ready for the crossing. It was pitch dark and a strong wind blew from the river. After sliding down the steep bank we came to the water's edge. I saw nothing at first, but then I overheard the splash of an oar in the distance; one boatload was already on its way. Quiet as a shadow the boat returned. One by one we waded in and crouched on the wet bottom as the guide, with quick, silent strokes, rowed us onto the river. We were nearly in the middle when something went wrong; the guide ducked, dropping the oars, and the boat drifted with the current. From afar

I heard muffled, hoarse commands. Looking toward the western bank, I saw a line of soldiers cocking their rifles. The guide, to forestall shooting, quickly turned the boat back to the German side. With a jolt we scraped bottom. After we had disembarked, the Germans lined us up and led us to a festively lighted estate where hundreds of soldiers sat at long clean tables eating *Abendbrot*. They searched us and confiscated whatever appealed to them; then, with nothing more than a few kicks and some spicy remarks about Jews, Poles, and other impure races, they released us.

When we reconvened at the guide's house for a second attempt at crossing the border, the moon had risen again, making the village and the other shore visible and bright as in daylight. But we could not wait any longer: our money and our patience were at an end. Once more we were seated in a rowboat, and soon we were again in the middle of the river – all silence but for the noise of the wild ducks in the reeds. We made for the other side in one swift diagonal, and when the boat scraped sand, we quickly disembarked. While we crouched among the reeds, the guide surveyed the undergrowth and listened for any suspicious sounds. He signalled and we followed him up the steep bank. In front of us was open country, sandy, spacious, flat. Two miles away was a sparse woods; if we could reach it, we would be safe. It was very quiet; even the barking of the dogs had stopped. We moved at a brisk pace across the denuded fields, across savage white moon-shine.

We were already close to the woods when, suddenly, shadows flickered past us and two Russian soldiers materialized out of nowhere, pointing the bayonets of their rifles at our noses. Wearing forage caps and long winter overcoats, they circled cautiously, then motioned us to sit down, all without uttering a sound. We began to talk to them, to explain, argue, and, finally, to implore and beg. It was useless. Someone tried to bribe them. *Molchat*, they snapped.

While one soldier stayed with us, the other moved off, knelt on one knee, bowed his head, listened. He loomed unreal against the green night until, triggered by a distant sound, he raced to the river. Ten minutes later he returned with more border jumpers, among them a young mother with a baby in her arms. Crying that she had paid her last money to cross, she begged the soldiers to let her go, but they repeatedly told her to sit and be quiet.

The baby slept peacefully, the woman sobbed, and the rest of us huddled together against the cold, watching the border in front of us. Through the mist rising from the river, flares and searchlights flashed like summer lightning. In the distance, rifle shots cracked. A slight frost set in, and on the nearby brook ice began to form. We rose to warm our stiff limbs. The mist was so thick we could see neither river nor woods. The wild ducks were gone, and a wind began blowing from the water. Dawn was approaching.

When daylight broke the Russians gathered us up and led us single file back to the Bug through a ravine thick with bushes. By prior arrangement among ourselves we started to elongate the line. Several times the Russians asked us to close ranks, but soon we repeated the maneuver. As we marched, every once in a while someone at the end of the line dropped to the ground. The Russians, unaware of what was occurring, marched on. Then, at one point when they again reminded us to stay close together, they noticed what had happened; of the original seventeen only nine remained. Silently, they looked at us. We were quiet too, as if unaware of the whole thing. Though tempted to go after the escapees, they realized that if they did, we, too, would disappear. So, one of the soldiers now brought up the rear and we marched on, slowly approaching the river. Soon the lights of a village appeared, clear of civilians but full of soldiers. We were led into a large square where a red flag hung motionless in the early morning calm. Lights blazed in the houses, and Russian officers shuttled in and out. Several hundred detained people sat about while armed patrols kept bringing in border jumpers from other areas. At the corners of the square, sentries stood with rifles at their sides.

We did not wait long. Two officers arrived and returned the pocket knives and razor blades the soldiers had confiscated. One of them lectured us about crossing the border illegally, then comforted us by promising that, within a week, the border would open and crossings would be lawful. Now, however, we must go back. To many, being forced to return home was a relief. Subliminally I felt it myself, for my dilemma remained the same as when Herschek asked me to leave with him. The Russians led us to the river, packed us into boats, and rowed us to the other side. We landed in dense woods and immediately moved on to avoid German border patrols.

My father was still in the village where I had left him two days before. He agreed to stay on while I went to Losice to reconnoiter. I reached home the same day to find the streets peculiarly deserted. The few people I did see quickly slipped into doorways and gates. The German command cars, however, were gone from the Square.

When I got home Mother told me that the Schupo had taken six men with them, and so far there had been no word from them. There was no reason to worry, I thought; they had probably been taken to a labor camp.

Next morning, however, we learned that all six men were dead. A farmer told us the details of the execution, which took place in a little grove two miles from town. One of the men had fought back and had been hacked to death. So ended the first visit from the official law enforcers of the Third Reich. Later we learned that this particular squad of the Schupo was a part of the special *Einsatzkommandos* entrusted, in the fall of 1939, with the liquidation of all Polish intellectuals. The six murdered Losice men had no claim to such distinction. None of them had finished grade school; two were illiterate. But they were Jews and thereby subject to any arbitrary classification, as long as it brought humiliation and injury to the victims.

iii

No one could remember such cold as during that winter of 1939. The air crackled with icicles and the snow gleamed like metal in the frozen, moonlit nights. The double windows were etched with fronds of ice, and the stove roared red-hot all day. It seemed true that the winters of war are the coldest of winters.

On one of these breath-stopping days, the first transport of evicted Jews arrived. Like the Poles, they had had to leave their homes in five minutes. Packed in boxcars they were shipped as far east as possible; here, near the Russian border, they were dumped into the open country. Some settled in the near-by town of Sarnaki, and the rest – about two thousand – came to Losice. They occupied all the empty houses left by those who had escaped beyond the Bug. When more arrived later, they filled cellars, lofts, and shacks; all the original residents had to share their apartments with these refugees. The young and strong clutched desperately at every sort of labor, however menial, fetching water, shoveling snow, chopping wood. The old and weak begged.

After several months of apparent anarchy following Poland's defeat, our role in the New Europe was finally formulated. Our portion of the country was officially named *General Gouvernement*, as distinct from the western "Ur-German" lands incorporated into the Third Reich. The newspapers, which I read regularly with my reluctantly expanded knowledge of German, explained that it was our function, as the *Nebenland*, first to serve the needs of Germany, and only second to consider our own. We were a sort of defunct appendix whose fate was yet to be determined.

In this Nebenland, the Poles were granted a local civil administration, Polish postage stamps, native policemen – and, for a governor, Germany's Commissioner for Justice, Hans Frank. Cracow was named the new capital, and on the Wawel, where embalmed Polish kings dreamt of past glories, a huge black swastika now waved. A lone newspaper appeared, the *Nowy Kurier Warszawski*, which, in simple-minded Polish, translated articles sent from Berlin. In the Nebenland the population was divided into three absolute categories. The Germans and the *Volksdeutsche* – the half-Poles, half-Germans – were the omnipotent masters of the land. Poles were permitted to exist as long as they remained deaf and dumb. Such tolerance did not apply to the intellectuals, who were exterminated in a deliberate and methodical campaign. Finally, there were the Jews, entirely outside the law, treated like bedbugs. There was no place for us in the New Europe.

After the brief and memorable visit of the Schupo, a single German was made ruler of our town. He was an *SS Obersturmführer* and he occupied seven rooms in the city hall. For a time we were not aware of his presence, but one day we heard from him. He asked to speak with the senior Jew in Losice, the Jewish Führer. This presented something of a problem, for we had never been

conscious of rank among us. But somewhere among us there lived
a certain Rozenzweig, a rosy-cheeked, tiny, clever Jew who thought
a great opportunity had arrived for him. In due time, he presented
himself to the Obersturmführer, who ordered him to organize a
Judenrat to handle all civil affairs for the Jewish community. This
was speedily accomplished, and Rozenzweig appeared a second time
before the Obersturmführer, now to introduce the "elected Jewish
representatives." Upon uttering these words Rozenzweig was
promptly knocked down and given to understand, amid a rain of
blows, that henceforth there would be no such thing as elections.

The Judenrat that came into being, elected or not, was a
peculiar institution. Its members were not collaborators; they could
not have been, even had they wanted that role. They told the Jews
what the Germans ordered them to say, but when force was to be
used it fell to the Germans, who would not have foregone the
pleasure in any event. As mere stooges, the Judenrat incurred
contempt and ridicule rather than hatred. By and large they were
greedy, middle-aged operators who did not realize whom they were
getting ready to serve – a pardonable imbecility, perhaps, when
greater men, national and international leaders, failed to assess who
and what Hitler was. No Judenrat member ever voluntarily added
to our misery; they never used physical violence against other Jews.
Isolated and dehumanized, they in time acquired blank faces and
false smiles, which enabled them to endure the ostracism of our
closely knit community. Mottel persistently refused the jobs which
his influential uncle Rozenzweig offered him, and my father did not
speak to any of them throughout the war.

Because of his black uniform the SS Obersturmführer was
called the Bat. Despite the ominous beginnings, we were to
remember his one-man rule as a sort of benevolent tyranny, thanks

to the magic of bribery. In his susceptibility to gifts and money, he could not be outdone by any Pasha. It was always a revelation to see these two men, the Bat and Rozenzweig, walk together, usually after curfew when they could be alone in the deserted streets: the tall SS man in his uniform, *Hakenkreuz,* and jackboots, and the bouncing little Jew, barely five feet tall. Slightly stooped, their hands clasped behind their backs, they sorted the affairs of state in low, confidential voices. If the Bat could not save us from the official blows, he spared us the supplements which more enterprising Germans would subsequently inflict on us of their own choice.

To keep us informed, the Germans gave us our own newspaper, the *Gazeta Zydowska.* It was to print no political or military news, or even pro-German items, but solely the ukases issued by various civil, party, police, and army offices – itself a full-time job. One morning the headlines declared all prewar currency invalid. Poles were permitted to exchange old bank notes for new, but not Jews. Another edict decreed that, with the New Year, Jews would be forbidden to travel by train. Still another ordered us to wear armbands of a prescribed width on the right arm, the blue Star of David branding us, henceforth and wherever we went, as Jews.

At the end of the winter the Bat's reign was augmented by thirty Schupo gendarmes who moved into a large building on Biala Street for the remainder of the war. Their arrival subjected us to additional rules. Jews were to tip their hats to every German and pass in an "appropriately wide arc." Hats had to be tipped even when the Germans rode by in cars. If hatless, the Jew was to bow. It required great dexterity, if not clairvoyance, to bow and tip hats when the Germans approached from behind. Somehow Mottel and I could not bring ourselves to conform. Whenever we saw a

German we turned away; and when we failed to avoid them, we accepted the inevitable slaps and kicks for not bowing.

We did not travel by train; we wore our badges; we bowed before the Germans; and we waited for the end of winter. We all knew the war would end in the spring. From the very beginning we nourished an imaginary world in which we made history conform to our fantasies. We were helped in this by Allied braggadocio. The French were promising to hang their laundry on the Siegfried line in the spring; Churchill sank the German navy several times weekly. When Chamberlain in one of his speeches predicted the war would last three years, the whole town became his mortal enemy; was he not a misanthrope and a fool? It was a difficult but not unendurable winter. It more or less conformed to our fathers' memories of war and persecution. Before the war, the Poles had made Jewish lives difficult, and now the Germans made Polish lives miserable as well – there was even some logic in that. And we were confident that the Germans themselves had a similar fate in store for them. We never doubted that they would lose this war. We were being kicked and trampled, but our preoccupations were still those of healthy people. I thought of Herschek in Bialystok, of his final exams, of the medical school he was going to attend. I corresponded with friends about books and school and postwar plans. When Mottel came back from across the Bug, as did many homesick people, we resumed our walks to Polinov and watched the farm hands cut ice on the ponds. On sunny days we played volleyball or gazed idly at the smoke rising over Losice's zinc roofs. It was still a white, peaceful town. We had dwelt insignificantly in time, and we were certain we would soon return to our insignificance.

As we expected, with the arrival of spring came the decisive moment of the war. The Germans first attacked Norway, then France. Norway the allies lost within a week, and we dismissed it as trivial. But when, on May 10, the campaign in the West ignited like a summer conflagration, we stopped in our tracks in a silent, breathless anticipation of the great decision, knowing only too well what its outcome meant to us.

But before we had time even to generate hopes or illusions, disasters mounted with the onrush of a flood. By the end of May, Holland and Belgium had been knocked out and the British expeditionary corps was driven from the Continent. The Germans had reached the Somme. But there they halted, and for three days their communiques had nothing to report. There were no bulletins about newly captured towns and hundreds of thousands of prisoners. On the streets of Losice one could hear laughter. Our eyes gleamed, for we remembered our fathers' stories about the German fiasco on the Marne in 1914; in 1940 it would be the Somme. Behind shutters, in the dark, we prayed and waited for Allied victory.

But on the fourth day the French front cracked and, soon after, folded. Beaten, the French armies fled. German tanks raced through the gash like wolves reaching for the heart of France. On June 14, the Germans took Paris. On June 19, France surrendered.

I sat on the balcony of our house staring at the gigantic crimson headline, two words on the entire front page: FRANCE SURRENDERS. It was past the curfew hour, but a crowd still filled the square, waiting, as had those six widows last November who would not believe their men were dead. A full moon had risen; it seemed to shine over a desert. Then the stillness was shattered by a wild cheering from the Biala highway – the Germans were celebrating the victory of the millennium.

iv

The defeat of France stunned us. England was continuing the war, but their war was not our war and her planes that dropped a bomb here and there had no message for us. We lingered in numb apathy, not knowing where to look for new hope.

By the end of August German troops began to arrive back in Poland. At first it was not too surprising: they were coming for a rest, for more eggs and butter. They were the Germans we knew so well – young, handsome, cocky, stupid. They were bedecked with medals: *Ritterkreuze, Eisenkreuze*, ribbons, and laurels. For a few days they did not molest us, were even polite, and returned salutes whenever, according to precedence, we tipped our hats. Then everything changed. Someone must have explained to the innocent soldiers that the population of Losice was not German, and immediately they were transformed. Their *Sie* turned to *Du*. They made us polish their boots, clubbed us for not tipping our hats promptly. When, with more troops arriving, the question of quarters became acute, we immediately realized that matters were about to get worse. One day half the Jews living adjacent to the square were ordered to clear their homes and businesses within six hours. Whatever the residents had not managed to remove by the two o'clock deadline, soldiers threw on a pile in the middle of the square and set afire. Then they rounded up a hundred Jews and told them to clean, disinfect, and prepare the place for the new troops.

Due to this resettlement we were forced to share one of our two rooms with a family from Poznan named Mordkowicz. This move was their fifth displacement since the war. There were three sons, all tall and thin. The oldest boy, Zalus, had been an engineering student before the war interrupted; the other two, Shmulek and

Boris, had attended Gymnasium. All three played the piccolo. When they weren't playing, we discussed Feuchtwanger's books, which dominated Losice's literary scene that summer, and we argued about war and Germans and Jews. Their little room, packed with pots and suitcases and a miniature stove, became our head-quarters, where we smoked endless black-market cigarettes and carried our ponderous arguments late into night.

But we were not given much free time for such activities. With the arrival of German troops began the grim chapter of forced labor. When my turn came, I was assigned work at the Schupo quarters. While our "employers" still slept, we polished their boots, cleaned their uniforms, emptied their garbage, and swept their floors. From one of the town wells we transported water in a large two-wheeled barrel which one of us pulled as two others pushed. Before we could break for lunch, there was the pavement to sweep and wood to chop. Afternoons we worked till four. Like all forced labor, we earned no pay.

More troops arrived, and the hasty construction of huge barracks outside the town presaged still more arrivals. Niemojki, the small railway station near Losice, swarmed with troops enlarging the ramps, building new tracks, and erecting vast depots. One hundred Jews were taken to work there, another hundred for a drainage project on the river Liwiec. Every night, the two huge diesels that hauled the workers back and forth to Niemojki discharged cripples with broken legs, ruptured kidneys, and severed fingers. The first fatalities were brought back from the Liwiec, where each week playful guards drowned at least one laborer in the muddy river. All Jewish craftsmen were mobilized to help build the barracks, and fifteen-year-old boys were dragged to the unskilled jobs on construc-tion and highways.

When my stint at the Schupo was over, I was ordered to another job, this one to help the Wehrmacht build roads around the barracks. The saving grace of this job was that we worked alongside German soldiers, themselves not eager for hard work. It was here that, for the first and only time, I heard a German soldier doubting the outcome of the war. In the midst of shovelling dirt he looked at me sideways and said, rather strangely, "Don't you think that Germany is going to lose this war?" I did not answer and he did not pursue it and we went on gravelling the road in silence.

Later on another boy and I were moved to a quarry near a little forest where we loaded gravel onto carts. To spare their horses, the peasants came only once or twice, and we had most of the day to ourselves. It was fall by now. Wind and rain tore over the countryside. We would dig ourselves a cave in the sand and light a fire. Billows of smoke would rise into the gray air while we squeezed close to the fire, trying to keep warm. Whenever I looked out, there in the valley was Losice, and next to it a new city, a city of barracks defacing the landscape. I thought of Herschek. This was his last year at the Gymnasium. He was probably already filling out his application for medical school – while I was here piling carts with dirt, huddling in a cave. And I asked myself the devastating question: What am I waiting for? Suppose, I thought, the war lasted a long time and I survived it. What would I have survived it for? Sitting there in the gravel pit, I decided to resume my studies, regardless of the Germans, their barracks, and their war.

Schooling under the Germans was, of course, non-existent, even prohibited, not only for Jews but for Poles as well. But even for home study there were difficulties – no textbooks, no people in Losice who could help, and, worst of all, no free time; we were at slave labor twelve hours a day or more. But no sooner had I made my decision than a twist of good luck made it possible. The Wehrmacht set up a laundry for the troops and I was assigned work there. It was an ideal job for me. Once I lit the six or eight stoves and supplied water for the washerwomen – which took no more than a couple of hours – I was free for the rest of the day.

The supervisor of the place, a Westphalian named Tyska, was, one might almost say, kind to me. As long as I kept the place going he did not care when I came or left. He liked to discuss various harmless subjects, procured books for me from Germany, and even invited me occasionally for a snack. Our circumspect discussions occasionally stumbled upon touchy subjects – an atrocity or two, Jews – but the smile never left his face. He disarmingly admitted that the quality of his rationed marmalade was of greater concern to him than what his compatriots did in Poland – or anywhere else, for that matter. He said that for his comfort he, too, would be prepared to do a thing or two. In fact he was so much enamored of his comfort that he rarely left his room. I had puzzling moments when I first started to work for Tyska. At the laundry, he slept in a little office. Upon my arrival in the morning he would hand me a neat package to throw into the garbage bin. I deposited the bundles as ordered until my curiosity got the better of me one day. Halfway through the unwrapping I was alerted by the smell of Aryan excretion and quickly rewrapped the package. Too lazy or frightened to go out at night, he defecated in his room. In addition to dark outhouses, he was afraid of the rats in the laundry, and he fired at them with his pistol, making big holes in the walls and floor, to the despair of the landlord who lived above. But Tyska's love of comfort suited me well for it allowed me to proceed with my studies, the beauty of physics and Mickiewicz's poetry providing some antidote to the swastikas fluttering over the city barracks.

V

Thick clouds of dust hung over the highways, marking the German armies' route eastward. When the spring of 1941 came and they overran the Balkans, we thought this deployment had some connection with the fighting in the South. But the battle there ended as quickly as the Polish and French campaigns, and their troops continued to pour in. It was impossible to sleep nights. The roar of engines filled the town, flashlights flickered, soldiers knocked on locked doors asking for directions to the east. *East – why, when the Russian border was only ten miles away?* All through those warm nights the military convoys rode on and on, their dimmed crimson headlights like the eyes of blinded animals.

Tyska left Losice with his troop and I lost my job in the laundry. Just then two hundred men were requested for work at the railroad in Siedlce, and I was immediately reassigned. To continue with my studies I had to rise at five to give myself a couple of free hours. At seven two trailer trucks arrived in the square and I would join the other workers in front of the Judenrat office. There a few Schupo men and the *Arbeitsamt* chief, a small bespectacled German who ran the labor office in Losice, waited for us to be counted; then we had to run for the trucks in order to avoid the whips and kicks that were an inseparable part of the ritual. The highway we traveled on was new, built by two hundred Jews from the Warsaw ghetto who, in two months, had been worked to death; near the town of Mordy, halfway to Siedlce, were the empty shacks where they had lived. The trucks moved on, passing small groups of emaciated, half-naked workers from another camp. The Germans from the cab threw empty cans at them or cracked whips over their heads. The Jews did not even bother to dodge and continued their slow walk, dragging their shovels along the dusty road.

When the trucks had halted and we lined up at the edge of the loading ramp, we had before us the huge railway hub of Siedlce. It buzzed like a metal beehive. Freight cars filled with troops and guns shuttled back and forth, convoys of trucks loaded ammunition at the depots, and heavy Junkers circled overhead as they made their approach to the nearby airfield. A row of Luftwaffe men in silver grey uniforms appeared, hats nonchalantly askew, silken kerchiefs around their necks. They looked us over; then, voices synchronized, they yelled a short, shrill *Los!* On the tracks were long flatcars stacked with thousands of telephone poles. Someone snapped the chains, and they cascaded onto the ramps – long, heavy logs coated with tar. We had to load up, two men to a pole, rush to the warehouse with the load, then rush back to the ramp. Down we bent, hoisted a pole to our shoulders, staggered about three hundred feet beneath this burden, stacked it, and then rushed back for another pole. Within an hour the body started to rebel. The poles grew heavier, our shoulders and arms stiffer; on our necks, where the tarred posts rubbed against the skin, bleeding sores appeared. Our steps faltered. As we sagged they ordered us to run with the load. Then we began a sort of exotic dance, jumping into the air, down, up again. One after another fell under the weight; the poles rolled over our legs and heads, and the Germans swung their clubs in a rising frenzy. In the evening we crawled back onto the truck on our hands and knees and lay on its floor without stirring, clutching our lunches which we had not had the strength or the desire to eat.

Breaking the monotony of the "matches," as we dubbed the poles, there were carloads of cable to unload – huge steel rolls weighing one hundred sixty pounds apiece. We didn't quite know how to handle these spools. At first we wore them over our necks like yokes. When the neck swelled, the spool was shifted to the back, propped against the left side, the right side, the stomach. Or it was cradled in the arms like a baby. But no matter how we carried it, it always weighed the same one hundred sixty pounds. The heat thickened, our lacerated necks bled – and all around us Germans, Germans. Drinking cold lemonade they sat in the shade and, like mad dogs, kept yelling a slangy *Hol up.... Hol up.... Los, los, los!* Very often soldiers from the passing trains would gather around us. They always found the sight hilarious. When one of us fell under the load, they burst out in roaring laughter, these innocent boys from Westphalia, Saxony, and the mild Rhineland. Once a general showed up, a neat rotund German with a white, professorial goatee. The Luftwaffe went berserk with zeal. They slugged us with such fury they soon exhausted themselves. Many workers lay unconscious on the ramp; all of us were bleeding. The distinguished guest walked calmly through it all, the faint smile on his scholarly goatee intimating, "Yes, I can see you are hurting, but that is precisely what was intended."

While we toiled on the depots and on the highways, the German army poured steadily in. Men who had lived through several wars could not recall an army so exquisite – in its flair, its precision, its spirit. Eastward! Eastward! And yet, for the first time since the fall of France, hope stirred in us. True, the thought of the Germans invading Russia brought pain and apprehension: we had friends and relatives on the other side of the Bug, and many of us felt a bond with the Russian people, their language, their literature, their character. Still, selfishly, and desperately, and cruelly, we wanted this war. England's clean and gentlemanly war was not our war; we could not afford it. In the East, we foresaw, Germany would reduce the fight to such beastly simplicity that there would be no room for the kind of military games played in Libya. Although we saw and were overwhelmed by the Germans' military might, we were confident that they would get stuck in Russia. And then, out of the steppes and villages, would come no *Herrenvolk,* no goose-stepping robots, but peasants fighting for their land and home; and we knew the Russians would win.

The German army trooped on, covering all highways and country roads. A wall of dust hung over the landscape for days. Since all available quarters were crammed with soldiers, the new divisions camped in the open; under the trees the muzzles of guns gazed hungrily into the bright sunshine. A neighbor, returning from work in Niemojki one day, told us he had seen the soldiers being given German-Russian dictionaries. Outside the town, anti-aircraft guns were emplaced and the infantry dug trenches in the field. All vehicles were equipped with the wooden meshes the Germans used to build their corduroy roads across swamps. Sleeves rolled up, their blond hair blowing in the wind, singing and playing flutes and piccolos, infantry divisions headed day and night for the Bug. We recalled Mickiewicz's epic about Napoleon's invasion of Russia, and even though the roles were now reversed – then the hope was that Napoleon would win, now that Hitler would lose – the poet's lines were still as palpable and pregnant with hope in 1941 as they had been in 1812.

Work in Siedlce came to an end. We were immediately transferred to Platerow, a station near the railroad bridge over the Bug, where the Germans were building tracks for rail artillery. Hundreds of Jews toiled there like ancient slaves for fourteen hours a day. Two boys died from beatings; another, pushed under a railroad car, lost both legs. After ten days the job was completed, and the monstrous gun was pulled into position.

On Friday, a sunny and cool day, we saw tanks roll through the town for the first time. That evening the flood of marching armies peaked. Field gendarmerie standing in their command cars flagged the columns on – faster, faster. The next day, all resident troops left town; only military police in steel helmets patrolled the half empty streets. Then, from some mysterious source, news came that it would start tomorrow. Sunday, the inhabitants started to leave town and disperse into the villages and farms. I resisted my family's wish that we move to Jozefowa's farm, where we had stayed during the Polish campaign, and we all remained in town.

An immense quiet settled about us. The barracks and the blocks where the soldiers had stayed all winter were empty. In the open windows abandoned laundry still dried in the sun. Only puddles of oil remained where the thousands of cars and trucks had parked for nearly a year. The afternoon lingered in a vast, disturbing silence, its gloom intensified by a sunset that splashed the sky with morose, purple shadows. Here and there one could hear the slamming of a door, the cry of a child. Just before dark, a single reconnaissance plane flew low over the town and vanished over the Bug. Then night fell, the night of June 21, 1941.

It was 3:15 in the morning, just at the break of dawn, when a blast of guns tore us from our sleep. We stumbled out of our beds and, dressing on our way, fled town. The earth shook under our feet, and in Polinov the ponds were red with the glare of the fires to the east. Infantry, bayonets mounted, lined the edges of the grove, watching us with sharp, nervous eyes from beneath their strapped-down helmets. Soon our ears caught a taut, vibrant flutter that overwhelmed the roar of artillery. We looked up; filling the entire sky, an armada of airplanes headed for Russia. Much lower, other planes were towing gliders which they would drop behind

Russian lines. Now and then a sudden flash lit up the debris of an exploding bomber.

Being so near the front we expected a prompt reaction from the Russians, and as soon as we reached a farm we started to dig a trench in the field with tools lent by the farmer. The dugout was only half finished when I heard the anti-aircraft guns in Polinov open fire. Through the crack of firing I caught the drone of oncoming planes; they were coming from the east. Before we had time to understand that these were Soviet planes, the sky turned over and toppled on us with a shrill, deafening crash. Losice disappeared in fire and smoke. We flattened ourselves in the wheat fields, our hearts pounding with fear and rejoicing: This seemed the beginning of the expected Russian counterattack. We lay in the field and waited. But nothing more happened. The cannonade weakened, the fires in Losice subsided. Even the front calmed down. In the deepening calm one could hear the crickets again. "Tsik-trrrr... tsik-trrrr..." came their haunting song.

On Wednesday, three days after the Germans crossed the Bug, we thought the expected Russian counterattack had finally materialized. At noon a sudden barrage of artillery erupted in the east, subduing all other life around us. The sun disappeared, and it got as dark as during a full eclipse. Planes took off from the nearby airfield in rapid waves and vanished immediately in the smoking wall. On the highway, ambulances raced in herds, and runners on motorcycles shot through the smoke with lightning speed. From time to time, huge fireballs shot skyward from behind the forest and leveled into rolling, crimson trains. All night we sat awake listening, watching, hoping.

After two days it was all over. Friday afternoon fresh columns of trucks and infantry appeared on all country roads – German reserves were moving up. The fighting we had witnessed was the battle for the border fortress of Brest, which the Germans had originally bypassed and now subdued. It was clear that the Germans were pushing ahead. The front was already far away and the country was returning to normal – German normality.

On Saturday I went to see Mottel, who was staying with his mother on a nearby farm. I encountered German troops on the Miedzyrzec highway. When I passed the first soldiers, they noticed the Jewish band on my arm. "Take your hat off!" they yelled. I took my hat off and stared at them.

"What's the matter?" they sneered.

"You are great soldiers," I said.

"Oh yes," they shouted in unison, "in two weeks we will be in Moscow."

I met Mottel, and he showed me the first German newspapers about the fighting in Russia. Unlike the laconic official bulletins, the pages were loaded with literary descriptions of the new campaign. Long columns of POW's, scorched villages, gutted cities, executed commissars – the crisp taste of a new orgy. We had prayed so long for this to happen; it had happened, and now what? Mottel said that it was too early to tell, that we had to wait, that the Russians would surely counterattack, and so on. But it was not too early to tell, and we could not afford to wait. If the knockout of France within a couple of weeks was the most traumatic event of the war, for us the rout of the Russian armies at the Bug was a close second. Here there had been no concealment, no surprise in the invasion; any child in Losice had known not only the day but the hour when it would start; the German soldiers had told us on the Saturday they left town for the Bug. Yet, aside from the three suicide bombers that blundered over the Bug – and all three had been shot down within minutes of crossing the border – there had been no response from the other side. Not a single artillery shell. No shred of evidence that, across the Bug, millions of Russian soldiers stood awaiting the onslaught. At dawn the Germans assassinated the sentries on the Bug bridges, crossed the river, and rolled at full speed toward Lvov, and Minsk, and Kaunas, with the Russians fleeing in complete panic, as if some malevolent Nazi God had gouged sight and sanity out of anyone the Germans had decided to cannibalize. Subsequently, newspapers reporting the Russian disaster were to confirm everything in multifold fashion – but we had already sensed it in the very first hours of that Sunday morning. And with it went the last of our hopes.

vi

When, after a week's stay on the farm, I returned home, I found a notice to report for work in the Siedlce sandpits. The Führer of the sandpits was a middle-aged German who, in contrast to most of them, at least did not look normal. He welcomed us the first day by walking along the line of men and stepping on our bare or rag-covered feet with his heavy boot. He counted the group, several hundred assorted wretches, by tapping our heads with a black, shiny leather knout. Then he led us down the embankment. The railroad station disappeared, the heaving of the trains faded, and of Siedlce only the red towers of its many churches remained. Soon we reached a vast, empty sandbowl. The only things seen in this desert were two stationary red railroad cars and a short stretch of track. Other than that we saw only sand and sand.

Our work on the first day consisted of moving the makeshift tracks closer to the steep sand cliffs so that the loading could be done more efficiently. On the commanding shout, *ooo-rook*, all of us, armed with long crowbars, strained and tensed to move the tracks, inch by inch, closer to the high banks. In the sticky heat we steamed and sweated like exhausted cattle. After the tracks had been shifted the real work began. An engine shuttled in a long line of flatcars and the digging got under way. When the cars were full, the locomotive came and took them away. Another locomotive then brought more cars and the digging resumed. Eventually two tracks were laid so that work could continue without interruption. They stopped giving us time for lunch, and we ate our lumps of bread while crossing from one track to the other. When, for some blessed reason, no new cars arrived, we were supposed to let down the sand. This meant forming on the sandbanks large protruding capes which would then collapse and roll down toward the tracks. The heat and glare were intense and in the rare breaks we got it was a sensual pleasure to lie down somewhere in a shady cave and stare into the blue of the sky until all sensation of reality was gone.

We walked to work in the early dawn when everything along the road still slept, even the birds. As the locomotive came to pick us up at seven, we had to be up at five to cover the four miles to Niemojki. When fall came and the days shortened, we started when it was still dark. The workers emerged each day from their shacks and cellars with sacks thrown over their shoulders, their pants and wooden clogs held up with pieces of string. Like perambulating scarecrows they streamed toward the railroad station, feet shuffling, naked limbs peering through the tattered clothes. When passing farms, they dug potatoes from the fields, stole a few beets, picked apples which they ate in haste or hid in sacks to carry back to their starving families. In the boxcars that monotonously bore us to work, they stretched on the floor, famished, half asleep, and utterly silent, the two years of slavery having cleansed them even of the custom of groaning.

On the desert of the Siedlce sandpits we huddled together like a leper colony, mute, remote, rid of all hope or expectation. The world had its beginning and end in this wasteland. Occasionally we would spot a lizard staring at us with mourning eyes. Now and then, larks chirped under a sky that seemed to turn yellow with the glare of the sand. We listened and searched for them in the sulphurous glare of the sun and frequently took a beating when, instead of digging, digging, digging, we waved to them in our loneliness and abandonment. They would fly away when the crack of whips and the screams rang out in the desert. Then all we could hear was the gloomy tooting of trains. And when this too died out, there remained only the silence of the sandpits and the noise of a grain of sand rolling down the steep banks.

As night fell we lay on the wet grass near the tracks waiting for the locomotive to take us home. Shivering in the cold we would watch the German searchlights ride the blacked out roofs of Siedlce, and when they expired we were left in a double darkness, a reinforced night. It was ten, eleven, and sometimes midnight before the locomotive with its drunken driver showed up. We crouched on the floor of the rocking boxcar, watching through the tiny window the flying sparks and the pale stars, to our tired eyes indistinguishable one from the other. It was only by instinct that we piled out of the train when it reached Niemojki. Then we trudged four miles in the darkness, reaching home a bare few hours before getting up for a new day of toil.

Yet, bleak as was our slavery in the sandpits of Siedlce, I was glad to be away from town, for it was sinking fast into unspeakable misery. Deprived of all source of income the people of Losice starved en masse. The houses left empty after the Germans embarked on their excursion to Russia were not returned to us. In the overcrowded slums, epidemics began to spread. Typhus flourished as in a hatchery, crossing from house to house and alley to alley. In accordance with the Germans' deliberate scheme, our life was seeded with miseries only professional torturers could invent. It was a monument to their industry that they were able to think about us in such detail while involved in a global war. Instinctively, we sought a rational explanation for every new disaster, trying to justify what they were doing to us. We searched for proof that our misery was of some benefit to them, that they were not doing it merely for fun. Events crushed our illusions time after time. We looked for a proper way of reacting, but whatever we did was wrong. Submission was not sufficient; loyalty was not even asked for; resistance was a farce. And so our story evolved at an accelerating pace. The ghettos of Lodz and Warsaw, packed with one million Jews, were being starved out, and the dead were systematically replaced with Jews from neighboring towns. In Ostland, after the invasion of Russia, the Germans took out tens of thousands of young Jews who were never heard of again. We heard a strange hammering in the night. Something terrible was being prepared for us, but we were prisoners, forbidden to travel, to communicate, to talk; our hands were tied, our vision barred. Like dumb animals we spun our ears in panic and darkness trying to guess what it meant. We did not know and no one would tell us.

As October rolled in – and with it the first long persistent rainfalls – the Germans who had been stuck in Russia for some time made a last desperate attempt to defeat the Soviet Union. At the beginning of the month, a proclamation from Hitler to the

Army and the Nation announced that "gigantic operations designed to annihilate the remnants of the Soviet Army" were under way. Then followed his chilling promise that "the enemy will be defeated before the onset of winter." The following day the papers related that the Wehrmacht had launched a decisive attack, that the center of the front was unhinged and two Soviet army groups were surrounded near Briansk. The next bulletins told of three hundred thousand prisoners, of Guderian's Panzer divisions rolling into the flanks of the capital. Kalinin and Kaluga fell and the Germans were at the gates of Moscow. The Soviet government fled to Kuibyshev. The papers heralded the impending end of the Eastern campaign.

In these foreboding days I left for work in the early dark, torn by the sickening fear that, when I returned home, everything would be over. An early autumn had set in and the mornings were quite cold now. The dunes turned soggy and gray, making the desert more depressing than ever. After the nightly drizzle the sand clung to the feet and water collected in the caves. We worked all day in the wind and the rain and then lay in cold puddles along the tracks waiting for the locomotive to take us home. We never saw Losice in daylight; we left in the dark and returned after midnight. Yet we were at a point where all this did not matter; we forgot our agony, forgot the peril facing us. Starved and beaten we lay in the mud, the wind ate at our half-naked bodies and the rain slashed our faces like whips, but we did not feel a thing for, in the East, the end of the Third Reich had begun.

Winter came and the German failure was clear. First a crushing silence froze the German press. Then came the news that the "remnants" of the Soviet Army, under the command of a "remaining" general named Zhukov, had launched a counterattack. The Germans evacuated a post, a village, a town, a line. Finally, the OKW officially announced that, due to the early winter and certain other difficulties, it had been decided to withdraw the German spearheads which were conquering Russia, and that the *Grossdeutsche Wehrmacht* had settled down to defensive warfare.

In the German press the silence deepened. Neither the Führer nor any of his henchmen had anything to say. What about the October announcement that only remnants of the Soviet Army were left? That the enemy would be beaten before the onset of winter, or was already beaten? How much can a Führer bamboozle? And how gullible can the most gullible be? How about the soldiers at the front? In each trench was posted the Führer's promise of an end before Christmas. What were the Germans waiting for now?

Perhaps some such thoughts occurred to the Führer. So one day he stepped up before his beloved *Volk*. And while Germany's young men were perishing in the snows of Russia, he brought his people a speech. He could not talk politics, for the Sudetenland was now German and Chamberlain was dead. He could not talk about the war, for there were no more blitzes. But he did talk about the genius of the Party, about his mission in Germany and Germany's in the world; and, most important, about the lousy Jews. First he repeated his old theory of the bonds between communism and capitalism. The identity of the two ideologies stemmed simply from the fact that, in both systems, the rulers were Jews bent upon world conquest. Churchill, Roosevelt, Smuts, and Stalin were mere puppets dancing to the tune of our Chassidic pipes, and we Jews – the professors in Germany, the shoemakers in Poland, the grocers in America, the kibutzniks in Palestine, all of us – had decided to conquer the world, and for that reason we had started the war. And here he delivered his apocalyptic words, "I prophesy that, in this war, it is not the Aryan mankind that will be destroyed but the

Jew himself who will be exterminated [ausrottet]. Whatever the struggle may bring, and however long it may last, this will be its final result. And only then, after elimination of these parasites, will a long era of international understanding and, with it, true peace, come to a suffering world." He spoke these words, but no one grasped their meaning; no wise man rose to listen; no leader rang the alarm.

Strange news began to reach us. The rumors, neither certain nor clear, were always incomplete. No one admitted that it originated with him; there was never a live witness. There was, however, one disquieting point: if these were mere rumors, they were bound to cease. Instead, they spread and multiplied with sickening persistence. We heard stories of mass slaughter, of caves filled with children into which the Germans threw grenade bundles, of trenches filled to the brim with old men, of whole cities wiped out, of entire age groups assigned to death. Poles who had travelled across the Bug repeated that "something" was going on there with the Jews. Soldiers returning from the front told us stories that made our bones shrink. We knew the Germans: a million Jews starving in the ghettos of Lodz and Warsaw; the slaughter of masses of Russian prisoners of war; murder and terror practiced for no profit at all. But even with all this, something new was descending on us. Not until Herschek returned from across the Bug half a year later did I learn what it was.

vii

At the beginning of the third winter of the war we were locked in a ghetto. Established on December 1, 1941, it was ringed with barbed wire; at its corners stood signposts: *Jüdische Woh-*

nungsbezirk. All administrative matters were handled by the Judenrat, which now ran also such essential institutions as a post office, sanitation, taxes. Internal order was maintained by the Jewish police, who were outfitted with ridiculous blue hats and truncheons. All signs had to be in both German and Yiddish, and we had to wear the arm bands, although they no longer served any identifying purpose. Laborers whose work took them beyond the confines of the wire had to carry special permits.

All the Jews of Losice — about eighty per cent of that town's prewar population — plus all of the refugees, were now squeezed into one third the town's area. Ghetto streets were so clogged that one had to push one's way through the teeming crowds. At the beginning the Jewish reaction to the ghetto was curious. Living in a purely Jewish community generated a deceptive feeling of strength, an illusion of safety. We thought we had been given *Lebensraum.* The ghetto seemed to be the last blow, a retreat where we could live or die undisturbed. It was a pathological variant of sovereignty. We realized food and space would be scarce but we failed to grasp what the Germans intended: we were sure we would at least be able to talk with a Pole near the ghetto limits, or buy a newspaper from the other side of the wire. We understood that we were not to stroll leisurely outside the ghetto boundaries, but we did not think that one or two inches beyond the yellow signposts would make much difference. Calmly we prepared for winter.

One of the orders accompanying the establishment of the ghetto was to hand over all fur garments; the punishment for non-compliance was death. We were not going to be very warm that winter, and that bit of Teutonic thoroughness in asking us for our rags that might help us endure did not bring the Germans any furs. Instead of handing them over, we preferred to burn them.

Warming ourselves over their cinders, we enjoyed a rare hour of comfort in our cold, icebound homes.

If we started off with illusions about the ghetto, the Germans soon straightened us out. On a certain Friday, while buying a paper from a newsstand just across the wires, I was told that six people were arrested for fetching water from a well in the Polish section. We did not make much of the incident, for the people were caught not deep in the Polish neighborhood but just across the boundaries. In their zeal to keep the size of the ghetto to a minimum, the Germans had neglected to include a single well in it, and we thought they would have to recognize our need of water. The next day with dawn barely breaking through the ice covered windows, we overheard a faint wailing. A full-scale blizzard was raging outside, and it was uncanny to hear that quiet sobbing through the roar of the storm. Later, through a thawed peephole in the windowpane, we saw a group of lost, frostbitten children and women huddle like a heap of rags at the corner of the snowbound ghetto. We did not have to inquire why they were out there, or whom they were mourning. The six people were dead. They had been taken out and shot at midnight at the edge of the frozen river.

After these first executions, we realized we were locked in a jail without food or fuel; from now on, time would do its slow and inevitable work. Hunger became the greatest killer. The thousands of dispossessed refugees dumped, half-frozen and penniless, in our midst during the first winter of the war now made up the ghetto's two lowest social classes: the dying and the starving. The dying simply lay in their bunks or on the floors, expiring in a silent motionless battle. It took them miserably long to succumb, as if in their last moments they rose to a sudden defiant glory. The starving, removed from the dying by only a brief breath of time, swarmed the town like locusts. They stood in the middle of the streets, rocking back and forth as if trying to lull hunger to sleep; they knelt on staircases, vomiting a green sickening wash; they leaned against the walls, surprised at their own tenacity. On and on they came, begging for food. They never tired; when refused, they knocked with bony fists against locked doors, tore at the windows, clawed and cursed and threatened. Obstinately they lingered, believing that something must eventually happen, that it was inconceivable they could be hungry, continue to be hungry, and die hungry. At times this collective starvation became an explosive charge that threatened to annihilate the ghetto, the barbed wire, the entire town. But nothing of the sort happened. The starving joined the dying, and in so doing yielded their places to those next in rank.

The old residents of Losice tried to hang on by selling their furniture, their clothes, their utensils, and every tile, hook, and nail they possessed. They sold to the peasants for whom the war had brought little change. As before the war, they just subsisted; now, however, subsistence was all. The intermediaries in this trade were suicidal people who preferred a bullet in the head to starvation. Despite the death penalty, they went out at night into the villages, bartering, begging, stealing, picking up food when and where they could. At the beginning, those who were caught were killed on the spot. Later, in some new sadistic refinement, they were brought back to town and jailed for a couple of days until they became delirious. For some reason most of them were young girls. Sitting in our cold, dank homes, we were forced to listen to their howling. Those of us who had food were unable to eat; those who had a fire could only sit and shiver. Usually at dusk, we would see a pair of beefy, red-necked Germans walk down to the jail; half an hour later two or three shots would ring in the frozen deadly stillness. That same night others would leave the ghetto in search of food....

The children spent the winter in bed, and as they lay there, they chirped and smiled. The men and women, with shoes of wood and clothes made from bedspreads, chair stuffing, and paper bags, walked the streets in a Mephistophelean dance, hating to touch the earth, galled and sulphurous with suffering. We never reported our dead so as not to forfeit their ration of three ounces of bread. These dead emerged regularly from silent winter nights, greeting us each morning with their stiff limbs and swollen bellies, forecasting a fate none of us would escape. They lay a long time; even in the cold they stank before they were removed. When finally collected, they received a new outfit – a brown paper bag. Our cemetery was beyond the ghetto, so we could not bury them ourselves. We could only carry them as far as the wires, where the town janitor threw them on a cart and carried them off without tears or candles.

Deep in the pit of agony as we lay, we still had occasion to witness the horror inflicted on the Russian POW's left over from the previous summer's mass exterminations. Among many executions that winter, the symbolic death of one young Russian soldier stands out. It had been a particularly blistery, frostbitten day. The evening before, we learned that the Germans had caught an escaped prisoner. With daylight, a cavalcade of three men moved across the frozen town. The Russian walked in front. Clad in nothing but a thin shirt open on the chest, he was barefoot, and his feet skimmed the ice as if he tried to walk on air. The temperature must have been minus forty degrees. As he walked, the man kept turning his head to stare at the ice-covered locked windows of the strange town. Behind him walked the town janitor with a spade over his shoulder. And behind the janitor, in a fur-lined coat and carrying a rifle under his arm, walked Leopold Puradt, a Schupo man familiar to us from a number of other executions. For some strange reason the prisoner was not killed at night near the jail as was customary; instead he was being paraded the length of the town in bright daylight. They had traversed the square and strode down Biala street. After a desolate, silent five or six minutes, two shots rang out over the polar landscape like metal whips. The name Puradt remains in my mind because, of all of Losice's Germans, he was the only one to stand trial after the war in a West German court. I was a witness at that trial and, among others, testified to the killing of the Russian prisoner. Puradt was acquitted.

viii

The devastation caused by cold, hunger, and epidemics reached its peak at the end of winter. Every day there were four or five deaths. Practically every family had its typhus cases. When the two Jewish doctors fell ill simultaneously, the ghetto was without a physician. Many people died after they recovered from the disease because they lacked food. The toll was about six hundred dead, almost ten per cent of the population. Sarnaki, Siedlce, and Miedzyrzec reported deaths of fifteen per cent.

In the midst of this catastrophe a new hope flashed. The Germans, we heard, had decided to employ all Jewish craftsmen and skilled workers. The *Gazeta Zydowska*, our official newspaper, published reports about the establishment of extensive shops and factories in which, it was said, the workers lived and worked in humane conditions. Speeches of the German *Kreishauptmanns* plastered the walls: we were guaranteed life and food if we remained loyal and obeyed orders. These events augured more than a mere improvement in our economic situation; they represented a fundamental change in our political status, an end to the deliberate starvation to which the Germans had exposed us.

Orders arrived for all furriers to report to work – my sister Manya's husband among them. Despite the prevailing optimism, my sister paled when the draft notice arrived, but she calmed down when Ignatz was granted permission to travel in a manner and at a time of his own choosing – things unheard of ever since the ghetto had been established. He was asked to bring his sewing machine if he had one, so we all thought he would stay in Warsaw, where most of the shops were allegedly located.

A week later it was the turn of the tailors; taking with them the tools of their trade, they departed in the same confident spirit as the furriers. When, with spring, rumors circulated that all unskilled men would be taken to labor camps, the craftsmen became even more enthusiastic over their future shops. Many others sought to learn a trade and tried to volunteer for work. We, meanwhile, waited for a letter from Ignatz.

The letter took a long time coming, and when it finally came it was neither from Warsaw nor from Ignatz. It was from Lublin, and from a stranger:

> We feel obliged to tell you that the entire transport of skilled workers, including your relative, landed in a concentration camp. We are writing this to you because among the arrivals from Losice there is also a relative of ours, a friend of Ignatz. Our relative asked us to inform you about the situation. All we can say is that you should try to get him out of there....

A few days later, we received a letter from Ignatz himself. Smuggled out of the camp, it was so scratchy we could hardly decipher it, yet the message was clear: a cry of terror and a call for help. We decided to send a man to Lublin, where the camp was situated, to see what could be done. We chose the father of Ignatz's friend, the one with the relative in Lublin. We waited four days for the Judenrat to obtain his travel permit, then a few days more for his return. A bribe of four thousand zlotys, he said, would release a man from that camp. As soon as they secured the freedom of his son, his Lublin relatives would get Ignatz out.

Ignatz's friend was back in Losice in about two weeks. We sold everything of value, including Manya's wedding ring, and sent the money to Lublin. And we waited.

Days passed. We watched the sleds arrive from the railway station, each time expecting to see Ignatz. Some delay was understandable. Such arrangements took time, we told ourselves. Perhaps Ignatz stopped in Lublin for a few days. Then a whole week passed, and still Ignatz did not arrive; and no letter, either from Ignatz or from those who were arranging for his release. The post office assured us the money had arrived at the proper address. We wrote letters every day, sent telegrams, utilized every avenue of contacts. No answer. The camp, Ignatz, all of Lublin, were mute as stones.

After weeks of this, we became certain something had gone wrong, and our uneasiness turned to anxiety. Manya gave us no peace: we could not sleep; Ignatz filled our entire lives. Again we sent an envoy to Lublin, another friend of Ignatz, a certain Noyman. He undertook the trip, carrying with him our admonition not to return without Ignatz. But on a dull and chilly day we sighted Noyman returning from the railway station, alone. Ignatz was no longer in Lublin. Lublin was empty of Jews.

Manya collapsed on the couch with a single terrifying shriek. Noyman tried to assure us there was no reason for despair. Most of the Jews from Lublin had simply been resettled, he explained. And Ignatz had been shipped with them. It was true, he added, that the Germans had killed six hundred while administering the deportation, but Noyman was certain that Ignatz was not among the dead. Wherever Lublin was, there Ignatz would be found.

That started our terrible and heartbreaking search for the deported. A letter from Warsaw mentioned the presence of Jews from Lublin. We immediately alerted our Warsaw relatives to look for Ignatz. They answered that, except for a handful of escapees, no Lubliners were in the ghetto. One wrote that they had been resettled in Kishynev, Rumania. When Kishynev proved false, it became Andrzejow, then some village in Belgium, another in Czechoslovakia, another in Galicia. In each we drew a blank until, finally, we came full circle: someone inquired of our Judenrat whether there were any Lublin Jews in Losice.

One day we received a post card that made us shout with happiness. Manya's friend from Piaski, answering one of our inquiries, wrote: "Shortly we too will be moved where Ignatz is." We wondered why she did not mention the place by name. We wrote again for precise information, but there was no response to this second letter. The Jews of Piaski, too, had been deported.

One day the *Warschauer Zeitung* wrote an article about the Lublin Jews, telling its readers that all had been moved to Majdanek Tatarski. But we knew for certain that in this suburban community there were only about thirteen thousand Jews, whereas the number of people taken out of Lublin was over fifty thousand. Why did the paper write that all the people were in Majdanek Tatarski? Where were the other forty thousand?

ix

One April day I sat with the Mordkowicz brothers. Zalus had been taken to a labor camp in Siedlce some time before and the old smoke-and-song-filled atmosphere of the room was gone. While Boris read a book, Shmulek practiced maniacally on his mountain flute. I asked him to stop the irritating wailing, but he only glared at me with his haughty eyes, not even bothering to answer. I got up and left.

In our room I unexpectedly found Herschek's father staring blankly out the window. He was quietly sobbing.

"Ignatz?" I called, muffling the word so that Manya would not hear me in the kitchen. He shook his head, stammering:

"Herschek is back."

A thousand wild questions flooded my brain, but I asked none. I rushed down the stairs and ran toward Herschek's house. There it stood with its crooked roof and squeaking gate unchanged; I had not been there since Herschek left. His mother and sisters were all in tears, and this should have given me some hint of what to expect, but I did not stop, did not look. They indicated to me that he was in the bedroom and I slipped inside.

He rose uncertainly, reluctantly, against the early dusk, and what I saw was the face of an old man with transported misty eyes. Then his hand grasped mine, and in the strength and warmth of this hand I recognized Herschek. We fell into each other's arms.

Releasing his grip, Herschek stepped back and stood for a moment, taut against the window; then, to avoid my shocked look, he turned away.

"Are you ill?" I asked.

Briefly he turned towards me and smiled, then relapsed into himself and his silence.

"What happened?" I persisted.

Looking at me with eyes that bore no resemblance to the eyes of Herschek, he whispered: "I came to say good-bye."

Under our feet a cat was playing with the table legs. Herschek picked him up and threw him into the other room, then returned to his former position, head down, hands on the table. Outside, rain fell. As he spoke, shadows deepened and eventually engulfed him, leaving only his voice, the irreversible timeless voice of death:

It was raining just like this when I took off across the Bug two and a half years ago. I was back in Bialystok, back in school.

At graduation I was the happiest man on earth I had been accepted by the medical school in Moscow; I even counted on getting there on the 'old goat.' On the last Saturday there was a graduation ball. We danced, we drank. There were Russians, Jews, Kalmuks.... I don't know how long it lasted, or when it ended; I only remember finding myself alone in the city park. I swear I talked to the stars. I was so drunk and happy.

But the next day was Sunday, June 22.

Escape the Germans! That was the one and only thought, and I hit the road. Everywhere masses of people were in flight eastward, and so was the Soviet Army. German planes sprayed us with bombs and bullets, just as in September. There was not a single Soviet plane in the air. The whole Bialystok-Minsk highway was choked with massacred civilians and routed armies.

I was on a truck with Russian soldiers when, at some village, a peasant told us the Germans were already ahead of us. Many Soviet troops were sliding into the woods to form guerrilla units. I begged our soldiers to join them, but they decided to break through. We were still driving on when a farmer motioned us wildly to turn back. The truck went on, but I jumped off. A minute later a blast from several machine guns wiped them all out before they even had time to see the Germans.

With two other Jews I stayed in the farmer's barn until the Germans arrived. When I first saw them through the walls of the barn, the world collapsed before my eyes. Since my companions looked like Jews, I separated from them and went on alone trying to get to Slonim, where my sister Matla lived. The first patrol I encountered asked me if I was a Jew; nearby lay a pile of about fifty corpses. I said no, and they let me go. Two weeks after the outbreak of war, instead of the medical school in Moscow, I ended up with my sister in Slonim.

About two weeks after my arrival in Slonim, the city filled with Schupo. They were rounding up young men, so everybody thought it was for work. Even so, I suggested to my brother-in-law that we hide, but he was afraid. The Germans came and led us to the square, where they had collected all the others. Huge trailer trucks arrived and the loading began. The packed trucks drove off, but only to return in about fifteen minutes, ready for a new load. I began to move back, trying to be the last possible man to mount the truck. The gendarmes looked at us with strange cold eyes, and on their lips floated sneers that made me shiver. Back and forth, back and forth shuttled the trucks. My brother-in-law was gone, and only a handful of us were left. The gendarmes counted the last groups; then, by some miracle, they told the rest to scatter away.

From Slonim they took about a thousand young men. Ii was the same in all neighboring cities. Where the men were taken, nobody knew.

Months passed. The front shifted way beyond Smolensk, and a civilian administration took over the country. To escape a labor camp, I worked at the Wehrmacht as a carpenter.

About that time the Germans, with their Lithuanian auxiliaries, began to go off on mysterious expeditions into the country, taking with them trucks and plenty of ammunition and vanishing for whole days. At first we did not pay any attention to it because they often went out against Soviet partisans, but after a while these expeditions began to intrigue me. Against partisans the soldiers went grudgingly; here they departed in jolly spirits, singing and joking. Besides, from partisan skirmishes they returned the same day; here they would be away several days, and they never brought back any prisoners for the customary hangings. I asked the soldiers where they were going, but the answer was always the same: partisans. I could perhaps have learned something from the less disciplined and illiterate Lithuanians, but soon after the start of these expeditions they were isolated from us. Once, after an unusually long trip, we noticed blood on the trucks. We stood there and watched with frozen eyes until the Germans landed on us with yells and kicks, ordering us to wash the blood off quickly. I told Matla about it, but after her husband's disappearance nothing interested her any more. That night I forgot all my personal problems, the university, medicine.

Close by there lived a respected Slonim family. I knew the daughter and was a frequent visitor in her house. The father, an official translator for the Germans, was on very good terms with the Oberleutnant of the local Schupo. I was there one evening when this officer showed up. He stood outside vainly trying to find the door. When we opened it for him, he plunged inside, barely managing to stay on his feet. He was dead drunk. With closed eyes and a swollen red face, he began to circle the room. After a while, however, he stopped, opened his bloodshot eyes slightly and, milling violently with his arms, began to snort.

Moses, he roared, nimm dein Gold, dein Frau, deine Kinder, und Moses, Moses, ich sage dir, lauf in den Wald.... Lauf Moses... laaaauuuf!

At first we felt like laughing, but we soon stopped, chilled by the tone of his voice. And he continued to yell hoarsely: Nimm deine Frau, dein Kinder and lauf.... Lauft!

He opened his eyes wider and, realizing where he was, shook his arm angrily and headed for the door. From far away, we could still hear his warning cry: Lauf in den Wald.... Lauf, Moses, lauf!

It was the night of November 12, a quiet winter night.

When I came to work next day, the soldiers told us to go home. Bewildered, we stood and looked at them. All troops were out of the barracks, the trucks were warming up, the soldiers carried ammunition and hand grenades; it looked as if they were going away on another expedition. When, astonished by the order to go home, we did not move, the soldiers began to yell, Heute gibt es keine Arbeit.... Los.... Nach Hause! *Some soldiers laughed at us, others shook their heads, but most just looked at us through cold, half-closed eyes. When, despite the yells and the threats, we still remained in place wondering what had happened, the Germans dispersed us with kicks and rifle butts.*

I walked slowly home, where I found Matla. She, too, had been told to go home.

Then, as we stood talking about what might have happened, the troops were let loose upon the city.

Dragging Matla with me, I ran out of the house. I did not know where to run, but I knew we must get out of the city; we headed for the woods. Suddenly a gun fired, then another and another. Still we ran over the open fields, but the firing drove us back into the city. There we heard the roaring trucks and the crack of gunfire. We hid in a loft. Trembling women and crying children were lumped in all corners. We were soon in a panic again and crawled down. There was a latrine in the yard, and Malta and I and another girl got inside. But it was a cold day; our ears and our fingers were freezing. We tore the latrine seat boards open and entered the shit, crouching with only our heads sticking up. They would come and have a hearty laugh. Jews sitting in shit up to their necks. They would fire and the Jews would drown in shit.

They were nearing our street. We heard them milling around the walls of the house. Raus, they roared. Alle Juden raus. We could see them through the cracks. Children showed up in doorframes and then they were gone. People revolved in place, lifting their hands, jumping into the air, covering their faces; then they lay quietly, like collapsed bags. Trucks drove off loaded to the brim, dripping blood as they moved on. New trucks arrived. Morning passed, noon passed while the slaughter progressed. They came to the loft where we were first hidden and threw them all down onto the cobblestones. I was watching them fall when they appeared in front of us. Raus, they yelled. They stuck in the gun muzzles and fired. The latrine was full of fire and smoke. The rifles disappeared, leaving two small holes in the rear wall. The Germans were gone. The roars subsided. The trucks drove on, and they did not return. Dusk was settling.

It was becoming still in the city. The only sounds were the muffled noises of the Diesels and of firing. Occasionally machine guns opened up as if a battle were being fought in the distance. And then this, too, stopped. The houses stood empty; nobody closed the open doors. The corpses lay where they had fallen. Nobody moved; nothing stirred. You want to know where Slonim is? Well, Slonim is where Vilna is, where all the eighty-six thousand Jews of Vilna are, and the hundred thousand of Minsk, and the sixty thousand of Kiev. They are dead, and Slonim is dead too....

X

With the arrival of summer, the Germans began to pull all remaining men out to work. Over three hundred workers were taken to the Siedlce camp, and more were demanded. One day the Germans resettled with us all the Jews from the nearby town of

Sarnaki, about a thousand in all. Only a work camp was left in Sarnaki, to which Losice had to contribute additional men. To avoid being sent to either of these camps people tried to find work on the various construction jobs or in the villages where there was a shortage of farm labor. All winter and spring, using the grimmest tactics, I bitterly resisted being taken to these camps; then, one day, the Judenrat offered me a job on some landowner's estate. It was presumably a great favor. Yet, distrusting the Germans and their motives, I hesitated until I at last let the arguments of parents and friends persuade me to accept.

With the sun rising over the Myeyski forest, about sixty of us in a rather jovial mood set out of the ghetto in the direction of the estate. The joviality was brief. We were still at the edge of town when, suddenly, from both sides, Schupo men emerged, and before we had time to realize what had happened we were surrounded. Whoever tried to move out of line was knocked back into place with a rifle butt. As we were marched off, it was clear we would no longer be going to any estate or village.

Further on we met a gang of Jews working on the road, and I managed to tell one of them to inform my family what had happened. In an hour we reached the railroad station. A short freight train was waiting, and we were packed into the boxcars. The doors were locked and sealed. We soon left Niemojki. The station's red buildings disappeared, a semaphore numbly dropped its arm, and the locomotive gained speed rapidly. We were on our way east.

After a short trip we stopped at the border station of Platerow. The doors opened and we were disgorged. Three Gestapo men stood before us, the death skull on their caps blackening the May sunshine. We lined up and were marched off to join another group of Jews working on the tracks. These men were from the

Sarnaki camp and it soon became clear that was where we would end up.

Sarnaki was probably the most benevolent camp under the Germans. Set in the middle of the now empty town, it consisted of one long barracks and three private houses, with a spacious yard between. The single wire around the camp boundaries was more a formality than an actual barrier. Thanks to the intervention of acquaintances, I was moved into the "club" instead of the general barracks. "Club" was the name given to one of the three houses quartering the "aristocrats," people who secured the better jobs and had access to extra food. The camp's lenity was due simply to the fact that all administrators and police were Jews. The Germans, short of men, let the camp run itself, but they of course made frequent visits. My job, officially, was that of a camp orderly or janitor, but it really consisted of watching out for arriving Germans. Not long before my arrival they had shot three men caught inside the camp during working hours; according to them, everyone, including the dying, was to be out of the barracks, working.

The camp rose to the sound of a bugle every day at six. At seven all workers were out in the yard, where they were split into work gangs and sent to various jobs, some located as far as ten miles from the camp. Next, those with individual jobs left, and a deep, vast quiet settled over the camp. The quiet lasted all day, broken only by the clucking of neighboring hens and the buzzing of flies. A shadow of some person would fleetingly sneak past the barracks, making the silence even deeper.

After the workers had gone I would sleep another few hours, for we stayed up rather late in the "club." I slept in the loft, where I could watch for unexpected visitors. I read some books that floated around the camp, or I carried food to the sick in the barracks. It was a relief to be away from Manya's tears and Herschek's savage tales, and from the terrifying suspicions of what the Germans were doing with the deported Jews. Our camp was peaceful, and so was the town. After removal of the Jews from Sarnaki, all houses remained empty; the town looked like a colony of hollow tree trunks. Sparrows made nests in the houses, flying in and out open windows, and flocks of crows nestled in the chimneys. Poles tiptoed among the empty houses looking for a place to live; youngsters searched the dumps for valuables, scaring away starving cats. A cart would occasionally roll down the streets, its rattle reverberating loudly in the settled silence. The countryside was splendid: vast meadows splashed with lilac and heather under a sky shimmering a deep blue that was almost purple. In this blooming garden of fields and forests, Sarnaki was a disintegrating log.

Toward evening the workers began to pour back into the camp. Exhausted and hungry they gathered in long queues around the kitchen waiting patiently for supper. The food was given out according to a list so no one would get two portions; if any remained, a refill was given. The suppers were relatively good; there were no Germans to make them deliberately bad. The workers finished their meal on the spot and then stood by, hoping for more. When the kitchen window closed, meaning nothing was left, they shuffled off toward the barracks. The workers immediately went to sleep, the lights went out, and it was still again in the camp.

As it was quite dangerous to stay in the camp during the day, I joined one of the work brigades clearing the railroad tracks of grass and weeds. From where we worked we could see the dim outlines of the railroad station of Platerow; toward the east the tracks vanished in the dense forests of the Bug. I sat and looked at the gleaming rails for hours. Something was happening to the Jews of Europe, and these tracks were somehow part of it. Over these tracks whole cities vanished; these tracks had carried off Lublin and Ignatz. After each deportation an alarm rang from one end of the country to the other, a million voices asking the same frightful question. And the only answer was the fading lament of speeding trains. Their thundering roll was like a stampede, as if hordes of people were being driven barefoot behind the forest. As long as the blaring of the trains hung in the air, as long as the rolling of boxcars echoed over the land, there still seemed time to go to their aid; it was not yet too late. I had a sudden vision that all the deported Jews had disappeared into that steaming, silent forest and I waited for hours expecting them to come out — singly, in groups, whole cities of them. I pricked up my ears. The forest stood blue and silent. Mist rose from its back, blurring its features, holding the secret of a vanishing people.

One day a farmer told us that a train filled with Jews had stopped in Platerow. While we talked, we heard the blare of a locomotive. I ran toward the tracks and climbed the embankment. The train had just left the station and was moving so slowly I was able to get a good look at the cars. They were passenger cars, and I would not have known there were Jews inside had it not been for the yellow rags they were wearing. As I stood and watched, the people inside waved to me. My arm went numb; I could not wave back. In the last car I noticed the green uniforms of the Schupo.

The train reappeared behind the bend. It accelerated wildly and shrank as it approached the forest, leaving behind a thick trail of smoke. When it disappeared beyond the steaming forest, a long jubilant blast cut the silence of the summer afternoon. There was victory in it, and murder. The cry hung in the air, resounding over the meadows and villages. Then it, too, died out. I kept my head turned as I walked down the embankment and looked at the mist over the forest. No sound came from there. Near the tracks I found empty food cans marked MADE IN AUSTRIA.

A few days later a second transport of Austrian Jews passed Platerow. It resembled the first: passenger cars, comfortable conditions, and a car with Schupo at the end. The camp people who worked in the station later told me that the train had stopped there and they had had a chance to talk to the passengers. The Austrian Jews seemed well off. They said they were being resettled in Minsk.

The time was July, 1942. With Germany's summer offensive in Russia in full swing, heavy transports of troops and materiel rolled continuously to the eastern front. On this day the traffic was particularly heavy. Every twenty minutes a train passed, loaded with guns and soldiers. A number of troops camped in the open for lack of rolling stock. And then, through this rush and congestion, rolled trains filled with Jews. There was something uncanny in it. German reserves could not reach the front because of the lack of trains, and yet here was a train with Jews going to Minsk.

Before the end of the week I saw a third transport of deported Jews. This time, however, the Jews were locked in cattle cars, and the train moved so fast that it was difficult to tell what the train contained. But in one of the tiny windows was the face of a boy. Just that: the white face of a little boy – and a dangling tea kettle. In the last car, a passenger car, were the inevitable Schupo.

Shortly thereafter we heard about the deportation of the Warsaw ghetto, the blackest news possible. Then more news arrived that the same was happening in Biala, only thirty miles from us. Disaster was striking close by, and if anything were to happen, I did not want to be separated from my family.

It was not too difficult to get out of the camp. I had stayed this long because there was less gloom here than in the ghetto. But now fear ate at my bowels over what might happen to those in Losice. So, one dark night, I picked up my bag, crossed the wire of the camp, and headed back to the ghetto of Losice.

xi

It was a lovely summer, lovely even in the ghetto: the days clear and warm, the evenings cooled by brief electric thunderstorms. The acacia trees blossomed, and not even the Germans could deprive us of the blue luminous sky. Children played in the streets, beggars mused in sunsoaked yards, and people gathered on the staircases exchanging good news and bad. My grandmother pored over the Bible, shedding tears over the fate of Sarah who bore no children, and over Joseph, sold into Egypt. With all the sharpened senses of the doomed, we perceived the town's little glories, the coolness of its shaded alleys, the smell of the first apples wafted across the wires. In turn, there evolved a new flush of health, false and fatal as the fever of consumptives, and with it delusions that it was all a long, slimy dream, that we were on the verge of awakening. We had visions. A voice from somewhere would speak to us. Airplanes in the sky would tip their wings and drop leaflets, white floating leaflets telling us that they knew. A mysterious messenger would give us weapons, or, at the least, press our hand in a last goodbye. But the days were quieter than ever; the fronts had never been, and were never again to be, as distant as that summer. Whatever voice came was the voice of disaster, and what new voices would join it were of death.

That summer, beginning with Lublin and Ignatz, deportations swept the entire country. Of these the liquidation of the Warsaw ghetto in July was the most shattering, for its half million Jews had been the nation's backbone. A railroad track was built right into the ghetto and, amid destruction and murder, half a million people were shipped out. When the people of Radom were deported, some of us saw them stop in Siedlce, where a hundred smothered corpses were thrown out on the ramp, the very train shuddering with the collective howl of thousands dying inside the locked boxcars.

We watched and listened but did not know what it all meant. The normal processes of thinking and reacting, the horror of our suspicions and the confusion deliberately planted by the Germans produced a frightful weariness, a wish to get it all over with, whatever it entailed: deportation, resettlement, concentration camp, death. And whether one concluded that the deportations led to life in some remote part of Russia or to collective death depended only upon the point of departure. When we heard the rushing trains, we cried instinctively, "We are all perishing." But that knowledge, once assumed, became impossible to accept. We went back to our daily routines – even slept peacefully and humored each other – until the trains were heard again and we started from the beginning.

In the wake of these deportations, a new craze swept the town. Everybody wanted to work for the Germans. This passion started with a postcard from somewhere informing us "something" was going on there, and only those who worked escaped deportation. From other places, too, came news that, when deportations occurred, only those who worked for the Germans remained. It was difficult to imagine how the General Gouvernement could exist without us. We toiled everywhere and did everything: fixed roads, lugged provisions, raised and erased buildings, cleaned the Germans' latrines and polished their shoes. If we all worked and obeyed orders, we would be safe, we were told; so all of Losice plunged into work. We worked where we were needed and where we were not; the young and the old and the crippled worked. Everyone hugged and cherished his working card like a life certificate. At home everyone insisted that I, too, choose a job. But I refused and contemptuously watched the crowds pile out each morning for a long day of slave labor. I did not try to dissuade others from grabbing at this illusion of salvation, but I stayed away.

Early in August the Germans imposed a levy of six hundred thousand zlotys on Losice. Asked why, suddenly, such a punishment, the Germans gave evasive answers. Most of the levy was to be paid at once, the rest in December. The deferral was most surprising as the Germans usually did not fool with installment plans. This time, the Germans said, they would wait until December.

Following news of the Warsaw deportations, I hastily began building a hiding place in our apartment. It was not yet finished, but on the day the levy was imposed, my mind was too troubled to allow me to work, and so I decided to visit Mottel. His father had died before the war, and now, a week prior to my visit, he lost his mother because an operation she needed could not be performed in the ghetto. Mottel, who had always been on the verge of seclusion, became completely indifferent to life. I found him at his usual place near the window, unshaven, half-dressed, chain smoking, staring into the square. I sat next to him. Here all was indifference and resignation, a relief from the rebellion of Herschek who wanted to live at any cost. But this time even here I found no peace.

I was with Mottel half an hour when a military truck drove up; besides two Germans, it brought Mottel's cousin from Sokolow, who worked for these soldiers. He came up to see us, and then, into the silence of the room, he dropped the story of Treblinka – a name I heard for the first time. He told us the soldiers once offered him a trip to Treblinka, a newly established place not far from Sokolow, where, the soldiers said, Jews were being killed off. "But Jews are being killed all over," he told them. This was something different, they insisted; this was a special place with permanent gas chambers. As he was talking to us, the soldiers in the truck honked the horn. The boy left his story unfinished.

I did not sleep all night, and in the morning I went to see Herschek. I walked around the house and waited on a bench in the little vegetable garden. Herschek came out and sat next to me.

From the corner of my eye I kept watching him. Then, without lifting my head, I told him the story of Treblinka.

"You heard it yourself?" he asked.

"Yes," I said.

"Where is this place?"

"North of Sokolow, on the Kosow railroad line."

"That's where the transport from Radom went," he spoke to himself.

We were quiet again. Then he said, "When I hear of one more deportation, I will leave the ghetto."

"Where will you go?"

"There!"

I looked in the direction of his stretched out arm. Along the horizon, sunk in a gathering storm, was the Myeyski forest.

"And then what?"

He spread his arms and shrugged.

Part Two

Immanitas

August — November, 1942

It was the dawn of a clear hot Saturday, August 22, 1942.

I awoke early and was still dressing when, looking out into the deserted streets, I was startled to see a policeman across the square with his rifle slung over his shoulder. Nearby, a German gendarme paced up and down. I heard steps, and two young men emerged from a side street. One was the Judenrat clerk who dispatched the laborers each morning; the other, a boy working in Niemojki. They walked on, their wooden shoes clomping loudly in the early morning. The gendarme, motioning with his arm, began to move towards them. It was difficult to tell what he meant. The two waved their permits at him to show that they had to report to work, but the German paid no attention and unslung his rifle. The two boys backed away, slowly at first, then at a run. It all happened very quickly. They bolted; the German raised his gun, and I heard the crack of a shot.

From the street rose a single muffled groan. One of the boys lay on the sidewalk; his hand came up stiffly once, then it dropped.

The gendarme walked slowly toward the killed man. He stopped, prodded the body several times with the tip of his boot, then shoved it off the sidewalk. Two more gendarmes showed up at the corner of Biala Street. Suddenly, as I looked beyond the cluster of roofs, at each corner and gate of the barbed wires of the ghetto, stood Germans – helmets low over their eyes, guns cocked, waiting.

In an unconscious pathetic reaction I backed off, away from the window, out of the room, out of the apartment, until I found myself walking down the stairs. Neighbors huddled on the steps, clutching small bundles. They spoke in whispers, telling each other to stick together, not to lose the food or the bottles with water. On the floor below, my grandmother recited Vidu, the prayer of the dying. An old man wrapped a tallis around his body and buttoned the coat over it. I was near the door leading outside when I heard guns firing from up the street, and I began to retrace my steps, upstairs and back into our room where I saw Father, hollow-eyed and waxen, clad only in his shorts, mumbling to himself, "What is it? What is it?" Belcia lay in the corner trembling while mother, practical as always, packed food and clothing for the "trip."

Outside, the sun continued to rise, shimmering off the acacia trees and glowing on the brick walls, forecasting a long, hot day. The dead man lay peacefully in the gutter, his lunch bag beside him. From various parts of the ghetto, shots cracked while, beneath our balcony, a group of gendarmes conferred in subdued voices. A car drove into the square and five Gestapo men stepped out, tapping their boots with folded white whips. They spread out in a semicircle and waited. The Arbeitsamt chief arrived, dressed in party uniform. Then came the Landskommissar with a group of SD men. All Germans were out, armed and ready.

As the firing thickened and the siege made certain that this was the fatal day, we began to crawl into our hiding place. It had been constructed by boarding up a small attic and masking it with the same wallpaper as covered the rest of the room. A hinged flap under the couch served as the entrance. Under this couch we now passed, one by one, into the attic. The last person closed the trap door behind him.

Around noon we heard Polish policemen march down the street shouting: "Cease firing.... Cease firing...."

The echo in the empty streets repeated, "Cease firing."

"All Jews outside.... All Jews outside...."

For a while it was very quiet, stubbornly quiet for one eternal minute. Then, like a rearing sea, came the roar of the disgorged population. The city turned on its axis and released in its fall a sob from eight thousand throats. All of Losice, its men, women, and children, wept in unison.

I looked out the little loophole of the cell. People poured in streams from all yards, doors, side streets. They congregated in the square carrying bundles bigger than themselves. Families tried to keep together, the strong carrying the bedding, the winter clothing, and the children. The young supported the old, and the sick were carried on make-shift stretchers. A cripple on one leg jumped quickly on his crutches, afraid that he might be late; old men prayed under the walls. And above the collective unceasing lament rang the threat of the Germans: "Everybody out. Those found in the houses will be shot."

Under the impact of this announcement, and seeing that the entire populace was out on the square, most of the group got up to leave and join the rest. Those of us who were determined to avoid the deportation first argued with them, then told them that, if they were going to leave, they had better do it now and quickly, for later we would not let them out. A volley of gunfire interrupted our talk, then another, and another. As if hit by the salvos, we all dropped to the floor, and in that dreadful instant all conversations ceased.

We heard horse-drawn carts roll in the streets, hundreds and hundreds of carts. The firing rose steadily. Machine guns flickered, stopped, flickered again. Then came the German commands, and eight thousand men, women, and children began their last journey. We heard them for some time: the rattle of carts and the stamping of feet. Then the noise receded, fading into the sigh of a distant sea. Then it died out.

Twenty-seven of us were hidden in the attic: five of my immediate family; Uncle Yankel, his wife and three children — Berko, Rivkah and Itzek; Uncle Erschel with his wife and child; a third uncle, the rabbi from Konstantynow with his wife and his son Mordecai. There was the Mordkowicz family with Mrs. Mordko-wicz's old mother; a woman from Sarnaki and her two small boys; a lone aunt from the Warsaw ghetto who had come to us after her husband had starved to death, and two tenants of ours, Gdalus and Saul. The youngest was Uncle Erschel's six-year-old child; the eldest, the eighty-year-old Mordkowicz grandmother. My own step-grandmother refused to hide and left with the transport.

The attic was small, the sloping roof prevented standing, and the only source of light and air was a small hole the size of two or three bricks. It was a scorching summer day and the zinc roof above our heads glowed like a hot plate. Soaked in sweat and filling the entire attic, we marked time. We expected that, as had occurred in other deportations, some people would be spared and would remain in town; we could then merge and become a part of the saved. We listened for the sound of conversation, steps, the slamming of a door. But no sound broke the deadly silence. Outside, the windows gazed dully at each other, not perceiving what had happened; the stricken houses appeared to be whispering inquiries.

As hours passed and no life stirred, hope for anyone's return waned. In the cell nobody spoke. Our twisted limbs ached, and the blood in our temples throbbed feverishly; some of us began to faint. I opened the trap door and crawled into the apartment. The fresh air and flood of light left me dizzy, and I lay for a while on the floor. Then I leaned against a wall and looked at the town. All windows and doors stood open, breathing the emptiness that had settled in place of those who were gone. The square and all the streets were littered with bundles, packages, suitcases. Bedding, discarded jackets, and shoes filled the sidewalks and cobblestones. Here and there fat puddles of blood glistened in the sun. I looked toward the place where I had seen the policeman that morning. He stood in the same spot. On Polinow Street, too, guards were stationed at the barbed wire. We were trapped and alone in the ghetto.

Dusk settled slowly, gently. In the blackness of the cell nothing could be distinguished. Nobody asked what had happened, nobody suggested what to do. The little window was first blue, then gray, then it disappeared. We still listened, but nothing stirred. Only a trembling sob hung above the dead town, and our lips followed it in silent mourning.

As night fell there was a stirring in the corner of the attic. Whispers – someone was speaking to me. I recognized Gdalus. He had a strange voice, which seemed to arrive from across an immense receding distance. It was a short summer night. We had to get out of the empty ghetto, and Gdalus and his brother were the first to attempt it. I saw them climb over the heads of the others, felt their hands on my shoulder, and heard them open the partition into the apartment. They had to descend two flights of stairs, step into the deserted ghetto, and cross it. We sat counting time, and as it passed without any commotion we thought they might have succeeded.

Suddenly, the clatter of boots; the flash of a shot lit up the bricks of the window. Someone shouted in German. Then a second gun thundered. We lowered our heads and closed our eyes. Quickly stretching out a hand, I pulled the trap door to the apartment shut.

Sunday arrived in a burst of brilliant sunshine. On this second day, the discomfort and physiological needs called us back to life. Our cramped limbs began to swell. We were hungry and, worse, thirsty. To alleviate these conditions some decided to go down to a second hiding place on the floor below us. Both uncles, Yankel and Erschel, with their families – eight people altogether – sneaked out of the attic and made their way on tiptoe to the lower cell. The transfer was accomplished without incident. Silence continued to reign in the deserted city.

In the attic the rabbi got to his feet, took out his tefillim, wrapped himself in the tallis, and, bent under the hot sloping roof, began the morning prayer. In the lifeless town his whispers thundered like the voice of a giant. With hands crossed on his chest, he lisped: "O Thou who revivest the dead, raisest the fallen, freest the jailed... who can stand Thy might and who equals Thee...." In the distance the steps of the German guards continued to knock patiently against the hard pavement.

Before noon we suddenly heard a human voice. Somebody was weeping. I looked through the tiny window. In the middle of the street walked a young girl followed by a policeman with a lowered rifle. I heard her begging: "Let me... let me.... I'll go where the others went." A jolly laugh answered her: "We will send a special limousine for you." The steps died out; a shot was fired and the sky replied with a ringing echo.

In the afternoon Shmulek and Boris decided they would attempt to get out that night. Their father – small, yellow, large nosed – had not shifted position since he entered the attic. After hearing the plan, he looked at his sons for a while, then turned his head back toward the window. When they handed him his coat early in the evening, the old man said: "No, no, I am too old for that."

Shmulek told him to stop talking nonsense. But he went on with a faint smile on his lips:

"You go.... I want to die here...."

He refused to do anything, and sat looking at the darkening sky with the enigmatic smile on his face.

The Mordkowiczs were leaving the cell. They had forced the old man to come with them by threatening that they would not leave without him. But he watched the preparations impassively, without lending a hand or uttering a word. They were rather careless and wanted to get it all over with quickly. The boys put their shoes on. I told them to go barefoot, but they ignored me. They would try to get to Siedlce, they said, and perhaps find Zalus, who was in the labor camp there. I asked where I could get in touch with them in Siedlce. Shmulek waved his hand, "Don't be a fool." He lent an arm to his father and pushed him toward the exit; then he, too, turned to leave.

They stayed in their room quite some time. We heard their movements and pricked our ears uneasily. Belcia knelt near the door and begged them, "Take off your shoes.... The shoes...." They did not answer. Everyone prayed that they would go. The thought of their walking out into the ghetto into the arms of the German guards made us stuff our ears and cover our faces. We wanted them to go through with it outside of our consciousness.

Then night came, dark and misty. It had been quiet for some time in the apartment, but now we heard them again, moving towards the stairs. I crouched near the window. After a while I began to distinguish the outlines of the houses and the stretch of Polinow Street. A mild breeze came and fluttered against my face; I opened my mouth thirstily and drank the coolness of the night.

Suddenly the knock of boots sounded around the corner, stepping briskly, then running. Beams cut the darkness, and a yell. *Wo kommt Ihr her?*

Several torches joined their beams, and in their yellow light I saw the muzzles of guns.

"Ooooh, don't shoot.... Don't shoot."

It was the woman's voice. *"Nicht schiessen,"* she whined. She spoke rapidly, with the voice of an animal. A gendarme hit her in the face, the slap coming sharp as the ring of a bell. She fell to the ground but rose with lightning speed, jumping between the Germans and her two sons. Each time she was hit with such force she landed on the other side of the gutter. But she was back on her feet, bleeding, spitting, and yelling in an insane voice, "Don't shooot.... Ooooh don't...."

Slowly a shadow detached itself from the group and I saw Shmulek advancing towards the Germans. He stopped and grinned at them. The Germans moved back a little. The woman shrieked and lunged toward the guns, but she was hit again and rolled onto the pavement. Then came the crack of a shot. Shmulek slumped forward, fell. He was still alive, and he lifted himself off the pavement. A second shot exploded with a flash of fire.

The Germans pulled Shmulek's body to the telephone pole. They removed his watch and took his billfold. Then, with kicks and blows, they got the Mordkowiczs going. For a while we heard them walking down the sidewalk; then their steps died out.

In the attic we awaited the inevitable. Soon we heard the distant knock of boots head in our direction and stop in front of the house. The door downstairs opened, and we heard them walk up the first flight of stairs. Sitting near the little window, I saw the flashlight beams fall on the wall of the opposite building as the Germans searched the lower apartments. I listened for any unusual commotion to indicate that they had found the lower hiding place, but it was quiet. Perhaps they would miss the third floor, I thought, but soon their steps were on the stairs leading to our apartment.

They entered the kitchen with a stamping of boots and the clatter of guns. Marching into the room where the Mordkowiczs had lived, they moved the chest of drawers and overturned the bed. We heard their steps near the entrance to the attic. They moved the couch away. For a while the light beams cutting through the hairline cracks of the trap door fell inside the cell and rested on someone's pale face like a knife edge. Then they left, the stairs creaked, the steps receded.

The haze of the night bathed the town in an acid green shimmer. An icy moon sat in self-contained contemplation, spinning a new reality. Death had always meant the end, but the ghosts of the night laughed at such an unsophisticated vision of it. It became a universe in itself. It was a world of the subtlest and finest vistas, a stretch through which one could wander throughout eternity without exhausting its secrets and promises. It was an infinity of hallucinations where one could dwell on and on, arguing and admiring some of the finest tests of insanity.

There was only one real object that night, and that was Shmulek's body under the telephone pole. He would float away in pools of green light, then come back hugging the cobblestones. He was not a corpse but the silhouette of the murdered city. He seemed to lie there and talk with himself, spitting out the stars that collected in his glossy eyes. Eventually the moon began to roll down the sky, and the shadow cast by our building lengthened. Other shadows also grew, touched and crossed until Shmulek disappeared in a lake of darkness.

Strange movements crisscrossed the town. All night we heard the marching patrols. Walking in pairs and singly, they emerged from the darkness and disappeared around corners. They all stopped at the telephone pole and looked at Shmulek's corpse. It seemed as if they regretted he was dead; then it seemed they were going to kill him once again. They lit their flashlights, whispered among themselves, and pointed to our house and to the little window where I sat. One of the gendarmes went into the house across the street. Another one sat down on the steps of our house, a rifle between his knees, his metal buttons gleaming in the blackness.

The third day in hiding. All food and water were gone. Covered with sweat and dirt, doing our physical needs inside the attic, relapsing into feverish dreaming as we roasted in the blazing heat, we were dying a slow and miserable death. Had anyone offered us a drink to surrender we would have accepted it, but the Germans probably would have refused us this last wish. And had they shot me without first giving me some water, I had a vision that I would take this thirst with me, remaining thirsty for as long as I would be dead.

Our discipline was deteriorating, and now, without need or reason, I crawled out and wandered about the apartment. In the Mordkowicz room, Shmulek's and Boris's clothes lay scattered on the floor, and on the table, near an old issue of *Die Literarische Blätter*, lay the old man's spectacles which he had not even bothered to take along. On swaying legs I moved into our room. The French doors of the balcony were wide open; through it fresh clear air flowed like a stream of crystal water. Below, Losice lay white, calm, and dead. It seemed to me that this was the end of life on earth, that only pure spirit remained, breathing silence and eternity. The room was shaded, cool. The sky looked in, blue and alluring. I had hidden to escape the gas chambers; I succeeded, and now I was left with nothing. It would be good to remain in this room, within sight of the woods where we had played volleyball in the summer with Shmulek and Mottel. I lay down on the sofa. Sparrows played on the electric wires in front of the window. In my swirling head I had visions of water – cool, wet water. Fog blurred my eyes and I could not see the sky. "Water, water," I mumbled. On the painting above the couch the peacock came to life, fanning me with his long, regal tail. "Water," I begged him. "Ssh...," he cautioned me and stuffed his tail into my mouth.

Like the Mordkowiczs the preceding night, we, too, prepared for the breakout as soon as it got dark. To be less conspicuous we at first split up into two groups; I was going with Mother and Belcia; Manya was to accompany Father. But just before leaving we decided against separating. Huddled together, barefoot, with small packages in our hands, we descended the upper flight of stairs. We were already on the lower staircase when a gun was fired next to the front door. We ran back upstairs and climbed the loft so that the Germans would not discover the attic. There we waited for them. The door downstairs opened and we heard them move about. But the door slammed shut and all was quiet again.

Back in the cell I sat and listened to the flow of time. The attic and the mocking moon contained all that was left to us. There was no way out from our trap. I stared at the lamplight across the street of shadows, the ghosts in the doorframes. Occasionally I slept, a sleep full of feverish dreams. I awoke every few minutes and each time rose and looked out at the slaughtered city. It was a phosphorous marsh, calcium houses, moonshine, moonshine....

Before dawn the night turned misty and we made another try. We pushed out our bundles, we crawled into the apartment, and we stood and shuddered and waited and listened. Out on the landing we looked down and saw two policemen across the street. Another was sitting on the steps of our house. Soon, over the Myeski forest, the sky began to flicker with the first flush of dawn which in half an hour brought a new hot blistering day.

The failure to get out that night, and the fate of those who did venture forth, made it clear we were doomed. All reason, all discipline broke down. We talked loudly and crawled unnecessarily into the apartment, subconsciously wanting to be discovered. Then we returned and collapsed once more on the attic's hot, dry, dusty floor. At one point the woman from Sarnaki grabbed a pot and put it to her mouth; several others lunged for the jug, tore it from each other's hands, and drank. It was not until the fourth person had had his share that he took a look at what he was drinking, put the jug away, and sat down with a groan; the jug was filled with urine collected in the attic for the last three days. Later, however, the people returned to the urine and drank until it was all gone.

The first to lose control over himself was the younger son of the Sarnaki woman. He leaped to his feet and screamed at the top of his voice with such fury that it probably carried over most of the town. We threw him to the floor, stuffed his mouth, and held him tightly until he quieted down. His mother, with a sudden impulse, began to dress him: "Go, get out of here." The boy did not understand what she meant. Nor did we. But she ordered her son to leave the attic and told him that, if he managed to get through the ghetto, he should head for Sarnaki, where his father worked in the camp. No one said a word. No one tried to interfere when she crawled out with him into the apartment. It was a mad plan to let him go in bright daylight, but he could perhaps be mistaken for a Polish boy crossing the ghetto. As time passed and no firing was heard, we assumed that he had gotten through.

When I walked down to the lower hiding place and told them that one of the two Sarnaki boys had probably escaped, my aunt decided to try the same with Berko and Rivkah. The two children wept and begged to be left alone, but she ignored them. Like the Sarnaki woman's son, they were tempted and encouraged by the promise of water. They were given money and pushed out of the hiding place. Through the cracks in the wall I later saw them out in the yard. Barefoot, tiny, the girl holding onto her older brother, they stood squinting in the bright sun and staggering. They were the only live creatures in the vastness of the silent houses and dead streets. Every few steps they stopped walking to look fearfully in all directions. Then they disappeared around a corner.

That afternoon, I noticed the Polish police slowly taking over the guarding of the ghetto. One of them was an acquaintance of Yankel; perhaps, I thought, we could get him to help us. The plan was desperate, but we could not lose much. Another day in hiding without water and it would be too late. The problem was how to contact the policeman. I thought of Belcia: dressed as a peasant girl, she might sneak through the ghetto to the policeman's house.

On a piece of paper I wrote: "A group of us are hidden on Miedzyrzec Street, No. 2. If you wish to help us, enter the building from the rear, come up to the second floor, and repeat three times: Yankel. We will pay you for your help." I signed Yankel's name. I gave Belcia the note and told her how to walk through the ghetto. After delivering the note, she was to leave for the village of Swiniarow and wait there for us at the farm where we had stayed during the Polish campaign. She listened without saying a word and, trembling, crawled out of the attic.

We walked down the first flight of stairs together, but I stopped on the staircase and motioned for her to go on alone. She fixed the kerchief on her head, took the white jug in which she was supposedly carrying milk, and without looking back continued down the stairs and into the yard. When half an hour had passed without hearing shots, we let ourselves hope that she got through.

It was after midnight when a shadow appeared at the end of the alley leading to our yard. It stopped, then moved noiselessly toward our house. I sat rigidly, my eyes glued to the approaching silhouette. A crushing silence hung about us for a long time; then we heard "Yankel, Yankel, Yankel."

We got out and stood on the staircase, talking. For payment the policeman agreed to help us get out of the ghetto, but he refused to take all eighteen of us at once. Instead he would take half of us that night and the others the next. In the event we were trapped by the Germans on the way out, he said, he would pretend that he had just caught us. He told the nine of us in the first party to be ready in an hour; then, promising to bring some water so that those left behind could last through tomorrow, he left to make the necessary arrangements.

It was a long wait before the policeman returned, a rifle over his shoulder. In a whisper he told us the details of the plan. He and a fellow policeman were guards at one of the corners of the ghetto. We would attempt to get through at that point. The most dangerous spot would be at crossing Miedzyrzec Street, where Germans were posted. He implored us again not to betray him if we were caught.

We descended the lower staircase. The policeman crossed Miedzyrzec Street and slinked into the gate of the opposite house. Barefoot, with little bundles in our hands, we crouched near the exit and waited for the signal. A flashlight flickered. Yankel with his family moved first. In the moon-soaked night we saw their hunched bodies roll across the pavement. The light flickered again, and we followed. From house to house, flattening ourselves against walls, crouching near fences, we slowly left the ghetto behind.

At the edge of the ghetto we waited a long time. We heard the guard's steps and the clank of rifles. Finally the policeman reappeared and motioned to us to move. We cut across Polinow Street past the barbed wire. We saw a sentry in the shadow, but he did not stir. The policeman led us to the Biala highway. He stopped near the bridge, looked around, and signaled us to continue. We climbed the embankment to the highway and lurched across. We were in the open fields.

xiii

We walked in the direction of Swiniarow, staggered by the cool air, the limitless space. Drenched in dew, the earth was a shimmering lake of moonlight, and in the valley only Losice's two church spires were visible. We walked fast, as if towed by the whispers and gleams of the throbbing summer night.

Soon Swiniarow appeared, buried among orchards and groves. We intended to stay in the village overnight and then, with the help of a farmer, get to a place where Jews lived. Over plowed fields we made our way to the low peasant hut with the red shutters where, three years earlier, an old man had told me that the Anti-Christ had arrived. Near the barn we noticed a large bundle on the ground, and someone remarked that other Jews must have passed here before us. We were among farmyards filled with the smell of steaming potatoes and fresh bread. Everything seemed asleep; only a dog barked, far away.

We knocked on the window. Evidently those inside were not asleep and had seen us coming, for it opened immediately. First of all, a drink. Jozefowa, the farmer's wife, silently handed us a pail of water and we drank. For a while the whole world was reduced to the pleasure of drinking.

Eventually we had our fill. Manya asked Jozefowa to let us into the barn.

"What are you talking about?" the woman whispered, crossing herself several times. "Don't even say it."

The door opened and the farmer strode out – wiry, tall, with only his pants on. Father explained that all we wanted was to stay overnight until we could find a way to get to Siedlce or Biala. When he did not answer, we at first thought he agreed.

But then he spoke: "I cannot let you in. There is an order not to hide or help Jews. If I were alone... but I have children...." He stopped for breath. "You want to go to Siedlce? There are no Jews left there either, or in Mordy, or in Kaluszyn. They did the same thing everywhere. Even if I let you stay here overnight, what would you do with yourselves tomorrow? Where are you going to go...?"

The man kept talking, but I no longer heard him. My bones had melted. This was really the first time that we perceived the apocalyptic truth: that the entire Jewish people was being massacred, totally and for all time. Vaguely I heard Manya ask the woman whether she knew anything about Belcia; the woman said that she was probably around somewhere. We called her name. For an instant there was silence, and then the discarded bundle we had noticed next to the barn moved, and Belcia crawled out from under a potato sack. Shivering, she wrapped herself in the coat we had brought along for her. The farmer still stood waiting on the threshold; from the windows other people were watching us. The woman, pointing to the bundles in our hands, asked us to give them to her as we would not live much longer anyway. The farmer urged us to move on.

"I do not want you to stay on my land.... Go on. Go wherever you like, but leave us...." His voice rose to a threat.

We turned around. Ahead of us stretched a vast plain. The starlit sky joined the forests on the horizon. Behind us, as we left the village, doors and windows slammed shut and all the dogs joined in a prolonged howling. We walked loosely, aimlessly, bumped against each other. It was getting cold and we put on our coats and shoes. After a few miles we came to a fork. A wooden cross leaned over the road and the moonlight burned on the metallic figure of Christ. We picked the road to the right and went on.

The shattering news that there were no Jews left anywhere sapped our last strength. Father fell every few minutes. I only now noticed that the rabbi's son, Mordecai, was with us; he had left his parents behind. I wished the Germans would catch us and finish us off; I contemplated going back to town and reporting to the Schupo; and I had other, similar thoughts. After some time we saw a small wood in the distance. Falling and pulling each other, we made our way deep into its hushed undergrowth and fell to the ground. We were hot from the effort, but we soon felt cold. Shivering under our coats we all fell asleep.

The afternoon of the next day we met a shepherd in the woods, a small old man with bushy eyebrows. He told us the road we had been traveling led to Konstantynow. He knew what had happened in Losice and he confirmed that there were no more Jews in Mordy, or in Siedlce, or anywhere. He shook his head and mumbled,

"I am an old man and I have been in three wars, but I have never seen anything like it. After I heard the shooting Saturday morning, I stayed home and prayed on my knees all day. God will now surely send down another deluge."

He went on in this manner, relating various details of the slaughter: how a car followed the Jews, firing at them all the while; how they went insane from thirst; how the farmers along the road had to bury the dead. I asked him again if there were any Jews left anywhere. He claimed that there were none and that he himself had seen the Schupo go to Konstantynow for the liquidation. I moved away. Left alone, he went on mumbling to his dog of what had happened on Saturday morning.

Between shock and a deliberate daze, I lay and watched evening descend through the treetops. In the setting dusk the trees renewed their mysterious, hushed whispering and the woods grew hostile, malignant. We rose and moved on. It was only the second night of wandering, but we had by then already forgotten where we had started out and did not know where we were going. Not having any aim or purpose in this march, I walked and gazed at the constellations, their sickly palpitation so akin to the convulsions of my brain. Something had been pushing me on; but this urge was now gone. Each step was a superfluous effort, each movement filled me with disgust for myself. Why feed the curiosity of these forests and fields? Why let the stars mock us?

After an hour's walking we saw in the distance the outlines of an unknown village. The scent of straw and stables drifted over, and the dogs, detecting our approach, began to bark. In those days the Germans had organized farmer patrols to intercept escaped Russian prisoners, and we met one of these patrols as soon as we entered the village. Some of the farmers who knew us from Losice recognized us, and we stopped to talk. Repeating the story of thousands of people crazed from thirst and massacred on the road to Siedlce, they confirmed that there were no Jews left anywhere – although they gave conflicting reports as to when the Jews from the Biala district had been liquidated. They asked where we were going. We said that we would go on until we found some Jewish community, that perhaps some farmer would take us in, and a few other fantasies. They laughed at our talk. One suggested that possibly we could hide in the forest as some Soviet prisoners did, but then he looked at us – the crumpled women and the children- – and shook his head. We drank some water from the well and walked on.

Thursday we spent in some sparse, young woods a few miles from Kornica, a large village with a police station in it. Here, we felt, was the end of the road. We were all quiet; only Mordecai walked back and forth, groaning and torturing himself for having deserted his parents. Stretched out in the undergrowth, I kept looking at his oversized shadow flashing across the sun, the sky behind him turning alternately black and ashen white. When I looked at the faces of the others, I had the brief thought that they were all going mad.

At some point in the day we were startled by the noise of crackling branches. The bushes in front of us parted and two heads peeped out. The eyes in the immobile faces watched us for a long time before two men emerged. They looked like peasants, and mother asked them if they were from the neighboring village. They smiled faintly. "We are escaped Russian prisoners." Only then did we notice their rags and that peculiar fatal mist in their eyes, the same that Herschek had brought back from Slonim. They asked us if we were hungry and offered us some bread and cold potatoes. Then with a pale smile of recognition of our ultimate fate, theirs and ours, they got up, threw their bags over their shoulders, and moved on, their catlike, cautious steps increasing our loneliness and terror.

The sickening odor of doom kept rising. In its grip all of us became unbalanced, pathetic.... Mother took out Belcia's new dress and asked her to put it on. Mordecai ran back and forth, begging us to go back with him to Losice to his parents. Manya was mumbling something about Ignatz being dead for over half a year. Father, always aloof, became sentimental, whimpering, "What did I raise a family for?" Up to this point we had still hoped that there might be Jews in Konstantynow, but we were now only eight kilometers from the town, and two women we had met in the afternoon told us that it had been cleared of Jews. Our feverish imaginations began to feed us details of the last scene. When the shots rang out, I visualized, the cows grazing on the meadow beyond the bushes would just raise their dumb heads for a minute, and then continue to graze. I was thinking how, in a thousand years, our bones would still be here. But the worst was a feeling that I could not be killed; that there, under the darkness, I would forever remain conscious of my death, that I would forever be struggling with the earth thrown into my mouth and eyes while, above, there would still be these skies, these woods, this brilliant, shimmering, summer sunshine.

In the afternoon a peasant showed up on the other side of the grove. He hitched his horse and began to plow a piece of stubble field. Evidently the women to whom we had spoken had told him there were Jews in the woods because, after a while, he stopped the horse, looked cautiously around, and came over. He came to ask for our belongings, arguing that we did not need them any more. We promised to give him all our bundles and whatever money we had if he would take a walk to Konstantynow to see whether there were any Jews left. He refused; the Germans, he said, forbade any contact with Jews. I told him then to leave us. The peasant scratched his hip and did not go. He repeated that he was sure there were no Jews in Konstantynow. As proof he cited the fact that the Jewish workers who normally came from Biala to the village had not shown up the last few days. If we gave him our bundles, he stuttered, he would bring us some bread. "You would at least be full before they take you," he explained. When we again told him to move on, he looked at us reproachfully. He then walked away, whipped the innocent horse, and resumed his plowing.

After the noon siesta the woods again teemed with life. The air, filled with resin, grew hot and humid. All around us the groves and woods were turning black. Heavy clouds gathered over the horizon, their swollen bellies heaving a cold, electric breath. The first lightning that flashed seemed to set the woods afire, followed by peculiarly short splintering cracks of thunder. The storm somehow bared the absolute pathos of our presence in these woods. Father sat stiffly with a swollen cramped face, watching the women's hair torn by the wind. Belcia wept. Mordecai again began to pace back and forth. Father walked away into the bushes; a minute later we heard a heavy thump. I found him fallen on his back, his face blue, his hat and pince-nez thrown aside. Mother gave a short cry and tried to revive him. I held her back, and we left him there unconscious.

At that moment, between cracks of thunder, we heard cautious steps in the bushes. One of the women we had met in the morning stuck her head out and motioned us wildly to move on. When we did not react, she rasped, "For God's sake, people, run away. Germans are raiding the woods. Can't you hear the shooting? Quick, there are still Jews in Konstantynow. Quick, quick."

The news of Jews in Konstantynow almost blinded us with joy. I shook Father. He opened half-conscious eyes, but he could not move, so we grabbed him by the shoulders and dragged him into the thick bushes. We pushed on for several hundred yards and then flattened ourselves against the ground.

Now we could distinguish the firing that reverberated in the woods. Along the trails we heard the drone of cars and, occasionally, commands in German. The police raid lasted a long time, but we paid no attention to it. We kept thinking of what the woman had told us about Konstantynow. While German patrols marched on the sandy road and bullets whizzed over our heads, breaking branches and spitting sand into the air, we only knew there were still Jews somewhere and that we would perhaps join them.

As soon as the raid was over, we headed east again. The bushes ended and the road turned sharply to the right. In front of us was another large village. We passed the first houses and entered a wide country road lined with low, straw-decked houses and barns. With their bells ringing, herds of sheep bounced into open stalls; from the chimneys smoke rose leisurely, smelling of meat and potatoes; storks circled the village, filling the air with a dry clicking. The peasants, after their day's hard work, sat in front of their houses, watching us impassively while smoking their home-made cigarettes. As we passed the village, I could still hear, far, far away, the husky voices of the peasant women and the bleating of the sheep.

We walked without haste. Only five kilometers remained until we reached Konstantynow, and we had the whole night. Mordecai knew this part of the country well, so we had no fear of getting lost. As we approached the town, however, the tension grew. There was a police station in Konstantynow. Worse, it also contained Luftwaffe Germans: their task was to spot enemy airplanes, but they were actually busy murdering Jews, Russians, and other "eligibles." From their tall observation tower, they could spot us miles away. The terrain did not change – low, dwarfish brush-wood hugging waterlogged fields. The distance to the town was decreasing and the night was still young. Near a small brook spanned by an arched bridge, we decided to wait until the town was asleep. There was some kind of mound in front of the bridge; using it as a shield, we stretched out on the wet ground opposite the side where the moon was later to rise. We covered ourselves with our overcoats and fell asleep.

I awoke periodically, shivering from cold. The night was misty and wet, and a heavy dew was settling over the fields. A spray of diamonds glistened in the air and my teeth chattered from their cold gleam. During one of the frequent wakenings I saw Mother, wrapped in her coat like an Indian woman, pacing back and forth. She was weeping. The silence rang in my ears, and I went back to sleep.

Soon the moon rose and the night became clear as daylight. In a small grove some distance away, an owl lamented with all of earth's gloom. It was past midnight when we moved again. We came to the town brook. Rushes and young willows lined its shore; the grass and reeds reached to my belt. We crossed the muddy lowland listening to the bubbling water. Under cover of the riverside willows we could not be seen from the town, and so we pressed on, closer and closer. At some spot the mud pulled a shoe off Father's foot. We all stopped and took our boots off. When we started again, two German bloodhounds across the brook began barking. Their roar tore the night with a violent alarm. We waited, hoping they would stop. But their insane yelling grew until they became hoarse. Mordecai cautiously parted the ivy in front of us. Across the river, we saw the dark silhouette of the town and the German tower high above the clustered roofs. As long as we stood under the brushwood, they could not see us, but to reach town we had to emerge and cross an open field. We considered going over to a near-by grove and there await the next night, but then we would have to face the same problem. We had to take the risk now.

We walked on a little farther along the reeds, then turned sharply and forded the river. Once we were in the open, we broke into a trot. The first suburban gardens; a fence; and we flattened ourselves against the nearest wall we found. The dogs went on barking, but we heard no firing and saw no other suspicious movements. Looking over my shoulder I saw that we were near a new, unfinished house. I tore a plank off the boarded-up window, and we all crawled inside. I put the board back in place and we crouched alongside the walls listening to the night.

When a misty dawn began to seep into the boarded-up house, I rose and looked out. I watched and waited. Then I heard the creaking of a door: an old bearded Jew was opening the shutters. He gaped as we emerged through the window but he said nothing. Silently, he opened the door and let us into his house.

xiv

Konstantynow was a small town known to me from childhood visits to my many relatives. No more than a thousand Jews lived there, all in extreme poverty. It was a settlement of wooden huts gathered around an unpaved square, and the only break in its monotony of straw and sand was the white brick synagogue. Whatever little life it had once possessed had withered under German rule; not a shop remained open, and rarely was a vehicle seen in the square. The cemetery, lush with fruit trees and grass, seemed the most prospering part of town.

In their primitive, predatory struggle for survival, the inhabitants, like birds, flew into the fields every morning to gather food for just one more day. With their hands they dug out a few potatoes and some turnips and hurriedly took them home to feed their starving families. They collected stalks of grain from the fields, ground them on hand-driven mills, and baked themselves thin, pale breads. When the estate laborers drove through town with felled trees, all the inhabitants ran out with knives and axes and scraped off bark to use as fuel. Most of the Jews were forced to work on the Plater estate, taken over by the Germans, and they always brought something home with them. They lugged branches on their backs; they filled their pockets with barley; the women hung pouches around their waists and stuffed them with flour and oats. With all this, most of the town still went around bare and hungry.

Konstantynow learned about the liquidation of Losice on Sunday. Father had three cousins in Konstantynow. One of them was visiting Losice on that fatal Saturday; he, of course, perished. His two sons, Motl and Shmyl, ceaselessly kept asking us about his fate. Others, too, swarmed over us with questions about their relatives in Losice. We answered that they had gone with the rest, that we had seen this one or that one a few days before, or even on the very morning of the deportation, but we could tell them no more. They then walked off, weeping.

We settled down in Konstantynow, paying little attention to the conditions of our "resettlement." We lodged in three different places and cooked our meals in a fourth. Father and I slept in the loft of Cousin Enoch's house. The monotone pace of this half-dead town reinforced my state of all-pervading listlessness. The snoozing goats, the old man chopping wood in the yard, the sunken moss-covered roofs, the synagogue, white and calm as a morgue, blurred the boundaries between life and death until they became imperceptible. I wandered over the cemetery stones, old and new, and repeated a vow to myself: "Here will be my last stop." In calmer moments I laid down the plan very scrupulously. If and when Konstantynow's turn came, I would not resist. No more running, no crazy ideas about survival. I would just step out of the house and ask the nearest German to shoot me. They would fire and at last peace would come. Lying in Konstantynow's melancholy little cemetery I would bloom, years after, as a new apple tree. This final day, I prayed, should come suddenly, granting me no opportunity to undertake new escapades.

I slept wonderfully on the fresh hay in Enoch's loft and the warm sweet summer nights passed quickly. But each day, just before dawn, I would awaken with a start. Unable to go back to sleep, I would listen to the cautious dawn seep through the roof cracks. Then my internal surrender would collapse with a crash. Somewhere a dog barked, a door slammed; firing, crowds, murder.... In the slowly creeping light I could hear a strange thumping outside the town; every morning the singsong rhythm rose and fell, neared and receded. I was told it was the tractor on the estate, but when I heard the thumping at night, I knew it was no tractor. Other voices would wake me: the clatter of a cart, the thud of logs in the sawmill, the crying of lapwings on moonlit nights. I would then lie for hours, listening, watching, waiting.

About ten days after our arrival, Yankel's wife came to Konstantynow with two of her children, Itzek and Rivkah, bringing a tangled web of news about themselves and the other people who had been with us in the attic on that fatal Saturday. Rivkah told us that, after she and Berko had left the attic and made their way to Swiniarow, they, too, were driven from the village. The children, not knowing what to do, decided to get back to the hideout, but they were caught as soon as they entered town and put into jail. They waited all night for the execution. On Thursday they were taken out of jail along with other arrested Jews and brought into a few empty houses in the ghetto. There they were told to resume their lives. With their arrival commenced the story of what was later dubbed the "small ghetto" – a camp with Jews in Losice where the Germans concentrated all survivors. The Mordkowicz family, except for Shmulek, was in the camp, as were Herschek, his mother, and his two sisters. Herschek's father, however, had refused to hide on Saturday morning and walked out, the Book of Job under his arm to join the Losice transport.

Rivkah also brought the news that the policeman who had led us out of the ghetto and who was supposed to lead the remaining people out of the attic the following night did not show up; he had been transferred to a different post. The rabbi, his wife, and my aunt from Warsaw had been found in the attic, taken down to the lower apartment, and shot.

I listened to this news, then returned to my state of torpor, shock, or whatever it was. Like the goats on the square, I stared and gawked at the faded, September sun. Each morning I sat and watched the people going to work on the Plater estate – emaciated, silent beasts of burden, their eyes closed with sleep and exhaustion. Enoch's oldest son worked in the sawmill. Taking a few steamed potatoes with him, he walked off every morning for fourteen hours of labor. The rest of Enoch's six children – tiny, dirty fledglings – filled the house all day with gibberish and cries. I watched them with amazement. Such bubbling life was almost obscene to watch; that children could still grow in these times seemed a perverse joke. But there they were, pulling the potato pancakes off the hot stove, playing games in the backyard, and the older ones already sneaking off to the Plater estate to fetch grain and wood. The people of Konstantynow: a little gray pile of humanity which would presently be ground into transparent floating thin ashes.

Weeks went by. Tall grass covered the unattended square. In the patches of garden, ripened vegetables, and the first fruits of autumn. Behind Enoch's house one could see the pastures we had passed in our wandering, the brook we had crossed, and the first Jewish home we had entered. Every day women ran to the river to catch tiny fish and collect a few branches, even though death awaited them for overstepping the town limits. The Schupo from Biala occasionally came to Konstantynow to claim their portion of loot and blood. While these gruesome Angels of Death walked the deserted streets, we closed the shutters and held our breath. When the Germans left, the usual urchins returned to their interrupted games and we to our routines.

Rosh-Hashana arrived, and ten days later, sobbing its vanishing strains of Kol Nidrei, Yom Kippur. The next day, on Tuesday evening, a messenger arrived from Biala with the sentence; by Friday Konstantynow was to be clear of Jews.

The next day, Konstantynow was already on the move. Horse-drawn carts with shabby furniture and bedding clattered over the streets on their way to the station. High atop the miserable belongings perched old bearded Jews and bewildered children, their eyes huge and wise beyond their age. A mob of peasants descended on the town seeking bargains, asking for property, promising in the name of the Holy Trinity to return them after the war. Like a pack of wolves they circled the town, snapping at the hearts of the victims. Soon they were driving off the goats and cows the Jews could not take with them. The animals were saved and the Jews remained. Nobody came to force them out – the countryside stood open before them – but the Jews had nowhere to go, nowhere but down the same road that Losice had gone.

Our family had decided that, when the order to evacuate came, we would return to Losice. Having eaten our last supper, we gathered in Enoch's house, now littered with boxes and bedding, and said good-bye to thirty or forty of our relatives. Then we backed out of Konstantynow. Its huts, only yesterday full of lit stoves, steaming barley, and chattering people, were now aban-doned, shapeless mud pies. They were rapidly sinking into silence

and darkness. The synagogue, a white flat square in the black of
the night, stared at us until we turned into a side alley and it was
snuffed out. At the edge of town we passed the house that gave us
our first shelter; it was empty now. As if undoing our struggle of
a month ago, we recrossed the brook and the meadows over which
we had come to Konstantynow. A haunting September night
glittered over villages peacefully asleep while we stumbled through
thickets and forests and, behind us, a whole town was being led to
its death.

xv

At dawn on September 24, one month after the liquidation of
Losice, we were back among the one hundred fifty survivors who
lived in the small ghetto. The most striking thing about this zone
was the leniency its inhabitants received from the Germans. The
space was ample; there was no barbed wire; and we could go into
the Polish part of town for food and water. Later, even the guard
posted at the entrance was removed. We could live any way we
liked.

The Germans kept us working at various jobs. The few
craftsmen among us produced furniture, coats, and boots for the
Schupo; some worked on the railroad in Niemojki. But most of the
people in the camp were employed at "cleaning," that is removing
the property left by the Jews. Inevitably, the day came when I, too,
was assigned to this cleaning. Several SD men came in the morning
to the ghetto and mustered us in rows of three. I stood near Mrs.
Mordkowicz, waiting for the order to march out. As the SD counted
us, the woman said to me, "Here is the one who killed Shmulek."
I raised my head. In front of me stood a young, good-looking,

grinning man. He was a picture of health, I thought, but then I met his eyes and there it was.... "Los," came the order, and we moved out.

As we entered the vast silence of the former ghetto, all talk ceased, all heads sank. In the empty streets we could hear the echo of our own steps. The square seemed to have expanded in its destruction; the streets had stretched into boulevards, infinitely long promenades. We rubbed our eyes, believing that the lifeless site was a screen, that a man would emerge from around the corner, two men, a crowd, that soon all streets would be filled with people. We waited for a window to open, for a boy riding his bicycle, for an old man on his way to morning prayer. Somewhere a girl was to clean the rug, a market woman was to hawk her vegetables. Here were supposed to be the fruitstands; there should have been the smell of fresh bread; over these sidewalks, over these streets, in these windows there were supposed to be people, people. It seemed that life had not been destroyed but arrested, halted. Some trick had cut it off; one had only to find the terrible switch and flick it for life to come surging back into the dead city. We waited. All was still. Huge bells tolled in space, the sun rocked under a blue sky, and the empty houses of Losice stared at us with their hollow, perforated windows, silenced forever.

After assigning us to various blocks, the Germans left us alone. No one worked. Some walked from house to house, picking up clothing, photographs and books, and throwing them back on the floor. Others stood motionless for hours, watching the dead town. The impression persisted that the owners of these apartments and houses were hidden somewhere. Surely the shoemaker whose tripod stood in the middle of the room and whose hammer and pliers lay nearby sat somewhere behind the stove; somewhere there must still be the grandmother who read the Khumash, or the child whose scooter leaned against the kitchen wall. We searched for those who looked down at us from the portraits on bookshelves and chests, for the people whose bread remained on the table. But there was only silence. The beds were cold, the ersatz coffee unfinished, and the bread thick with mold. This was Losice, but it belonged to no one. Nothing but disembodied shoes and jackets and hats and shirts....

Only starving cats remained among the ruins of the ghetto. They sat on the cold stoves watching us with phosphorescent eyes, menacing and repulsive. Dying slowly among the ruins, they did not retreat, and when we appeared they stood up and hissed like snakes. Hungry and crazed they miaowed thinly, hysterically, arched their backs, and, raising their bristle, spat at us. When we approached they slid noiselessly away, hid under the beds, and watched us with eyes that flashed fear, hate, and revulsion. After we went on our way, the cats reassumed their perches, stubbornly awaiting their owners' return.

In the afternoon, the SD would usually show up for an inspection, and then we had to do some work. Work consisted of emptying the houses of all the things that could be moved. Furniture was supposed to be lowered from the upper stories with ropes, but we just dumped it out the windows and over balconies, breaking it to pieces. Within minutes we were gripped by a mania of destruction. Sewing machines, chests, mirrors – anything that came into our hands we flung down and smashed; all windows were broken, tiles cracked, bedding ripped open.

Before we were led back to the little ghetto we took for ourselves any clothing we may have liked and all the food we could carry. Life suddenly became prosperous, carefree. After an ordeal of starvation and misery, we had plenty of everything, ice cream and eggs and butter and cake. After three years of filth and stench – during which, like scarecrows we walked about naked in snow and wrapped in blankets on hot summer days – we rolled in luxury. The women dressed in silk to cook meals; we went to work in striped suits. The dresses our girls had been saving for after the war we used to wash floors. When we changed underwear, we threw the worn ones out the window. Obviously, what had constituted poverty for eight thousand people was wealth for a few hundred survivors. I wore the clothes of a dead man and ate the food that a hundred others did not live to eat. In the apartment where we lived still hung portraits of the previous owners; over the bed there was a picture of twins whose carriage we had removed to the cellar. There were even storm windows available which the meticulous owner had already prepared for the coming winter.

"Cleaning" soon became unbearable. The first time I went into the former ghetto, it seemed something I had hallucinated. But with time the place became real. The first blow came when I found myself in Mottel's home. I was still on the stairs when I suddenly became aware that all this was familiar. I entered the apartment and sat on the floor. Through the wide open windows the late summer air floated into the room like incense. It was the same room – the same wallpaper, mahogany chest, yellow rug. On his night table lay Feuchtwanger's *False Nero*, the book I had given him on our last Friday together. A packet of cigarettes lay upon its pages. In the drawers were his books, his photographs. Everything had been left behind except the portrait of his father who had died when he was a child. The large old clock that had always ticked with such regularity now stood still. The copper disc seemed huge in its immobility. On the untouched calendar was the fatal date: August 22, 1942.

And then our own house – large, white, deserted. All its doors and windows were wide open, and when a breeze blew they turned on their hinges with a screech. Through the gaping chest of the building one could see the disemboweled interior. A hushed silence met me on the staircase and followed me up into our apartment. I sat down on the floor in the middle of the living room. Swallows flitted past the open balcony while the late afternoon sun poured into the apartment like molten brass. To my left on a shelf in the open closet sat Ignatz's hat, the only thing left of him. Along the windows the flower pots stood lined up as in the past, the plants now shrivelled and dead. On the wall hung Herzl's portrait, alone on the entire bare wall. In the bookcases lay my notes, books, scribblings, drawings....

The next day, I was demolishing our own apartment. From the third-floor open balcony I let fall tables, chairs, dishes. Piles of glass, wood, and iron littered the sidewalk below. The work progressed rapidly and soon the apartment was empty. The whole ghetto reverberated with crashing thumps, cracks, and knocks; Losice groaned as if the intestines of a cadaver were being pulled. I strode up to the books and yanked them from their shelves. Down they went by the hundreds: books in Polish, in Russian, in Hebrew; textbooks, dictionaries, poetry; Mickiewicz and Heine and the Talmud and Marx. On the way down they were caught by the slipstream, stopped in midair, opened and fluttered like injured birds. Then they somersaulted and plunged downward, landing on a heap of trash. I looked around the apartment. There was nothing left in it. Only the door to the hiding place stood open, a blind, black hole, staring into the room as if it were the fatal wound that caused the town's death. Something else still remained: Herzl's picture on the wall, the large eyes sad and bitter. I took the picture off the wall and threw it out the window. It fell face down and shattered like a bottle. This was the last time I went "cleaning."

xvi

Soon after we had returned to the small ghetto, the number of survivors rose to two hundred and stopped. They ranged the widest assortment of character, age, and physique. Logically one would expect the survivors to have been the cleverest and the strongest, but that was not the case. All kinds of mediocre and feeble individuals survived, most of them unwillingly. Although we avoided speaking of what had happened – and when the subject did come up, we talked not in words but in symbols, in raw violent gestures – slowly, inexorably, there emerged the full story of where Losice went on that hot Saturday of August 22, 1942, and how it died.

Losice's fate had been set for a Saturday, in conformity with the German practice of picking Jewish holidays for such executions. In the preceding weeks, the Germans adopted two lines of policy, a strategy. They tried to give an illusion of normality by creating new working posts, by issuing new identity cards, by setting a ransom to be paid in December, and by assuring each community it would remain intact. Simultaneously, they raised terror to such a level that the mere sight of a German triggered a paralysis of mind and body.

On Friday, at eleven at night, a telephone call from Siedlce put the Germans on the alert. The Polish police, who had been kept in the dark until the last moment lest they betray the secret, were awakened after midnight. Messengers went out to the neighboring villages ordering farmers to appear with their carts in

Losice. At 1:00 a.m. on Saturday one hundred German and Polish police encircled the sleeping ghetto.

The Jews at first did not realize what was coming. That morning, whoever ventured outside or stuck his head out of a window was shot at, but they thought it was one of the Germans usual wild parties. As the siege continued, however, something ominous became clear deportation. The Jews began to prepare for "the trip." Since it was expected that the Germans would not allow them to take anything along, people put on whatever good clothes they still owned: underwear, overcoats, indispensable items for the coming winter. Babies were wrapped in pillows; the sick were put on makeshift stretchers.

At ten o'clock came the command to start. The police were told to tour the town and order all Jews outside. Eight thousand people left their homes, crying and saying good-bye to each other. Although at the beginning hundreds hid in various places, the sight of the entire populace gathered on the square made most of these people join the transport. In the end only thirty-eight people, including the twenty-seven in our attic, remained in hiding in Losice.

At eleven o'clock the women and children were ordered to mount the carts which had arrived from the villages. The men, lined up in rows of seven, with the Judenrat in front, were to make the journey on foot. Several old men refused to leave or hide and remained in their houses.

In the violence that accompanied the dispatch of the women's transport, many children, separated from their mothers, were left on the sidewalks and the steps of houses. As the Germans accompanying the transport passed them, they methodically kicked or shot them to death. Older men afraid of being trampled pulled over to the side and were immediately killed. All sick people were executed before the transport had left town. Other gendarmes combed the empty side streets executing the wounded and stragglers. On this first leg of the trip one hundred seventy people died.

At the edge of town the highway divides: one road leads to Niemojki, the other to Siedlce. When the crowd was ordered to turn in the direction of Siedlce, a spark of hope flickered that this might indeed be a resettlement. The carts with the women and children forged ahead and soon disappeared. The men had to travel the road to Siedlce, a stretch of thirty two kilometers, on foot. Polish policemen marched on both sides of the transport; the Schupo, a lieutenant and two gendarmes, rode behind. A machine gun stood mounted in the middle of their command car, surrounded on both sides by cases of beer and ammunition.

It was the hottest day of the season. When the transport reached the highway, it was already noon and the sun blazed with blistering heat. A cloud of dust rose from under the feet of the shuffling men and stayed with the crowd. Immediately, thirst flared up, but no one was allowed off the parched, dusty highway. In the command car, the lieutenant operated the machine gun, firing brief salvos at regular intervals; the other two gendarmes fired from rifles. Of the Polish police, only one used his gun, a man who later explained that he had done it because the Soviets had deported a relative to Siberia. Most of the killed and wounded were trampled. Those wounded who remained alive after the transport had passed were left on the highway.

Near Majowka, a village seven kilometers from Losice, the procession halted. The Germans were having lunch. They got out of the car, spread a tablecloth on the grass, and began to eat and drink. Here the endurance of the men broke down. First a few individuals rushed toward a nearby well for water, then the entire crowd surged toward the well. Some used their hands to drink from the pails and the cattle trough; others fell to the ground sipping the spilled water, moistening their lips in the puddles and the mud. The Germans, interrupting their lunch, hurried back to the car, and the machine gun opened fire, killing several hundred men at the well.

In the late afternoon the column reached Mordy half way to Siedlce. The town that had housed about two thousand Jews was empty. It was the first sign that Losice was not the only town to be struck that morning. Up till then the transport had been leaving their dead and wounded behind them. Now the road ahead was covered with the bodies of the Mordy people who had been driven to Siedlce a few hours earlier. The wounded sat or lay in the middle of the road. At the sight of the oncoming transport they made convulsive attempts to get out of the way, but they all eventually perished under the feet of the marching thousands.

In the calm of the approaching evening, just as the sun began to set, a Red Cross car left Losice and drove up the Siedlce highway. In the car sat two Germans who had waited all day to perform their mission of mercy. As the car drew near a wounded person, it stopped and one of the Germans shot him through the head.

Just before Siedlce the command car that accompanied the marching men drove ahead to the moving carts. Without saying anything the Germans opened fire, driving the women off the wagons. The farmers were told to turn back home. When a cloud of dust announced the approach of the column of men, the women were told to march on. Finally, in the gray shadows of the evening, the roofs and spires of Siedlce appeared on the horizon. Here the transport of men and women was taken over by Siedlce Gestapo and a troop of Ukrainians. The car of the Losice Schupo, firing their last volleys, turned around and drove back. By the time they had returned to Losice, they could count on the road eight hundred people they had killed that day.

In the outskirts of Siedlce, populated by Poles, the streets were filled with a gay crowd of week-end strollers. There were lights in the houses; children played in the yards. And when the Jews, hit by the sight of this ongoing life, averted their eyes, they saw water flowing in the gutters; the water was stained with blood. In Siedlce, too, something happened. The Poles fell silent as the procession of doomed men and women filed past, while German soldiers who lingered on the sidewalks commanded in sneering voices *Eins, zwei... eins, zwei, drei....* At this point some Jews managed to escape the transport and head back toward Losice, but most met the Red Cross car on the highway and were killed.

Eventually the transport reached the barbed wire of the Siedlce ghetto; no Jews remained there. A large square was situated between the synagogue and the old cemetery. Around ten in the evening, the Jews were driven to this central space. Thousands of Jews had already been packed into the enclosed area when the additional seven thousand from Losice were shoved in. On this one square were collected all the Jews of Siedlce, Mordy, and Losice – twenty five thousand people.

High walls surrounded the square on three sides; the fourth was closed off by a line of Germans firing into the crowd. The Jews were forbidden to lift their heads, to talk, or to move, and they had to relieve themselves where they sat. As the night progressed, the place filled with feces, blood, and corpses. The Germans kept changing shifts, but with the square bathed in darkness and the crowd silent, the thrill of killing evidently waned, for, later in the night, the shooting stopped. From the railway station, the Jews could hear the uninterrupted clatter of shuttling trains.

Through late Saturday and Sunday the Jews from Mordy and Siedlce were shipped away, and on Sunday evening the Germans drove the Losice transport to the railroad station. Several hundred exhausted and wounded people were shot when they could not stand. At the station, the Germans ordered everyone again to sit on the loading ramp. The Losice people, now two days without water, moaned, shrieked, begged; some blindly charged the Germans. The guards, laughing at this ridiculous desperation, mowed them down. Some Germans and Ukrainians walked among the Jews, collecting rings and money and asking them for their hidden gold.

On Monday morning the Germans began to load the remaining five thousand Jews from Losice; one thousand had been shipped earlier and two thousand had been killed. Two hundred fifty to a car, they were packed into boxcars jammed so tightly the last ones had to be thrown on the heads of those already inside. Then the doors were slammed shut.

Within minutes, gripped by the convulsions of asphyxiation, the people inside went insane. Fighting broke loose over access to the little windows; they stripped naked, bit their neighbors, themselves. Their yelling could be heard miles away. While the day grew higher and the sun blazed, the train stood on the ramp. Hours passed while, inside, clusters of naked bodies whined, fought, died. Then the doors of one of the cars burst open and a mass of naked delirious prisoners lurched onto the ramp. The machine guns opened fire and mowed them all down.

After this the train left the station. It sped over the country, carrying the moans of five thousand people slowly smothering to death. With each turn of the wheels more lives extinguished; with each kilometer the whining became weaker. It sped through fields, forests, villages and stations, not stopping anywhere but emitting from its locomotive every now and then a triumphant cry, the familiar elongated lament that had swept the land so many times before Losice's turn had come.

Not far from the Bug, northwest of Kosow, was a small railway station, Treblinka. There, amid brushwood and dense groves, in a place not found on any map, a new city had sprung up. The transport had reached its destination.

When the train stopped, a line of Germans stood waiting along the ramp with submachine guns slung from their shoulders, long white leather whips in their hands, and snarling dogs straining on leashes. They watched the Ukrainians unlatch the boxcars. Through the open doors, the cars disgorged the dead, flooding the ramps, overflowing the walks. Most of the living cargo that had been stuffed into the wagons was now transformed into a mass of swollen black pouches. A mere five hundred had survived, and from this remnant, two hundred men were picked to carry the dead from the ramp. On this day, it so happened that a Jew in Treblinka had stabbed a Gestapo man to death; as punishment the Germans shot all the regular workers in the camp. Consequently, it was necessary to employ new people. After the two hundred who were selected had carried off the dead, the Germans shot them all into the same ditch. Then, of the three hundred now left alive, the Germans chose fifty as permanent camp workers.

The remaining two hundred fifty were led away. From afar one heard thumping bulldozers. Smoke rose constantly from behind a tall solid wall. The group walked to that wall. There they read in huge letters: BAD, followed by a list of instructions on how to behave during the disinfection and bath. "1. Take off your clothing.

2. Put it together so that you can find it. 3. Hand money and papers over to the cashier," etc. They undressed; they gave away the papers; they tied the pairs of shoes together; they received soap for washing. Then they were led across the wall.

In a huge lot stood a huge structure from which rail tracks led off into the distance, ending where smoke and fire rose incessantly from long ditches. Near the woods a bulldozer dug new ditches. Groups of workers waited silently near big lorries. A line of tall Germans stood alongside, impatiently swinging their whips. The doors of the building opened. Inside were many cells, and the group was led into them. Then the doors were closed and locked.

They stayed inside fifteen minutes. In the meantime the workers moved the lorries close to the gates. The doors opened, the dead were thrown on the lorries and rolled away to the ditches for burning.

After three days and nights, the agony of Losice had come to an end.

It was on Sunday night, while the bulk of population was still awaiting shipment to Treblinka, that the Germans decided to create small ghettos in Siedlce and Losice. An order was issued not to kill those that hid or escaped but instead to concentrate every Jew in the new camps. This was the reason those captured in Losice after Saturday, including the Mordkowiczs, were spared. The deadline for a safe return to these camps was set for September 1.

The administration of the small ghetto was given over to the *Landskommissariat*, a semi-civil office, and at first the Schupo kept away. The Germans were tolerant. When a Jew came wounded from "the road" – the exterminations, transports, and other brushes with the Germans – we were allowed to call in a Polish doctor, even make use of the Aryan dispensary. And we were allowed to provide ourselves with all the food and clothing we cared to have.

The week following our return, the small ghetto received its first Treblinkan, a man who escaped from Treblinka itself. We soon had three of them, and Losice was later to boast of one who had escaped twice. By then the stories and the numbers these men cited were a history no longer of the death of Losice but of the end of a nation: of twenty thousand Miedzyrzec dead piled on Treblinka's ramps while, next to them, the naked crowds of Sokolow and Kielce stood waiting for the Germans to finish gassing the people from Warsaw and Vienna and Prague. And new and bigger gas chambers, these escapees told us, were being erected in Treblinka.

We listened, then returned to our drinking, the one human reaction we still exhibited. Money was no problem, health no concern, and so we drank prodigiously. We gathered at Mietek's; this lone remnant of a large family lived with ten other survivors in a posh apartment that once belonged to the richest man in town. It was a spacious salon, ablaze with chandeliers and littered with stuffed armchairs, and on the tables there were always the sleek transparent bottles of vodka. Anyone at any time could come and join in. A few girls were always in the kitchen frying sausages or eggs, and in the corner an old phonograph played some tunes. When it was cold or it rained, the stoves were lit and we all drank while the mirrors on the walls multiplied our devastated ranks into infinite crowds. We drank ourselves sick, and we danced and collapsed in the corners with hysterical laughter. Often we remained slumped over the tables or sleeping on the floor through the night. With each new day, the drinking would start again.

As dawn begins breaking on
September 1, 1939, German
bombers head for Poland.

Losice between the two World Wars.

My older sister Manya, shortly before the war.

I, flanked by two cousins.
Herschek is on my left.

Our house, seen from the Square. We lived on the top floor.

Above: August 22, 1942.   Losice's Jews, herded into the Square.
Below: Seen from hiding, scattered groups driven toward the Square.

The tail end of the populace as it leaves town.

Losice, empty except for the Jews' abandoned bundles.

Left: The men being driven down the Siedlce highway.

Below: A woman killed by the side of the road.

Above: Some of the 30,000 Jews waiting in Siedlce for the Treblinka trains under the spires of a nearby church. *Below:* Waiting for the end in Siedlce.

xvii

Workers were being sent to the villages, and as I did not want to be separated from my family, I found myself a job building a new headquarters for the Schupo on the outskirts of town. There were ten of us originally, including Herschek, whom we soon lost. One afternoon he said we had rested enough; now we must fight for our lives. After the liquidation of Losice, he had stayed some days in the Myeyski forest and barely escaped with his life; several others were killed there. I asked him where he wanted to go. He did not know. "Are you coming?" he asked. When I refused, he turned away embittered; that same night he left the ghetto.

Like many others before him, however, he was back within a week. It may seem puzzling that men returned to the ghettos knowing their fate. But it was infinitely safer to be in the ghettos – while they existed. In the woods the chances of survival were about one in a hundred. Most people perished within two or three weeks: they were caught in raids, betrayed, or massacred by the farmers. In the camps and small ghettos, except for the terror that claimed a couple of lives now and then, Jews lived on. The best strategy was to live in the ghetto for as long as possible, then either clear out a day before the trap sprang or escape from the transport. Many people also came back to the ghetto determined not to live any longer – a decision often easier to make than to adhere to, for when the time came to face death, many of these people escaped only to find themselves going once again through the familiar cycle. There were of course opposite cases. One grabbed at life at all costs, ran into the woods and villages where the sense of loneliness, despair, and the memory of the dead was too much to bear, and then returned to die with the next shipment to Treblinka.

October passed in calm rueful days, its melancholy sun wandering over fields and woods as if on a last pilgrimage. We walked to work every day trying to keep our eyes off the Polish houses, the women cooking meals, the children playing in the yards. We avoided the highway, where we might have met normal people, and tramped along the river which took us past the Jewish cemetery. Its fence was gone, the trees cut down, and pigs and goats grazed on the lush grass. Near the end, where the cemetery abutted the river, a ditch of sunken earth marked the place where Saturday's ninety dead were buried. The water seeped into the graves, creating a downwash that was beginning to carry away some of the old bones.

The building we were remodelling lay near the Niemojki road; next to it was a large shed and garden. All day we lay in the shed on a pile of straw and did nothing. Nor did the two Polish bricklayers do any work, as together with most Poles they were usually off collecting "rags" in the city.

The Poles did not hide their feelings about the extermination of the Jews. They themselves, they said, would never have done such a thing. But since they could not be held responsible, they were rather glad it had happened. The massacre revolted them and they granted that it was history's greatest crime, but it was not a bad turn for Poland. Religious Poles regarded it as God's punishment for the Jews' betrayal of Christ; the enormity of the slaughter was such that only God could have brought it about. Even so, the act provoked a restlessness in them. They had not really known the Germans until now, and panic struck their hearts when they realized what the Germans were capable of. The thought spoiled considerably the half-festive mood of those days.

The attitudes of the Poles toward the few survivors was also of a double nature. The Poles had strong psychological reasons to desire our disappearance. We had seen too many of them involved in killing Jews, and the Poles knew we understood their reaction to our tragedy. In contrast to the Germans, the Poles did care about world opinion; they did like to talk about rights and ethics, and they knew that, as long as we lived, they might find it difficult to invoke these virtues for their own cause. They were sure of God – anti-Semitism was a part of the Polish catechism – but they were not sure of some of the "humanists" whose teachings they collected in their libraries and whom they revered in their aspirations to "Western" culture. On the other hand, they did not want us to disappear, because as long as we existed we were a better prey for the Germans than they.

There was also a very practical side to the relish of our neighbors, for they were the scavengers of our property. Our pots and pans and Bibles lined their entrance halls; our broken furniture piled up in their yards; our prayer shawls served as curtains for their windows and cloths for their tables. On all gutters and roofs lay our letters and photos; in their latrines hung our books. There was not a dump that did not contain our remains. There was not a household that did not inherit something. It is natural to want to acquire property, but rarely was any Pole disturbed by the circumstances of this acquisition.

xviii

I came home from work one day to find two men asleep on my bed. In their tattered clothes and with raw cracked faces, they were strangers to me until mother revealed out that they were Motl and Shmyl, our relatives from Konstantynow. They later told us that, after Konstantynow had moved to Biala, both towns were driven on foot to Miedzyrzec, from where, on October 6, they were all shipped to Treblinka.

The two brothers had jumped from the train, Motl leaving behind his wife and seven children. Shmyl's face was scalded with some chlorine compound sprayed inside the boxcars. They had spent a week on the road, and Shmyl repeated the familiar story of raids in the woods and of the farmers' hostility. Despite all that, they were determined not to stay in the ghetto. As soon as they recovered their strength, the two brothers threw sacks over their shoulders, stuffed loaves of bread into their pockets, and walked down the country road leading toward the forests. I watched them go with mixed feelings of envy and pity.

Indications multiplied that we would not last much longer here. We never doubted that the small ghettos had been created to lure and concentrate the remaining Jews and thus facilitate our extermination. Yet one could think that, for some weird reason, the Germans might want to maintain miniature ghettos: the Jews would perhaps be spared to work as slave laborers; as proof to the world that not all Jews had been exterminated; as objects of fun, as specimens for zoos. Possibly we had been spared merely because the handful of us who remained could be liquidated just before the war's end. But to apply reason to our situation was foolish. Our extermination was not a matter of logic or profit; it was not even an act of passion; and so we knew that end was only a question of time. We observed how, after we had been concentrated, the Germans began to tighten their grip. It did not come as a surprise; we had expected it. We visualized very clearly the day they would come for us. We knew exactly the road we would travel, the gleaming railroad tracks over which we would roll and roll with a monotonous thump of wheels; we saw the walls of Treblinka and we rehearsed in detail each leg of the journey to the gas chambers. We saw the smoke billowing against the sky after we had been put inside the crematoria, and then we saw ourselves returning to Losice as transparent clouds of ashes. Somewhere there lurked the last fatal hour.

It was exactly as Herschek had painted the picture of Slonim after the slaughter, the crippling psychosis of awaiting one's death. When too many carts appeared in town, we recalled the mission for which they had been mobilized by the Germans on a certain Saturday in August. When the Germans who were having suits made by the Jewish tailors canceled the orders, we expected the end to come the next morning. The nights were the worst time. The slightest movement outside brought us to our feet. When shots rang in the stillness, we ran out in our underwear, waking the neighbors and asking each other, "Is this it?" Various dates and deadlines were rumored for our extermination, and we lined up to await the gendarmes. When we left in the morning, we said good-by knowing we might be liquidated outside and the rest in the camp. At work we listened for any commotion in the ghetto, for firing, cries. Returning from work we prolonged the march, loath to enter the doomed camp. It was a box of death. Standing at its corners for hours, we peered at the Polish districts, where lights were lit, families gathered on the front steps, dogs played....

People did think about escaping the small ghetto, but these were absurd, futile, pathetic dreams. And they were ten times more absurd for me. I had a family, an aging father, and a tiny sister; I could not leave them. The chances of finding refuge outside were nil. People had tried to save themselves from the first slaughter, hoping that some Jewish communities would remain and that it would be possible to live among them. Faced with a common enemy, we expected that the Poles would have some sympathy for the remnants of such massacres, or at the least that they would stay neutral. It was never active support that we expected of individual Poles. We needed their assistance but could not ask for it because there was the death penalty for hiding us. What we did ask for was an absence of hostility. But this they were unwilling to give. In that respect there was here some parallel to the behavior of the humdrum German soldier. No one of us expected any German to endanger himself or to disobey orders. What makes the German record fatal is that, above and beyond the orders they were issued, they, individually and voluntarily, actively and tacitly, endorsed, enlarged, and enjoyed the official program. We had nothing and no one to count on, not even our own brothers and leaders overseas who, in other times and in other respects, had proved so resourceful and shrewd. One could only make a gesture, and thereby leave evidence of having tried to survive. But for whom the gesture? And at what agony? It was enough to recall our march to Konstantynow to shudder in horror. It was unthinkable for me to strike out on my own in order to save myself; indeed, I tried to stay as close as possible to the rest of the family. When others ran from the sounds of firing in the ghetto, I ran wildly toward them to be with my parents and sisters, afraid to miss the final moment.

Days and weeks passed while the liquidation of all traces of Jewish existence in Losice continued. For two months thousands of carts lugged Jewish possessions; yet the homes were still not completely cleaned out. Seeing that the job had to be finished, the Germans solved the problem in a radical way: for a nominal price they sold all Jewish properties to the Poles.

Under new management the liquidation of the ghetto proceeded with fresh zeal and efficiency. The buyers would appear one day with carts in front of the houses they had bought and empty them to the last rag, nail, and board. As most of the buyers were

farmers with no intention of living
could be ripped away. They rem
window frames, and yanked boa
mutilated walls remained after t
filled with water, the roofs sagg

Thereafter, the ghetto was ...
to could enter and live in it. A few grocers p
their stores; spinsters who had quarrelled with their families, an
as all kinds of thieves, tramps, and prostitutes, moved in. Some
grotesque situations arose when a single person occupied an eight.
room apartment or one family settled into a three-storey house.
Most of the buildings, however, remained empty. The Germans then
sold the houses for scrap. After such a purchase the new owners
appeared with axes and shovels and tore the building down. In a
few weeks all that was left were the foundations, raw and jagged
and filled with rain. The town was disappearing from the map.

There still remained the warehouses with the clothing of the
dead Jews. While the better clothes were shipped to Germany, the
rest were disposed of in public auctions. They heaped the "rags" in
the middle of the square and sold them. On days when these
auctions took place the farmers piled into Losice as on a religious
holiday. Preference was given to German informers, to prostitutes
who served the Schupo, and to collaborating officials. The rest was
grabbed by whoever had strong arms. Often the Germans just threw
the clothes into the crowd and watched the hands of the mob
tearing the things from each other. Sometimes they threw the
"rags" in a heap and, at a given signal, let the Poles run for it.

At work we watched the procession of farmers to these
auctions. It was like the holiday of Corpus Christi when, over all
roads and highways, the pious pilgrimaged to the holy rites. The

...ked on, heatedly talking and arguing among themselves, ...ing what to get, how to divide the purchased property, and ... it was best to go. They came with their entire families, ...ryone carrying a sack and a rope tied around the waist. In the evening they walked back, loaded with tables, beds, pots, and rags. As success at these auctions was a matter of luck, some returned doubled up under their acquisitions, while others, empty-handed, returned full of bitterness. When they passed us I always had the impression they were angry at us for their failure. One heard curses and threats directed against fellow Poles, against the Germans, and against the dead Jews. Quarrels exploded on the highway, and the women tore each other's hair fighting over the loot. At these fights, often vicious, tables would be broken, dishes shattered. Fights also occurred when time came to divide the spoils, and then fists and even clubs and knives were used to settle claims.

Then the auctions, too, wound to an end and a vast silence descended on the ruined town. We were now the sole reminder of the destroyed life, and events indicated that we, too, would not last. We went on drinking at Mietek's with ever growing abandon, and we now also began to drink at work. Not far from where we worked was a lonely Polish inn where, as the days turned cold and rainy, we would sit for hours watching the leaves fall from the huge elm trees along the highway and the crows as they hung in flocks over the treetops, crowing their hoarse, saw-like cry. We would turn our heads away only to stare through the half-open door at the owner's private quarters: clean beds, holy pictures on the walls, and, of course, Jewish furniture. We would see there the owner's daughter, a young handsome girl, studying Latin from a book in her lap. With our every visit, she inexorably advanced in her studies. Once when we had been told that tomorrow was "the day," we sat, drinking and waiting, while the girl diligently practiced: *habeo, habes, habet.* As I listened to her occasional errors, I thought that, when they buried us, she would be studying the third conjugation, and that when we started to rot, she would have mastered the *accusativus cum infinitivo.* I smiled at her. She smiled back and blushed. Then I smiled to the man behind the counter. He came over, offered us some recently arrived halvah. I told him we spent all our money on drinks. "I will give it to you on credit," he said. We all burst out in violent laughter. The man, thinking we were drunk, smiled uncomfortably and returned behind the counter.

xix

Winter arrived abruptly. On the tree branches, still covered with yellow leaves, hoar frost sat like a web of Christmas tree decorations. A dry frosty wind blew down the alleys, raising billows of snow powder and shaking the silver laces off the trees. On the window panes bloomed the familiar ice ferns. But instead of urging us into our homes, the winter drove us into the cold and snow. We wandered over the wintry country like dummies, not knowing what to do with ourselves. Herschek, in his riding boots and fur collared jerkin, was more of a phantom every day. Boris was twice his size; he had become a giant, and I wondered how they would manage to bury him. News of near and distant slaughters kept arriving. The drinking parties at Mietek's went on and on.

Then, with the tenderness of a kept promise, came the verdict. I was eating dinner when Herschek poked my shoulder. Turning, I saw the newspaper he held. There was news about an invasion, I thought, but Herschek did not let me read the front page; instead he showed me an announcement in the back of the paper.

On the territory of the Warsaw District, central Jewish communities are being created in six cities, among them Siedlce. All Jews who live anywhere else must move to these central places by November 30, 1942. Any Jews found outside these communities will be punished by death. The death penalty is also to be imposed on anyone hiding Jews.

Soon after this notice appeared in the newspapers, huge red posters with the same message plastered the walls of all cities and villages. We knew this was no move to Siedlce but a trip to Treblinka. Not only did the Germans fail to convince us this was a relocation, but they also unwittingly informed us of the date set for the execution. We had three weeks left. In the shadow of this deadline all life in the ghetto came to a standstill. We stopped talking to each other and everyone retreated into a shell to spend his last days in solitude. In the uncleaned, unheated homes we struggled with oncoming death in a repulsive and ridiculous way. Even the drinking at Mietek's ceased. Each day, we could hear a giant pendulum tick away our remaining time.

In this final stage, an opportunity for rescue appeared: we heard we could obtain falsified Polish documents, called *Kennkarten*. The evidence suggests that the Polish underground manufactured these papers: only they had experience in such forgeries; only they could have operated so widely and so efficiently. The motivation behind this offer remains obscure, even today. The scheme may have been conceived to help the Jews; if so, however, the stiff prices exacted for these documents went into the pockets of intermediaries. Possibly it was done purely for profit: the underground needed money, and the selling of Kennkarten was certainly safer than raiding German banks. Given the subsequent record of the Polish underground regarding the Jews, this latter version is the more likely. But whatever the motivation, the Kennkarten were the only effective and accessible help we ever received from any source.

As these papers seemed the only means of deliverance, the phenomenon soon assumed pathological forms. Anyone in the ghetto who had money purchased false papers, even though they were useless in effecting this metamorphosis from Jew to Pole unless one had the cooperation of Polish friends. The pronounced difference in appearance between us and the Poles presented an insurmountable problem for us. A German may not have recognized every Jew, a Pole could "smell" him through a wall, so sharp were their national talents on that score. So success required the acquiescence of the Poles. After the Kennkarten became available, some girls did make use of them; they were the first to leave the ghetto in a plausible attempt at survival.

Soon anyone with any plan, however far-fetched, deserted the ghetto. The Mordkowiczs were negotiating with a farmer about a hiding place. One day Herschek told me he would shortly leave the ghetto, adding, after a long silence, "I am deserting my mother."

I had no plans. Our family had no money, but this was not the problem. Had we been able to find a place, those with money would have been more than willing to join us and pay all expenses. We had scraped together seven thousand zlotys from our ghetto "cleaning," and we spent it all on a Kennkarte for Manya. But, with Kennkarte in hand, she sat at home, unable to find a Pole willing to cooperate.

November 9. A snowstorm woke us from a brooding, feverish night. I ate breakfast alone as the others stayed in bed, gazing at the ceiling with fixed, abnormal eyes. I walked to the end of the ghetto and watched the blizzard swirl. The wind lifted clouds of snow and deposited them in rolling, heavy dunes that blocked alleys and the entrances to houses. I did not go to work because, according to the last prediction, this was definitely to be the day of our liquidation. Whoever had the chance ran from the ghetto, leaving friend and family behind. About me flitted the wrapped shadows of those remaining, and I felt as sorry for those who were escaping as for those who were staying. Where were they going in this furious blizzard?

Frozen and shivering, I dragged myself home for dinner, but nobody had cooked that day. They were all still in bed. Mother nagged Manya to run away, somewhere. "You have a Kennkarte," she kept reminding her. Manya did not reply. It was cold in the house. I started a fire, sat down near the stove, and, staring at the flames, relapsed into a stupor.

After some time I heard someone run up the stairs. The door opened and the wind burst inside with a spray of snow. Someone touched my shoulder and I saw Herschek. "I am leaving," he said.

We went out. Herschek told me he and two other boys had found a hiding place on a farm in Shanikow. I waited outside his house when he took leave of his family. Herschek came back rather quickly, wearing his brown jerkin, a ski cap, and high boots. We struggled through knee-deep snow to the edge of the ghetto, where his two companions stood with knapsacks at their feet.

We waited for the cart that was to pick them up. We stood without looking at each other, blinking our eyes in the oblique, violent streaks of snow. When the cart appeared, it passed us without stopping while the two boys threw their knapsacks on it, and then followed a few paces behind the farmer.

"The cart...," I said.

I stretched out my hand. He did not take it. Without looking, he stepped out of the ghetto, and I watched his silhouette fade into the snowstorm, emerge at the corner of the street for a flicker, then disappear.

The same day, Yankel's little girl, Rivkah, left the ghetto. She was to go into hiding with a Polish policeman, the same man who had arrested her on the Tuesday she left the attic. During our stay in the small ghetto he used to visit us, saying he was never at peace for having arrested the little girl. This remorse, boosted by a need for money, made him decide to save the girl's life.

A few days later, Manya, too, suddenly had the opportunity to leave. An old friend, when told that Manya had a Polish passport, said he would find a place for her at his daughter's farm. We lit the room and for the first time in many days cooked supper. We treated our friend to a drink while Manya got ready for the trip. Then we said good-by quickly, swallowing our emotions. And she was gone.

Two days later, just as we were getting ready for bed, Manya reappeared. She stood for a while on the threshold, then came in. We looked at her with crazy eyes, and words caught in our throats. She behaved as if nobody were in the room. She took off her coat, the rubbers, the shoes, all without a single word. "Say something," shouted Father. Looking at him with a bitter smile she continued to undress. "Say something," he yelled. She was undressed and getting into bed. Before she went to sleep she turned around and said, "I cried more as I was leaving than when I was coming back." She pulled the blanket over her head and went to sleep.

XX

We still went to work during these last days putting the finishing touches on the Schupo's new quarters. To escape the cold, we started fires in the stoves and sat near them for hours. The smokestack would get red hot, radiating a pleasant warmth through the newly fixed-up rooms while, outside, the snow fell steadily, softly against the windowpanes. The mansion was beautifully renovated: bathtubs, recreation rooms, an electric kitchen, rugs. All this we would leave as fare for their transporting us to Treblinka. Those who were still planning to escape looked at the snow and the freezing windows with terror; those who had given up and were waiting for the end sang in gloomy voices.

Returning from work one night I bumped into Leyzor – a childhood companion with whom, once upon a time, Herschek and I had hiked, played soccer, and broken windows with our slingshots. I knew he had escaped from Treblinka to Sokolow, where he again fell into their hands. Now he had escaped a second time. I took his arm and turned him around. In his striped Belgian suit, gold watch, and silk tie, he looked like a sample sent out by Treblinka as an advertisement. Bearish, red-haired, he shook hands with his old imperturbable composure. He asked about Herschek. I told him he had left. "Good," he said. Then, stamping his heavy feet, he followed me into our apartment.

It was not my intention to talk about him or about Treblinka. He had twice crawled out from the flames, and I only wanted to touch him before he took a third trip there. But the story of Treblinka soon filled the room.

He talked about his father, whom he himself had carried out of the boxcar. He lifted his hands with their stubby nails to show how the Germans cut off fingers to get the rings and the diamonds. "It's done only to the dead," he reassured us. All this had happened when he was there the first time. Things had since progressed, Treblinka had a new giant gas chamber that could handle five thousand people at a time. With the precision of truth he described how the Germans had lined the *Himmelstrasse*, as they called the path to the gas chambers, with gravel; how a band played tangos and waltzes; and how the Germans rocked lazily in hammocks watching the parades of nude women. Leyzor put his small, puffy hands down on the table, looked at his fingernails with his small, pink eyes, and calmly related how the hair was cut off, the gold teeth pulled out.... He talked and talked; his words became chaos, sounds without meaning.

When I later moved away from the table, Leyzor was gone, the room was dark, and all the others lay on their beds. They were going to spend the night dressed. I put on my jerkin and walked out. There was no one in the alley. I had already started climbing Mietek's stairs when I recalled the drinking had stopped; Mietek himself had left for Warsaw with a Kennkarte. I stood at the outlet of the alley, looking into the suddenly clear night; my eyes ranged over the frozen river, the forest, and the scattered farms that were peacefully asleep. When I returned home, the dawn had broken and mother was already on her feet. In the last weeks she had often lost control over herself; she neither cooked nor slept, nor let us sleep. Now, as on many other mornings, she wrapped a heavy shawl over her head and left to look for help. There was something raw and animal-like in her empty attempts to save us, a repugnant, primeval motherliness. I went to bed and covered my head with the blanket.

I was deeply asleep when someone tugged at me.

"Get up," I heard Father call impatiently.

I turned my head and saw a farmer in the room, a wretched-looking, bewildered peasant with narrow, frightened eyes. Next to him stood Motl, gesticulating. A wild thought occurred to me. During Motl's previous visits we had talked about the chances of finding a farmer who, for money, would take in Jews, but the talk had been as real as the babble about the Messiah; now, evidently, he had come with just such a man. I gazed at the peasant. My first thought was that he intended to take us in and kill us, and yet this farmer who looked more like a poacher or bandit had my confidence. As I looked at his tattered clothes and hole-ridden boots, it was obvious that sheer misery had forced him to consider such a frightful deal, and I always preferred a deal in which we would not have to rely on kindness, or charity.

Motl's eyes sparkled as he came over to me. "Get up, every-thing is practically settled," he cried.

It was at this instant that the reality of it all dawned on me. Here was an escape – a sudden, searing chance of escape. We ourselves had no money to pay for such an exorbitant undertaking, but Uncle Yankel was coming with us, and he undertook to pay the entire cost. There was no argument about the price: the peasant got all he wanted. Many parts of this undertaking should have been resolved before we transferred to the farm, but we postponed them; many problems, we knew, never could or would be resolved. We didn't bother; the thing was to get out of the ghetto as quickly as possible. We agreed on the logistics of our escape and, after eating supper with us, the farmer left.

Of the ten people in our two families, three were not to be with us. Rivkah had already been sheltered by the policeman. Manya, who with her Kennkarte posed as a Polish girl, found work in the same village where our farmer lived. Yankel's youngest son, Itzek, a boy of about eight, was deposited with another farmer considered more trustworthy. The remaining seven were to stay with the farmer Motl had just found.

We immediately packed a minimum of our possessions. That night, three people, my parents and Belcia, were to leave for the farm. Another three – Berko, my Aunt and I – were to leave the following night. Uncle Yankel was to remain in the ghetto to gather as much money as possible for the deal. As the farmer who was to shelter us did not own a horse, another peasant – Wacek, Motl's long-time friend who was later to become a historic figure in our ordeal – undertook to transport us there. When night came he drove up with his cart and we heaped it with our packs. Wacek drove on alone, while Motl, together with my parents and Belcia, got out of town by back roads.

The next day, the frost yielded and the snow thawed on the streets. The ghetto filled with puddles and grew very quiet. Most of those with any chance of escape had already left; the rest were waiting for Treblinka. Nobody came into the ghetto any more – no Pole, not even a German. The remaining Jews were no longer being taken to work. The ghetto had a maximum of twelve days to live.

Then night came, the dark and misty night of November 18. Rain fell, then snow, then hail; then the sky cleared. A slash of yellow light atop the Myeyski forest reflected dimly on our house that rose white and empty at the edge of the square. My home! I was leaving it, the streets where I had played, the river I had watched each spring. I was leaving all Jews, the millions that floated in clouds of cold ashes, and those who would join them tomorrow. One step more and the ghetto was behind us. As we left the pit of the dying, we did not know that we were entering another pit filled with the screams of those who had survived their own death.

Part Three

The Silence

1942 — 1944

A still, flat land. Along the horizons, forests. Winds tumbled over fields and puddles and trees, their howl the cold, immutable voice of the country. Here and there villages huddled in the mud. And far off, all by itself, stood a lonely, small farm – a white-washed house, a shed, and an unfinished barn. In the loft of the farmhouse we lay hidden.

The loft was dark except for narrow bands of light filtering in through the eaves – just enough to outline the smokestack and our bodies heaped in the corner. Through the cracks we could see a trail threading from the house into the waterlogged fields and, to the west, a pine grove on a hill. From the living quarters below came the shuffling sound of a woman working: a pot rattled, steps emerged and receded. Unseen by us a peasant occasionally approached along the trail; a door squeaked and then came a greeting: *Blessed be Jesus Christ.* A hen clucked sleepily, and all was still again.

We lay motionless without making a sound, afraid to move lest we disturb this age-old melancholy, lest one word of ours explode like an alarm and upset the order of existence. The hay must not rustle, and no knock, cough, or breath must be heard as all around us lurked the vast stillness of a Polish village and the sharp ears of its peasants. Through the slots I watched the cold sky that

145

seemed to recede to unreachable heights. Beyond the forests, clouds gathered like powerful mountain ranges. I scanned these mysterious skies, and in my brain there was no thought, no reaction.

The first day of our makeshift stay was coming to an end when, towards evening, a cautious shuffling in the depths of the loft betrayed someone's arrival. We looked at the bulky silhouette and recognized the farmer. Motionless and silent, he leaned against the chimney. Although we could not see, we knew that he had troubled eyes. Why had he come? Why wasn't he digging the shelter for us in the shed? Why were we still being kept in the loft?

"Ghosts are in the house.... Ghosts," he said.

Ghosts in the house – a symbol of the terror we brought with us into this land, a promise of the day when twelve shots would ring out at the walls of this peasant hut and seven Jews and five Poles would be buried together in a common grave. The peasant stood immobile as a tree and waited.

I recalled the night we had come here: the woods, the pine grove, the hill we descended with our eyes glued to the dim light in the valley. A dull knocking had come from below, the sound of piles being driven into the ground. As we approached, the knocking had stopped. Motl, with a bag on his shoulder, had walked ahead, and we had followed him single file until we found ourselves on a meager farm. A dog had growled somewhere, stopped. The tiny light was near, a door creaked, and we had entered the farm house.

Whitewashed walls of a bare room, an earthen floor, a bench in the corner, and a big clay stove with eaves above it. In the kerosene lamp, its cover broken, smoked a feeble flickering light. It was cold in the hut, colder than outside. Motl stuck his hand into the big sooty pot on the stove, took out a few steamed potatoes, and ate them, smacking his tongue. The farmer, tall, gaunt and silent, leaned against the stove, gazing into space with a dazed look. Next to him, clad in a thin torn dress, her hair unkempt, a small woman slouched, scratching her head with jerky strokes. Barely able to stand on her shaking legs, she groaned, "Please, Jan, don't. I am scared. Don't...." She repeatedly crossed herself and implored, "You are killing us, me and the children...." The peasant stood glum and rigid and did not answer. Outside, beyond the blanket covering the window, lurked a heavy silence; only the dogs bayed, long and menacingly.

We sat on the floor with sunken heads, our faces buried to hide our pain and our shame and humiliation. I watched the soot-covered lamp with its sputtering little flame, asking myself why the farmer did not kill us. I raised my head and looked at him in wonder. He stood at the stove, cold as a rock, his jaws locked. Meanwhile, his wife lay in the corner, whining like a smitten dog. Here was man, surrounded by two monsters, death and destitution. The big, clumsy peasant was struggling. On one side were we Jews, who could one day cause his skull to be shattered by German bullets; on the other slept his hungry children. That first night, when, despite the terror in his eyes and his wife's panic, he had asked us to climb the loft, we thought that it was the final decision. But now, two days after our arrival, we had him in front of us, babbling in fright.

"Ghosts are in the house."

We did not answer. We had no answer. The farmer could choose, but we had no choice. In his hands lay our lives, lives whose masters we had ceased to be long ago. The deal was wholly based on money, and it was futile to attempt persuasion or to beg for pity. If he had changed his mind, we would have had to go back to the ghetto. So Mother told him that we wanted a clear answer from him whether he was going to keep us or not, and that, if not, we had better know it now while there were still Jews in Losice.

The peasant stood a while longer in the loft, then left as noiselessly as he had come.

The next morning, the farmer brought us breakfast, leaned against the chimney again, and watched us eat. He was fingering his tattered coat and scratched his head. Finally he said: *Kapota albo kaput* – he would either get rich or perish. Again he expressed in a short sentence all that could be said; in it lay not only the farmer's decision but also the very soul of the transaction. Misery won, and in its gloomy victory it sneered at death. The farmer lay down an additional condition; namely, that after the war we give him all our bedding. We promised him all we owned, here and elsewhere. Satisfied, he collected the dishes, brought us a gigantic loaf of black bread and started to dig a pit under the shed.

It was not a simple job. He had to be cautious so that neighbors would not see or hear him digging. He could not be at it all day, for this would awaken the suspicions of his cousin Antoni, who lived nearby. As he proceeded with his digging, the problem arose how to dispose of the dirt. It was late fall, a season when peasants do little work and spend their hours visiting and gossiping. While he surreptitiously worked, we slept, sometimes twenty hours a day. After the man had agreed to keep us, there followed a complete physical and mental lethargy. These days of waiting occupy no space in my memory. There remains only a sort of a hum, a rustle of sweet-smelling hay and the murmur of voices in the hut below us.

By Sunday night, four days after we arrived, we were ready to transfer to the underground shelter. There were quite a few packs, and it took some time to get them all down into the house. The farmer covered the windows and lit the lamp, then built a fire in the stove. We sat on the bedding and watched the dim light of the lamp, the shadows on the walls. In the adjoining room a tense silence hovered in the darkness; his wife and children were awake, listening to what was going on. The farmer occasionally lifted his head to listen, but the night was quiet save for the distant baying of dogs.

From our supplies we filled cups with vodka and invited the farmer's wife to join us. She came with mortal fear blinking in her eyes. We tried to calm her, stammering that perhaps it would succeed, perhaps she would be rich and have everything for her children, perhaps.... But we were short of words. We knew it was all a lie.

We drank the vodka. We put the frying pan on the low bench and ate the kielbasa. The woman reluctantly kept us company. We again tried to say something, but each word required a physical strain, and nothing could liven up this morbid celebration. We raised a toast that we might drink together again soon. The woman wept.

The lamp was extinguished, the fire in the stove doused. The farmer opened the door slightly and listened; we were told to move singly to the shed. Loaded with packs, we slid across the yard and disappeared into the shed. Then, one by one, we lowered ourselves into the pit.

xxii

Uncle Yankel arrived more than a week later, having barely escaped the last and final slaughter at Losice. On Friday, November 27, the Germans had surrounded the small ghetto while he was in the Polish Section. From the doorway of an empty house, he watched the remaining victims being marched to Treblinka. The small ghetto ceased to exist, and, for us, all links to the outside world ended. Our only contact was Motl, who, with his brother Shmyl, found a hiding place in the nearby village of Dubicze. There were five of them in a shelter very much like ours: Goldstein, who supplied the money, came with a nephew of his, and Motl and Shmyl brought in Enoch – the man who sheltered us when we were in Konstantynow and whose wife and six children had died with the Biala transport. These two brothers, Motl in his thirties and Shmyl only eighteen, both with alert blue eyes and short and stocky, were the pillars of our existence. For years they had dealt with the Poles and knew the peasants as intimately as the woods and roads of the countryside. While all of us, at least at the beginning, could do nothing but squat in our holes, they moved about. Farmers who would have nothing to do with anyone else talked to them and sold them food. Motl brought us the basic provisions we needed, as well as information, particularly about Manya, who, posing as a Pole, worked on a nearby farm, and about Itzek, who was living with the elder of Dubicze.

Afraid of being discovered digging, the farmer had built a cramped, minimal shelter just large enough to let a man slip through a square entrance overhead. It was not possible to stand, and in a sitting position our heads touched the ceiling. The pit, about five feet by seven, allowed each person just enough space to sleep on his side. Only the children could stretch their legs. The ceiling consisted of two heavy doors laid over logs. Boards lined two walls; the other two were bare earth. Along one boarded wall was a bunk which left a narrow corridor along the opposite wall. During the day four people sat on the bunk while the rest squatted in the corridor. At night we covered this passageway with boards, thereby converting the entire shelter into one large sleeping platform.

When we abandoned the small ghetto, we had taken along such indispensable items as bedding, clothing, and a few pots. All these things were to have gone under the bunk, but we discovered that the farmer, in his haste, had not bothered to remove the soil there. It was an unbearable situation, but our host ignored our complaints. He did only what was absolutely necessary, and he had no patience for what he considered troublesome details. So we were forced to rely on our own devising. Using tablespoons, the women busied themselves all day underneath the bunk, digging up earth which they then stored in a sack. If, as we hoped, the farmer were eventually to dispose of the sack, we would gain some space.

It was soon apparent that life could not continue under these circumstances. Trifles turned into insoluble problems. When the kettle with hot soup was delivered, we had no place to put it; when Shmyl or Motl visited us, one of us had to stay awake all night huddling in the corner to make room for him. After Yankel's arrival the difficulties increased to a point where we were forced to make changes.

Again we mentioned the intolerable cramping to the farmer, but he pretended not to hear. When we insisted he do something, he refused; his managing to camouflage the construction of the shelter had been a miracle, he declared, and it would be best not to tempt fate again. In a way we agreed with him, for we too felt that only through a stroke of exceptional luck could this shelter have come about. Yet we could not go on living in these conditions indefinitely, and so we persisted in our attempts to have the farmer extend the pit. He cited one impediment after another; he had no more boards; he could not dig too close to the foundations because the walls would collapse; the shelter might flood. Then it occurred to us to pay him for the job. At once, all his arguments vanished.

When we promised, in addition, to buy him two bottles of vodka, he immediately got down to work.

Yankel and I helped him. First, after shoveling the manure from the place where the pit was dug, we extended its top level. Once the earth had been removed from the upper portion, we replaced the ceiling and covered it with manure to disguise it from above. Then the farmer continued the excavation inside the shelter. I pulled the dirt out in pails and Yankel loaded it into sacks. Outside, the farmer's wife stood guard. From time to time she would run in to yell: "God, somebody is coming," and we would all tumble down as the farmer fled the shed. But soon he would be back and work resumed. By evening the job was completed.

After the pit was enlarged, we modified the arrangement inside. We dismantled the old bunk and converted half the shelter into a permanent bed. On top, we piled the bedding; underneath, we stashed all our belongings. In the other half we installed two benches, between which we rigged a board anchored to the two walls. During the day the board served as a table; at night, when lowered to the level of the benches, it converted the entire shelter into a bed. The farmer also built a special cover for the entrance which could be opened and closed both by us from the inside and by the farmer from the outside. Due to the digging, the floor of the shed had initially been uneven, but as time went on and the layer of manure thickened, nothing from above could suggest that seven people lived their lives under that shed.

At the beginning we had a watch with us. Given the perpetual night in our pit this watch assumed especial importance. One day, it needed repair, so we gave it to the farmer to take to Biala. We never saw it again. Many other items were lost in a similar manner, the farmer each time coming up with the most ingenious explanations as to how they vanished. Our intuition took the place of the watch. We woke with dawn – although in the shelter, of course, we never saw daylight. The squeak of the door in the farmer's house when he paid his first visit to the livestock indicated the start of a new day. The sound of filling the troughs and the farmer's cooing as he caressed the pigs signaled that it was time for us to get up. Someone lit the lamp and while all of us squatted in a corner of the shelter, Belcia made the bed. The shelter now resumed its daytime architecture. After half the pit had been reconverted into two benches and a table we more or less dressed and sat down. A white jug, which had accompanied Belcia on her trip to the police-man and which we had carried on our trips to and from Konstan-tynow, held the water that had to suffice for all our various needs. For washing we used one of our eating pots. One comb which was rapidly losing its teeth was passed from one head to the next. With this the morning toilette was over. A "normal" day began.

We waited for coffee. The farmer brought it rather early. With one hand he would lift the cover, and with the other, lower the soot-black pot down to us. At the beginning of our stay he made soup for breakfast, but later he said it was too much to cook twice a day, so he replaced soup with coffee. Made of roasted rye this coffee had only one virtue: it was always hot. We sweetened it with saccharine, then drank in shifts because we lacked cups.

Although dinner was the culmination of our daily routine, it was scarcely a feast. There was never enough, and all our pleas for more were of no avail. At first we handed the food that Motl bought for us in the village to the farmer to cook for us, but we soon realized that he was appropriating most of it for himself. Changing the procedure we then parcelled out small amounts to him for each day's needs. But this did not curb his thievery, and our complaints had no effect. So we had to be content with whatever the farmer gave us, which was not much. Still, dinner was the central event of our existence, for the satisfaction of physical hunger was associated with mental excitement. We developed such sharp senses we could tell how much lard the farmer had used, or whether there was a spoonful less soup today than yesterday. Yet, despite this shortage of cooked food, there was no starvation at that time. We had enough dry provisions and fats, and the farmer sold us as much bread as we wished. We would later recall these times as the period of prosperity, a golden age which was never to return.

After dinner we waited for dark. From the outset of our life in the pit the most longed for time was night. Night was our ally, the only friend when everything was our mortal enemy. The sound of livestock being watered intimated the approach of evening; when we heard the woman milk the cow, we knew it was already dark. The farmer would spread straw in the stall, give the cow some hay, and lock the door. We were not to hear him again until morning.

At night we talked in whispers while we shaded the lamp to prevent any light from leaking into the shed. Then we ventured out, cautioning each other to maintain absolute silence. Emerging from the pit was like leaving a hot bath. The sty was pitch dark, the livestock shuffled uneasily in their sleep, and from outside we heard the wind and the patter of the falling snow. We always felt an urge to run back down. Everything was frightening: the breathing of the animals, the phosphorescent eyes of the sheep, the distant howling of dogs. Panic sucked at our bones as we realized that we were separated from the outside world only by the thin walls of the shed, a distance which down below seemed infinite.

One of our last daily tasks was to air the shelter. The ventilation consisted of exchanging the hot air of the pit for the smelly but cool air of the shed. We turned down the kerosene lamp, opened the cover and sat, silent and motionless, feeling the waves of cold air descend into the pit. Then we went to sleep.

Our farmer's name, Karbicki, ended with a suffix that hinted of aristocracy, but there his nobility ended. He was a tall, young, crude peasant, strong as a bear. While Karbicki possessed the rugged common sense of the peasantry, his wife retained all its negative strains. She was dumb, petty, and stubborn. They had three children, all girls, ranging in age from six to ten years. These children originally presented the most serious obstacle. They had to know that seven Jews were hidden on the farm and it seemed to us that in such circumstances the deal was doomed from the start. Youngsters of that age could not possibly realize the seriousness of the situation, and we were convinced that eventually they would reveal our presence, intentionally or accidentally. But the farmer swore this was no problem. He said he had a foolproof way of handling it; when we asked what solution he proposed, he answered, "A whip." He laughed his short, squeaky giggle and added that his children would understand everything, and he would not even have to use the whip. We passed over it, not because he had convinced us but because we had no choice. It later turned out that the children kept the secret better than their father.

The farm was part of the village of Koszelowka, although the village itself lay about a mile to the east of us. To the left of us lived the farmer's cousin, Antoni. There were no other close neighbors. Behind the farm was a pine grove and the low bushes through which we had come. The farmer owned six acres of land which supplied him with enough bread for about three-quarters of the year, potatoes for him and the livestock, and a little money to buy salt and kerosene. He had built the house and shed himself but the barn remained only half finished because he did not have enough lumber to complete it. The whole family was clad practically in rags; the house was bare and primitive. His wealth consisted of a cow, two pigs, and several sheep, all kept in the shed above us. Unable to afford a horse, he worked his field with a rented animal or tilled the soil himself, pulling the plough harnessed to his powerful shoulders. He did not even keep a dog, and he could not afford a well of his own. This was the way he had lived before the war. Killing the Jews, the Germans promised, would buy him a new life, just as the Polish OZON had promised would occur when they expelled them. The Jews were exterminated, but the only elements of a new life were crippling requisitions of grain and livestock, which deprived the farmer of bread, even in the winter, and left no money for salt or kerosene.

Karbicki was made of hard, strong peasant stock. When faced with hardships and danger and his role was to stick it out, he endured them with blind, iron stubbornness. The decision to hide us, even though it could bring death to him and his family, fitted in with his cold, calculating tenacity. The motive force behind it all was money and nothing else. From the moment it occurred to him to undertake the deal, he realized that this was a unique chance to make money, a chance that would never recur. Initially he asked three hundred zlotys a week, but he later turned out to be a master of financial doubletalk with few scruples against lying or breaking terms. He shunned neither threats nor sanctions if they promised results. And so, instead of the three hundred zlotys, we ended paying a thousand. Furthermore, he asked payment for the entire winter in advance. This was the most disquieting aspect of the deal, for we suspected he wanted the money in advance in order to kill us later. Such things had happened more than once. Then, too, his appearance – hands like shovels and unusually narrow, totally white, icy eyes – did not inspire much confidence. But we could not afford to worry about it and went along with his various financial schemes. When Yankel arrived, Karbicki demanded an additional one hundred and fifty zlotys weekly for his presence, even though the original agreement had, obviously, included him. He also tried to make money in other ways. He baked bread for us, and though the flour cost four hundred zlotys, he asked for double that amount; though a meter of flour yielded a hundred and forty kilograms of bread, he gave us only half of it. When we complained, he very logically answered that if we did not like the arrangement we could bake our own bread, and he laughed jovially. To him we were exclusively a source of money; there was nothing personal in his greed, and we did not hold it against him. On the contrary, I often looked for some sign of hate towards us for bringing the threat of death over his head, but there was none.

The farmer's wife continued to demand that we leave. The possibility of success never entered her mind. She was angry at her husband and more than resentful of us. Karbicki would come over, bring food and tell us what was going on in his home or in the village. In our warm cozy pit, he quipped, we had it "like in America." He genuinely envied us for not having to do any work. Occasionally he would sit with us, telling long stories that began with Antoni's dog and ended with the fighting in Tunisia. The woman, however, never came near us. After the farmer had dug the shelter, he showed it to his wife. She fled, and never again came to look. Karbicki talked about her and treated her with contempt. They had frequent brawls at home and he often beat her. When he did she went on strike, or ran away from home, and then he had to do all the chores himself. Scenes also arose when she demanded money from him — Karbicki would rather have parted with an arm or an eye than with money. Our pleas that he live a more peaceful life with his wife were of no avail.

At the beginning we only knew about his children from hearsay. The little girls sensed what was involved and behaved admirably. They watched for visitors, warned about the arrival of police, and, when necessary, hid the food being cooked for us on the stove. They avoided the vicinity of the shed, particularly when the neighbor's children were around. The shed in their eyes became something forbidden, untouchable, taboo. They understood that if they did not follow all these precautions they would lose their father and mother and themselves. The children showed almost miraculous self-control in standing up to this formidable test.

Despite our fears that we would suffer from cold, it was actually too hot in the shelter. The earth insulated us and seven human bodies converted the warmth into oppressing heat. The worst was the humidity. Three times a day we got hot pots; the steam condensed on the walls, dripped, and, having no escape, evaporated anew. Hot kerosene vapors, sweat, and body odors made the air foul and nauseous. The only time we could get fresh air was at night. Throughout the day we had to keep the lid closed as the farmer often brought people to the shed to show them his livestock, and we had to prevent the steam from freezing above the shelter, for that would have been a clue to our presence.

Cleanliness was a major problem. Above all we lacked water. The farmer gave us one jug daily and this had to suffice for drinking, washing dishes and our toilette. Since Karbicki had to fetch his water from Antoni's well, he could not do it too often without raising suspicions. To wash to the waist we had to collect water for a week; by adding half of the daily hot coffee one of us could take a "bath." The matter of laundry was also complicated by the Karbicki woman's unwillingness to wash our clothes. Even with all the washing, it was impossible to stay clean as the dirt from the walls and the seeping manure made our attempts quite futile.

Our most important problem was keeping occupied. The question of mental endurance was no less important than keeping up our physical resistance. It was impossible to sit all day and gaze into the dim light of the kerosene lamp or stare at the four walls of the pit which we already knew down to each single crack. The most interesting occupation, at least at the beginning, was reading. The quality of the books was not too select, but whatever we had was priceless. During the first few weeks we read Sholom Aleichem. Jewish life passed in sentimental detail through the shelter like a puppet show, and it helped us endure our new existence. We also manufactured cards from old cardboard, and the women occasionally played with them, mostly solitaire. We played chess almost all day long. The game provided interest not only for the players but also for the kibitzers. To make the games more challenging, we played for stakes, for a potato or a spoonful of soup, food being the most precious of things to us. As the losing side had to yield part of dinner, we fought our matches with bitter determination.

Mother mended clothes and also read a little. Father, who knew most of the Yiddish books by heart, watched us play chess and specialized in stealing or rearranging pieces. This in turn provoked arguments and debates which killed time – a priceless gain. Only Yankel could not find any diversion. He smoked cigarettes, one after the other, and talked continuously about getting out of the pit.

One of the greatest diversions in our entombed life was the farmer's occasional trip to Biala. Karbicki now had money in his trousers and often rode to the city to shop. We would always ask him to buy some things for us too. After a while the farmer realized that even a trip to Biala could be a source of income, and so he never went unless we needed something. Certain items, like kerosene, salt, or saccharin, were indispensable to us, and we had to pay the farmer for a special trip to the city. I myself wished he go to Biala as often as possible because he brought newspapers back with him. Newspapers were the sun of our shelter. On days when the farmer went to Biala, we did not read, we forgot our chess matches, and we waited excitedly for his return; it was as if he were about to bring freedom itself. All our hopes for great allied victories were rudely quenched once we read the papers; even so, it was a treat to have them. We read them from first page to the last. One of my frequent nightly dreams was of the farmer's going to Biala.

And so, buried alive, we settled down to outlast the second World War. Each movement crystallized; each function settled; the tracks of our existence were cut with microscopic precision. We endured everything at the beginning with stoic patience. Nobody complained, no one sagged. We cared for the safety of the shelter and only its good concerned us. We were in a daze that eliminated memories and dulled reactions, two powerful forces that later began to rip the shelter apart. We rejoiced over the passage of time, confident we were being borne closer to the liberation that surely awaited us somewhere on this nightmarish road. Our undertaking seemed to work, and we did everything to endure and carry on. We grew roots; we became a part of the pit. It was all we had left.

xxiii

It did not take long for the first complications to arise. Some collected in an undercurrent until they floated to the surface; others came suddenly, causing little earthquakes. Hurrying to construct the shelter, the farmer had not bothered to build a new bunk; instead he gave us an old one from his house. One day we saw a bedbug on the wall. The next day we noticed two more diving into the wallcracks. Eventually they came in swarms. As soon as we went to sleep, they crawled out from the straw, fell from the ceiling, invaded us from all four walls. When we lit the lamp in the middle of the night, they ran for cover by the thousands. As soon as the lamp was doused they returned.

The second calamity was rats. The food attracted them. At first they scratched gently at the corners and we even had some sympathy for them. Later, however, they became obnoxious; they staged frivolous performances, catapulted over our heads, squeaked, did not let us sleep. There was one large family of them, a mother with many young. If we were quiet and dimmed the lamp, they appeared even during the day. The rats' preferred sport was to race around the pit. Then they began to cause damage; they spoiled the food, chewed open the flour bags, and spilled the cans containing fat. It reached a point where we could not keep any food in the pit. This problem was similar to that of the bedbugs. It would not stop with this single group; this was the nucleus of an army.

Seepage was another plague. As manure accumulated overhead, the pressure caused the liquid excretion to run down the walls of the pit and collect at the bottom in nauseating puddles. It stained sheets, soiled the linen, dripped on our faces, caused an unbearable stench. The smell was often so strong that we woke from our sleep with splitting headaches.

Several weeks into our subterranean existence the Karbicki woman burst into the shed yelling that police were heading in our direction. I told her to stop crying and get out of the shed. I tightened the cover of the pit so that it would not yield in case they stepped on it. I dimmed the lamp and we froze into silence, ready for whatever was to come. Yankel, who had a cold, began to cough. Stuffing his mouth with a pillow, we shoved him under the bunk. Then the rats came out, deceived by the sudden quiet and the dimmed light into thinking it was night. After scratching for a while at the logs, they came up to the edges of the ceiling, ignoring us completely. We stared into the rusty glare of the lamp and endured that peculiar tension in the spine and the collapse of muscles that usually accompanied these moments. The whole world was reduced to the contemplation of a single familiar image – our execution outside the shed. This lasted until evening, when the woman finally came with word that the police were gone.

It was the first day of a kind that later became quite common. Whenever police visited the village, whenever Germans arrived for requisitions, we had our "bath." Our farmer, like most peasants, accumulated manure throughout the winter, which left the entrance to our pit much below floor level. To fill in the telltale dip during police raids, the farmer would pile almost a carload of manure on the cover, sealing the shelter like a tomb. It got hot, and we undressed almost to the skin. The lamp was turned down to a flicker and we sat contemplating how it would look when they came for us. Because of some peculiar wish not to be led to the execution naked, we kept our clothing and shoes ready for that moment. The intensifying heat drove us to the floor of the shelter, where the air seemed a little cooler. Pressing our faces to the cool earth, we soon lost all sense of time and fell into a daze.

A moment would come when the lamp light would begin to flicker, jump convulsively, and finally go out. The first time it happened we lit the lamp again, only to watch the flicker repeat the same convulsions and die again. Finally, when we could not even light a match , we realized there was not enough oxygen in our cave. In the evening the farmer would open the shelter to find us on the floor, half unconscious, and it took a few minutes before the cool, fresh stream of air from above returned us to life. We referred to these experiences as "baths"; they were days of penance within penance.

In time our physical endurance began to fail. Mother succumbed first. Crouching near the slightly open cover, she gasped for air all day long. It was a dangerous thing to do and she had to be constantly on the alert. Then Belcia, complaining she was short of breath, could not sleep nights. We solved the problem by putting her down on the bottom of the pit. When the bed was made, she found herself between the boards of our bunk and the floor; there, prevented from sitting up, she had to lie flat on her back all night. Nausea, cramps, itches, and pains of all kinds began to plague us. We had to find some relief and we thought about the loft of the shed, where, when it was filled with straw, one could stay without being seen from below. We mentioned it to the farmer on the occasion of some new financial transaction, and this made him grant our wish.

The trip to the loft immediately became the day's major attraction. Each of us was rationed half an hour of it. On bright winter days the loft was full of sunshine and high blue skies, and in the vast quiet of the countryside, the sounds of the village in the distance were haunted melodies of longing and peace. Alternately, like the irregular diffused peal of bells, came the knocking of pails against the village wells, the whir of spinning winches, the rattle of a cart behind the woods, the husky lonely call of a peasant woman. I raised myself carefully on one elbow and looked through the hole in the roof. Over the snow I could see Koszelowka, its many chimneys trailing smoke, the windmill slowly spinning, and

next to the windmill, the house with the red roof where Manya
worked. Was she at the same moment staring at our bleached
lonely farm, shuddering each time she saw the police ride in our
direction? How much more difficult it probably was for her, how
much lonelier, how much deeper the bitterness. I knew she found
the task of attempted survival distasteful for, after Ignatz's death,
she had no particular wish to go on. I wondered how long she
would endure under this red roof. A hen flew up, noticed me, and
stopped in place, astonished; then she began to cluck hysterically.
She is raising an alarm, I thought, she is announcing to all
Koszelowka that I am here. Frightened, I rushed back into the pit.

Another great moment for us was a sprint to the farmer's
house. In the shelter where the slightest variation – a fuller pot of
soup, an extra loaf of bread, a new wick in the lamp – was news,
a visit to the farmer's house took on the weight of a historic event.
The women dreamed about washing their hair, we polished our
boots all day. Karbicki came at nightfall and opened the door of
the shed. A blast of fresh cold air hit my face and stopped my
breath. Snowflakes settled on my eyelashes. The farmer signaled us
to move and we followed him through a space that stretched to
edges of the sky. I slowed down to prolong the short walk, but the
farmer, restless, tense, urged me on. I bolted across the yard and
into the house.

I was in the room I had entered for the first time a few weeks
before. The same lime-bleached walls, the same eaves over the
stove and the black earthen floor. The farmer's wife joined us. She
had the same wild eyes as last time, but somehow she managed to
control herself. She told us about the last visit of the police when
Ludmilla, her youngest daughter, on being asked whether there
were any Jews in the vicinity, had answered that she did not know
what Jews were. One of the little girls appeared from the dark

alcove and, stopping in the corner of the room, looked at us with frightened but curious eyes. Gathering her courage she walked over to Belcia and pointed to the ribbon that my sister wore. Belcia took it off and gave it to her. She hesitated, but we encouraged her to take it and she ran off into the dark room to share the event with her sisters. The woman, clasping hands, sighed: "If I go, I go, but the children...."

Mother was frying lard on the kitchen fire while the farmer stared with stony eyes at the blacked-out windows. After a transient liveliness, the woman became uneasy again, scratched her head and groaned. The conversation ceased, and we all watched the crackling flames under the stove. With a lusty pleasure I sat on a low stool, stretching my legs and back and breathing the dry air of the room. Outside, Antoni's dog barked. Karbicki went out to take a look and reported that Shymeluk with his two daughters had just passed by, heading to the village for food. Shymeluk, a Jew from Konstantynow, was hiding in our neighborhood, although we did not know exactly where. "They are still alive," Karbicki said, shaking his head. Further down the trail, dogs had begun to growl and Karbicki explained that they belonged to Rataj, a rich farmer between us and the village of Wolki, where the Jews evidently went for bread. The dogs kept barking and soon all the dogs in the village joined in. Karbicki sighed, took the kettle of the stove, and said with a heavy voice, "You'd better go back."

And so, amid dark days and darker nights, in the incessant stream of time, Christmas arrived. Karbicki had been talking about it for some time. He was dreaming of that full, bright Christmas he had never really had. Even in the shed one could feel the holiday mood. The farmer slaughtered two lambs. The woman baked loaves of white bread. There was a lot of commotion in the yard, and we heard the children rehearse carols.

On Christmas Eve the world round our shed grew quiet and brooding. Farmers sat with their families at candlelit tables; none of them wandered far from their hearths. Thus it became a holiday for us too; we could move about the shed without fear of strangers. The animals, supposed to possess miraculous faculties on that night, behaved prosaically: the cow chewed its cud and the sheep snored in the corner. We lounged against the walls of the shed, gulping fresh cold air, and listened to the night.

Christmas Eve. The night was clear, and over the blue landscape flickered the sparks of farms and villages. The stars, high above the torn thatch roof of the shed, were cold and pensive; snow drifted off the edges of the rafters. Far away, where lilac lights glowed across the snow, trembled the tones of *Bóg sie rodzi moc truchleje....* God is born, power trembles. The night listened to the lovely song. A cosmic Hallelujah rang in the stillness and floated into the shed with associations as sad as the face of Christ.

For the first time memories flooded the heart. In times past we, too, had celebrated holidays. In times past our children, too, had sung songs. There had been a time when the brightness of these ancient rites had stepped over our thresholds, too, and we had all sat together at festive tables: grandparents, children, and our mothers. There were in those days white tablecloths and lit candles. Listening to the quiet flow of the carols, we sang all the Jewish songs we knew, songs which, once upon a time, had floated over this land together with the songs of Christmas.

The next day, for the first time doing something that was not dictated by monetary considerations, the farmer treated us to cake he had baked for the holidays. In return, we treated him to a bottle of vodka. We sat in the pit and raised toasts. Like all peasants, Karbicki became contemplative under the breath of vodka, philosophizing on the meaning of life and death. He searched his conscience, became almost tender. I watched him with surprise, for I had never believed that any abstract feeling could glow in those narrow slit eyes. He sat there, this time not against but with us, and told us about his poverty: how he had gone about barefoot all winter, how he had toiled for the rich farmers who made fun of him. Now that he had the satisfaction of having overtaken all others in wealth, he felt regret that he could not show it to them. For the first time he expressed pity for us and, looking at Belcia and Berko, he shook his head. "Such young children...." For the first time we felt and shared the commonness of our fate, the commonness of danger, the possibility of a common grave. He finished almost half a liter of vodka and, sipping the last tumbler, he mused: "Maybe I drink on my last holiday. Next Christmas I will be dead."

xxiv

Life dragged on. We stayed underground, unseen and unseeing. The village of Koszelowka was feeding us but the villagers did not know it. The windmill ground flour for us, the store sold us cigarettes, the farmers supplied lard – and none knew he had a hand in keeping us alive. Antoni on the next farm, who spent hours in Karbicki's house, did not have the slightest idea that seven Jews went on living only a few feet from where he stood. Karbicki made special trips to the village and stuck his ears into gossip circles and meetings trying to learn whether there were rumors or suspicions about him, but all was quiet.

Karbicki required maximum caution from us. During the day we talked in hushed voices, at night in whispers. In the farmer's house the family was always on the lookout, and whenever a cart clattered we immediately heard the door open; someone was out to see who was coming. If the steps approached the shed, we knew we had to close the cover, turn down the lamp, and be quiet. Whoever was in the loft at the time had to descend in a hurry and hide.

The farmer himself, however, was not so careful. He changed his way of life, ate better, and dressed more fancifully. When we told him this was an unwise thing to do, he became offended and ignored us: What right did we have to dictate how he should live? We also learned that he drank a great deal. One thing, though, saved the situation and blunted any suspicions. Karbicki had gone to Losice the day the small ghetto was liquidated and had returned with a cartload of Jewish "rags." A rumor spread in the village that Karbicki had found gold in the clothing he had bought, and his higher standard of living was attributed to this stroke of good luck.

We quickly adjusted to numerous minor and major difficulties. We might consume a pound of meat in one day only to then go meatless for weeks. We got used to the smell of manure collecting at the bottom of the pit. We devised ingenious ways of prolonging sleep. To fool time, we created tricks and games fit for children or morons. One of the most absorbing jobs was cutting tobacco leaves for Yankel's cigarettes. Hours were spent just trimming the lamp, and I endlessly tinkered with the two flashlights we owned. I also became the official barber of the shelter.

Above everything, I was hoping to fill out the time in the pit by continuing my studies. Yet I found myself incapable of methodical thought. I gave my books to the farmer, who proceeded to roll cigarettes with Slowacki's poetry and the laws of physics. Fiction proved to be a more fitting diet, and we absorbed it – mostly popular novels – with relish. We watched the supply of reading matter diminish with apprehension and eventually started to ration it. When our mood was black we read more; when good, we occupied ourselves in other ways. The only substantial book I read in the shelter was Darwin's *The Descent of Man*. For some reason my brain did not refuse to work on this subject.

My other non-vegetative activity was keeping a diary. I had started writing the diary with the outbreak of the war, and I continued it in the pit. But this, too, was a battle. Only with great reluctance would the farmer bring me supplies from Biala. To lug salt, rags, and even a newspaper was normal to him but to bother about ink and paper seemed a derangement. To economize on paper, I left no margins on the pages, and I squeezed the lines to such density that the diary was nearly all black.

Our condition affected everyone in radically different ways. The two sisters, my mother and Yankel's wife, alternated between long periods of mourning and flashes of hysteria. They would patiently do their duties, mend clothes, ladle out the food, or play solitaire; then they would erupt into brief, petty quarrels which I would watch flabbergasted. The quarrels were not over any serious matters but over trifles and subtleties. The confinement and tension of the pit made the small hurts and brushes more incendiary than they might have been under normal conditions. Luckily these flare-ups were short-lived for, seeing Belcia in tears begging them to be quiet, they would stop and go back to darning the rotten stockings or carefully dividing the yoghurt they had been hoarding for days.

Of the men, my father, nearly sixty, was the eldest, and he was shriveling up like an uprooted tree. Normally full of jibes and curiosity, he turned gloomy and extremely bitter. About the war, however, he retained an obstinate optimism. When the Germans reported victories, he argued that the boasts offered best proof that they were losing, and if they admitted the loss of one company, Father liquidated whole armies. Whenever I tried to dampen these exaggerated hopes, he fell into a rage and called me a black crow.

He never ceased citing the First World War, when the Germans, with all their *Im Westen Nichts Neues*, so splendidly lost it. He sat all day in his customary corner and stared at one wall of the pit. He was losing weight rapidly; pouches of skin hung from his once full face. His eyes sank deeper and deeper, and the nose sharpened. How long, I wondered, would he endure?

The most adaptable of us all was Yankel's thirteen-year-old son, Berko. To him the pit was nothing unusual – merely one other possible mode of existence. He never complained or argued, and he stoically endured all tribulations. He maintained an immunity we all envied, and when asked how he could remain so unaffected, he answered, "How will my feelings help?" He alone remained unperturbed during police raids, and he slept soundly despite the deluge of bedbugs, the fasts, the stench, and the rats. He could get absorbed in some maniacal occupation and be at it for weeks on end. He grew in the pit, and dreamt of Sundays when the farmer would cook potato dumplings for us – the royal meal of the shelter.

His father, however, was the exact opposite of Berko. In his forties, Yankel was a short-tempered, restless man who often became irresponsible and dangerous. He was the only one who could not find any occupation and his only interest was cigarettes. He smoked them continually. When the supply ran out, the shelter was in danger of blowing up. He owned a Kennkarte, and perhaps in anticipation of becoming a Pole one day, he grew a moustache à la Pilsudski. It was that moustache that suffered most. He kept plucking at it with jerky nervous fingers until the bristles coiled like springs. He usually sat against the wall with his bare feet on the table, and one would think from the many quiet hours he spent there that a lamb was snoozing in the corner. But we knew that his fuse was smoldering, and that the explosion was only a matter of time. It would start with his scratching his chest in quick, tiny movements. Even if the shelter was quiet and offered not the slightest provocation or reason for argument, he would suddenly sit up, begin to toss about, and complain that there was not enough room, that the lamp was too dim, the ceiling too low. Then he exploded. He would flail about, shout, threaten, swear. We slouched in trepidation, expecting the farmer to arrive any minute with the crushing news that we had been overheard. Miraculously this never happened. After each outburst, Yankel relapsed into his corner and resumed winding his moustache.

Long days dragged on. Time was a stream of tar, endless. The war was not coming to an end and the basis of our gamble was crumbling. The optimists had predicted Germany's collapse in a few weeks, and now these had passed. The pessimists had predicted a few months, and these, too, had passed. The newspapers were stagnant. We entered the shelter with the battlefield names of Woronezh and Stalingrad, and the same names were still in the communiqués two months later. The Americans, exhausted by their safari to Tunisia, had been basking in the hot African sun for nearly three months, resting. Our conversations about the war were like brush fire. After reading the newspapers, everyone would ask me what I thought of the situation. My grimaces usually sufficed for an answer, and then I would hear Father in the corner. "Black crow," he would hiss. "In the last war, I remember...," and he would begin again his old story about the German defeat in 1918.

When we got newspapers the farmer usually came down to hear what good news we had about the war. For him, of course, I was not a black crow. For him I mauled the German armies wholesale. His feelings were more important than ours, and we could not let him have any doubts about a speedy end to the war. We tried to paint as rosy a picture as possible, but it was becoming increasingly difficult. The longer the war lasted and the gloomier the news, the more interest Karbicki took in the course of the conflict. In time, he began to doubt our hopeful interpretations, for he tried to read the papers himself. Because he did not quite grasp what he read, he could not catch us in any outright lies, but he had a general notion how things stood and knew whether the Germans were winning or not.

The stalemate on the fronts had further repercussions. In the long winter nights, when farmers sat near the warm stoves and their women trailed gossip over their spinning wheels, the only substitute for rumors about the war was rumors about the Jews: about the majority which, perhaps rightly, had been eliminated and the few good ones who had not deserved it; about those who were buried near the village and those who might still be alive. Then the farmers in Koszelowka and Dubicze said that Motl and Shmyl, who had been seen still alive in November, had disappeared and were probably dead; that Shymeluk with his two daughters were still alive, wondering who could be supporting them; that here five Jews had been caught and there six of them shot; a tale about peasants in Sarnaki who had delivered twenty-five Jews and got twenty-five liters of vodka from the Germans; and many others. Some stories were true and some false, but their authenticity was of no importance. Each time, our farmer returned from these palavers depressed and apprehensive. After repeating what he had heard, he would groan: "When they tell all that, I just look at my house to see if it isn't on fire yet."

"It would not catch fire by itself," I assured him.

"Oh, there are mean people in the world," he sighed, watching the flicker of the lamp with strange and heavy eyes.

xxv

Some disquieting changes began to take place in our existence. The farmer ceased taking any interest in the war, rarely came down into the shelter, and avoided talking to us. When he brought food, he was brusque and almost angry, and when we told him about some good turn of events in the war, he waved his hand impatiently. He stopped bringing us the morning coffee and delivered less and less bread, explaining that he could not grind enough flour because it would arouse suspicion. When we protested, he growled: "You will do without it." He began to drop disturbing allusions, and as he scratched his messy hair – a sure indication of deep thoughts – he groaned and mused that we had not come to the right place, that we should have gone to a richer farmer, that it would have been better, perhaps, if we had hidden in Losice. He told us he was having dreams of our being discovered. Something had gone wrong.

One day the Germans raided our neighborhood. Someone had informed the Schupo in Biala of two Jews hiding in the Dubicze forest. They were found, taken out, shot, and thrown back into the same pit. Karbicki's sighs and groans became heavier than ever.

A few days later, two Jewish women who had been working as dressmakers in the cellar of some farmer were killed in nearby Kornica. A neighbor had spotted them and spread the news. Because Kornica had no German post, the Polish police handled the case, and thus only the two Jewish women were killed and nothing was done to the farmer. Nosow, only two miles from our shelter, hid two Jewish tailors. After they supplied the farmers with enough coats and suits for the winter, they were tied with ropes, thrown on a cart, and delivered to the Schupo.

Our farmer's tenacity sagged under the weight of these accounts, and he became glum and frightened as he recognized, perhaps for the first time, that the danger from his own compatriots might be greater than from the Germans. Yet, intimidating as all this was, everything was "all right" so long as only Jews were being killed and no Poles were harmed. But this, too, eventually happened.

One day, as I enjoyed my half hour in the hayloft, my ears caught the sound of a car engine. Suddenly several shots were fired. I slid down into the shelter and closed the cover.

Usually, when Germans were near, Karbicki warned us and threw more manure over the pit, but this time nobody came. Dinner time passed. The hungry pigs squealed, and even the usually stolid sheep began to complain, but nobody brought any food. Single shots continued through the afternoon. Toward evening we heard a violent exchange of rifle fire lasting for about half an hour. Then, at nightfall, the shooting stopped.

When I later went up and looked in the direction of the noise, I saw the darkness tremble with a red glow: a fire raged in Walim. The village was only one mile away, and I could see the burning dwellings distinctly. What was strange was that no one was attempting to douse the fire. There was not a sign of people anywhere.

The next day was Sunday. We were still dressing when the door of the shed opened. In the opening of the shelter appeared the farmer's long legs. With a thud he slid down into the pit.

Never before and never after did we see a similar expression on his face. It was the mask of an infuriated beast. His nostrils flared, his eyes were completely white. I turned my head away, hit by his murderous expression.

"You have been discovered," he said.

Belcia groaned. Yankel let go of his moustache.

"I warned you and warned...," the farmer foamed. "Motl was here yesterday, was he not? People saw him. They saw him go to Rataj for food. Then they saw him crawl into my shed...." He held his knuckled fist in the air.

Motl had indeed visited us the night before, and he had indeed brought us food from Rataj. None of us tried to say anything. We were all paralyzed by the black news.

"You must go away," he announced.

We heard steps outside. The farmer quickly got out, covered the trapdoor, and closed the shed. We were left with the words: "You must go away."

Where to? That simple question contained all our reactions and black visions. It was a question graver than death. Throughout the rest of that day none of us uttered a word. After several hours the lamp went out and we sat in darkness. No one brought food. From our provisions we ate raw yellow peas, and mixing some flour with water, we baked small cakes the size of buttons on the top of the kerosene lamp. Knowing that sleep was the best medicine against hunger, we turned in earlier than usual, but the bedbugs immediately invaded from all directions. Tossing from side to side, I felt a wild sense of revenge at the thought that this paradise would soon end for them.

Next day the farmer again came into the shelter and told us the story of Walim. Two escaped Soviet prisoners had been kept on a farm by a widow. In order to compensate the woman, they resorted to stealing – which eventually betrayed them. Because the Russians had rifles and, in defending themselves, had killed a policeman, the Polish police in the village sent for the Schupo in Biala. The Germans came with hand grenades, killed one of the Russians, and set the shelter afire. To avoid burning alive, the other

Russian shot himself. The Germans then burned down the rest of the farm and executed the woman and her daughter.

Karbicki was shaking as he told the story. It was the first incident in which Poles had been killed for such a thing, and the farmer was broken with fear. Threatening and furious, he asked us to leave. Trying to steer the talk away from the specter of leaving, we babbled that it was the second day we had not received any food, that we were hungry. He almost jumped out of his skin. "Here I am talking about death, and you, bread!" When we said that even pigs are fed before they are killed, he shook his thick powerful fist at us and left. All that day and the next, a dead silence reigned over the farm. It seemed as if everybody above had deserted. Every sound, each rattle of a cart or drone of a distant motor alarmed us. We sat holding our shoes ready for the execution. As the monstrous hours dragged on, I began to wonder whether death would really mean an end. I recalled a story Leyzor once related about Treblinka, where the Germans put pistols to their prisoners' heads and told them that they were going to be shot; when the victims had closed their eyes, they were hit with clubs. As they regained consciousness, the Germans, bending over them, gleefully taunted, "See, even in the hereafter there are Germans."

For days the farmer kept returning, sometimes with food but more often without, alternately ordering and pleading that we leave. He was being spied upon, he said; the police were raiding the village; all neighbors were whispering about his Jews. The pressure mounted. One night he breathlessly announced he was leaving, for he had just overheard the bailiff say the Schupo was to arrive next day to search his farm. After piling a load of manure on the entrance, he ran off.

For two days we waited for the Germans in the darkness, without food or drink and without relieving ourselves. With shoes and coats under our arms we waited for the call to get out. At the end of the second day, air in the shelter had been exhausted and we began to lose consciousness. But once these days had passed without a sign of the Germans or of anything unusual, we began to suspect the farmer's story.

Seeing that threats would not do the job, Karbicki began to look for more drastic means of forcing us out. He continued to starve us and forbade our going to the loft. He would not bring us anything from Biala; consequently, we had no light in the pit, and whatever food we had was without salt. For long periods he deprived us of water. Every hour he came with fresh stories about spies, Germans, and police. He began to wear us out. Realizing it could not go on like this we decided to take a desperate chance to resolve our situation, one way or another.

The next time Karbicki insisted that we go, I asked, "If we leave and the Germans catch us, don't you think that they would find out where we were hiding all this time?"

The farmer was dumbfounded. His white narrow eyes filled with the bewilderment of a trapped animal. Everything in his mind had been arranged, exactly as he had conceived it during the long nights of scheming and conniving. The shelter was paid for. What was the use of keeping us? As he saw, if he could chase us out, he would fill in the pit and emerge from the war a rich man. Had the crisis been as real and imminent as he claimed, the danger implied by my remark would have been a secondary consideration; the urgent thing still would have been to get us off the farm. But Karbicki did not act that way. Instead, he sat confused and frightened, not knowing what to say.

It then became clear that we had to adopt a strategy to deal with the farmer. To handle the situation effectively, we had to understand him. Yet, as we had just discovered, we knew him very little. He was cunning and shrewd; also he was a free man and thus had an infinite advantage over us. The fight to force us out of the shelter was an unequal one. Although the crisis had passed, we feared he would eventually win. Unless something happened to change the course of the war, he would force us to leave.

xxvi

Our most joyful moment in the pit came unexpectedly on a winter night. It had been one of our frequent days of fasting, and we were getting ready for sleep when a sheep bleated above us. A minute later the cover opened and Shmyl tumbled in. With an oversized hat fallen over his eyes and his face burned with sun and frost, he sat in the corner, breathing the cold of his snow-covered coat and boots into the shelter. His face shone with grim joy. He burst out laughing: A Soviet victory at Stalingrad!

And then he added that Miedzyrzec still had a ghetto with Jews in it.

We stayed awake all night. As the details Of the defeat ,and encirclement of the German Sixth Army unfolded, we permitted ourselves to hope and expect it would be repeated, louder and more lastingly, until our dreams became reality. Father sat next to Shmyl, wringing his shoulder to tell more and more while mumbling, "Just as I said – just as in the last war." Yankel was so exuberant we had to stuff his mouth with a towel. How spacious the pit became that night! The ceiling rose to make room for all this tenuous, exaggerated hope. Tired with happiness, we crouched in the corners and built our own tomorrow. That night we did not hear the rats or feel the bedbugs. The shelter was again what it had been meant to be: a trench in which to endure until the German collapse.

On the following day we told the farmer the news, but he was not surprised. He had evidently known for several days and had not informed us. Even so, he did not know as much as we, and he could not possibly generate as much hope as we had to in order to go on. Did he also know about the retreat from the Caucasus? Had he heard the latest about Woronezh and Tripoli? The Don we immediately connected with the Dniepr, and the Dniepr with the Bug. Didn't he realize that the Soviets were just across the river? The farmer listened attentively and tried to catch each word. Although it was still early in the morning, we told him to fetch some vodka. He complied immediately, and we drank to the victory of the Red Army and to British success. But after the vodka, as usual, Karbicki became pensive. Shaking his head, he keep repeating, stubbornly, "What is the use when you have been detected?"

Yet he treated us much better that day, serving dinner promptly and even giving us a loaf of bread. At nightfall he came down into the shelter again and asked if Shmyl would take us away. Though startled by his insistence in trying to get rid of us, we were not crushed. Shmyl was going to Miedzyrzec, we glibly told him, and upon his return we would leave.

More news of Soviet victories followed. In early February the papers reported that the Sixth Army had capitulated among the ruins of Stalingrad. A score of generals, including Field Marshall Paulus, fell into Russian hands. The Caucasus was cleared of German troops and the Soviets were at the Donetz. The entire front was back where the Germans had been in 1941, and it did not stop there, for the Soviets launched a fresh offensive. Woroszylovgrad fell, and Rostov. And there was the wild, drunken, happy night when, after breaking through the German lines at Orel, the Soviets captured Kharkov.

Given that the farmer kept insisting on our departure, we decided to take advantage of the favorable conditions and end this confrontation once and forever. Our suspicions that the farmer was inventing facts to suit his schemes about our stay in the shelter increased to a point where we were almost sure of it. With the Red Army marching towards the Dniepr – and with the Miedzyrzec ghetto as a back up, if indeed we had to leave – we, too, were maneuvering for a victorious battle against Karbicki. An incident near Sarnaki provided us more ammunition. A farmer who was hiding six Jews had decided, with his eyes on their money, to get rid of them. At night, while the Jews were asleep, the farmer, with the help of a few other thugs, poured boiling water over them, and when the Jews, all severely burned and some blinded, ran out of the shelter, the assailants jumped them with axes and clubs. Two of the boys, although wounded, managed to escape. They were eventually picked up by the Schupo. The two were, of course, shot. But the farmer was executed also, and a short time later, friends of the dead boys who lived in a nearby cave burned down the entire farm.

When, shortly after that incident, Karbicki again asked us to leave, we said we would go immediately. He looked at us with unbelieving eyes. We reckoned the time we had stayed and told him he owed us money for two months; as soon as he returned the money, we said, we would leave.

This exchange produced a complete retreat. There was little truth in all the stories he had been feeding us, and when pressed about returning the money – a thing he would never in his life have done – he abandoned his scheme. After that, conditions in the shelter improved considerably. The shortage of food persisted because he could not grind much more flour than required for his owl, use, and his supply of potatoes was coming to an end, but there were no more fasts. Having given up the idea of forcing us out, Karbicki returned to what he had been before – greedy, tough, but with a modicum of decency.

A permanent change, however, occurred in our own routines. The latest events had thrown us off balance. All interest in chess playing ceased and we discarded this pastime. I had completed Darwin and could start on nothing new. Only the women continued with their solitaire. Yankel kept torturing his poor moustache. Waiting had become our occupation, our mainstay. We did not want to be bogged down in any job lest we miss the magic call: "You are free." In our fantasies Karbicki was to be that heavenly messenger, and the rattle of Soviet tanks was to greet us when we emerged from the sty. After Kharkov we awaited the fall of Kiev, remembering that in 1920 Pilsudski needed only one week to run from there to Warsaw, and that tanks are faster than horses, even Polish horses.

With spirits raised by the confluence of Soviet victories and our success with the farmer, we declared war on the shelter's vermin. To rid ourselves of bedbugs, we tried to seal the cracks with glue, and then to burn them out of their nests, but they multiplied faster than we could kill them. At last we asked the farmer to get us some insecticide and organized an air raid on the shelter. In the evening we all went up, and after we covered the pit tightly, I filled it with a yellow, choking cloud of insecticide. We practically eliminated the bedbugs, to the last specimen.

We opened war on the rats with a trap on the floor, but it did not attract any. Then, discovering that the mother paraded on the overhead beams, we put the trap there. For a long time she sneered at us. She liked to dig and fling lumps of earth around her, doing it with such gusto that she sprang the trap from a distance. But one night a loud squeal woke us from our sleep. I quickly lit the lamp. The trap was tripped but empty. Though hurt, the rat had torn herself free and lay at my feet, large as a cat. Hit with the heel of a boot, she slid under the bank and died. Soon we caught fourteen of her young, and the shelter was cleared of rats.

xxvii

It was night and we were all asleep when Karbicki lifted the cover to let someone in. When we lit the lamp, we saw Manya in the corner. She told us she had been denounced to the police and had just managed to escape.

In the morning, the farmer appeared at the opening, frightened by the denunciation and worried over Manya's presence in the shelter. Before any of us had time to answer, Manya said to him: "Don't worry, I am leaving, tonight or tomorrow." Shymeluk and his two daughters, she told us, had given up and gone back to the ghetto. A Jewish tailor and shoemaker who had been hanging around the village also could no longer endure their life on the run and returned to Miedzyrzec. She, too, had enough. Calm, indifferent, she said she would go to Miedzyrzec.

The next night Shmyl came for her. Mother did not stop crying. Father sat in his corner, stiff and silent; I was afraid to look into his eyes. The farmer came urging them to hurry. Manya knelt at the cover, framed by the dim light of the kerosene lamp. "Goodbye," she said, "and live." And she was gone.

We tried not to think about what had happened that night. We waited for the end of the war. This was the thought we took to sleep and our first thought upon opening our eyes in the morning. Father sat numb all day except when Karbicki came into the shed. Then he pressed him for good news. The farmer passed on tales and rumors that the Soviets had captured Kiev and Vilna, and, to celebrate, the farmer gave us two full jugs of water. We gave one another "liberation" haircuts. We talked about how we would leave the pit. But the capture of Kiev was not confirmed; instead, the Germans reported their own counterattack. Yankel again began to scratch his chest. Berko put away the map on which he had been charting the progress of the Soviet armies. The shelter still waited, still hoped, but it was getting jittery. Suspicion slumbered on the floor of the pit. It was quiet. Too quiet.

On one of the routine nights in the shelter we lay slumped on the benches watching our shadows leap and huddle in the corners. It was very still in the pit now that the rats were gone, and all we could hear was the wind outside and the incessant strung-out wailing of dogs. I looked at Father sitting rigidly in his corner and realized for the first time that his hair had turned completely white. He sat and waited. He still remembered the last war. Above, the door creaked, the pigs moved uneasily in their sleep, the straw rustled, and we heard the farmer pass us the news that the Germans recaptured Kharkov!

We knew this was the end of the Soviet offensive, the end of our hope. We knew the feeling well enough from past experience; we knew the consuming hollow gloom that accompanied the end of all fighting. The lamp went out, and we sat all night in darkness in unchanged positions. It made no sense to go on. "Enough," I murmured to myself. "Enough!" This thought must also have occurred to Yankel, for he was up on the bench, pounding his fists against the wall and screaming: "To Treblinka all of us. To Treblinka...." The quiet country picked up his insane scream and rushed it over fields, forests, and villages, making a universal call to all struggling Jews to surrender; a last voluntary march into the gas chambers; a call to the dead to rise to be burned once more in the still-hot ovens. Ghetto of Miedzyrzec, you forever open arms of death, we are coming, we are coming.

The next day, Shmyl returned from about a month's stay in Miedzyrzec. Manya, he reported, got there safely and was "established." He gave us a few more details about the ghetto. Approximately five thousand Jews lived in it; there was enough food. Shmyl reported all this brusquely, huddling in the entrance of the pit. I noticed his tight lips and the impatience in his eyes. He wanted to sleep, he said, as he had walked all night and was drenched and tired.

Shmyl awoke at noontime and looked at me with ill-boding eyes. "What is it?" I asked. He shook his head to indicate nothing was the matter. I packed a few things and cleaned the accumulated manure from my shoes; I was getting ready to leave for Miedzyrzec with Shmyl. I felt his piercing eyes on me again. "Nothing, nothing," he mumbled, and then he blurted out: "Herschek is dead."

Herschek had stayed through the early winter in a shelter in the village of Shanikow. In search of food and an occasional view of the outside world, he and his two companions would venture into the countryside along remote roads and only in the darkest of nights. But, as everywhere, the stealth of the Jews was no match for the sharp ears and tongues of the peasants. The farmer who kept them was warned, and he told them to leave. They left the shelter for the snowdecked, frosty land and roamed the forests. But this gained them only a few more days of life. One evening in January, a party of Germans rode down the country road of Shanikow, and there, between thickets, they spotted the three boys. The Germans were on sleighs when they saw them. They unhitched the horses, mounted, and galloped across the clearing – troops of German cavalry charging three half-frozen Jews. Halfway across the clearing – the horses still some distance off – Herschek stopped, raised the collar of his jerkin, and put his hands in his pockets. They fired one single shot and snuffed his life.

On that afternoon, after hearing Shmyl's account, I underwent my first bout of claustrophobia, anxiety, or whatever it was. It began with a sudden police raid. The farmer's wife dashed in, shouting: "Police! Police are coming!" She heaped a load of manure on the entrance, stamped on it with her weight, and left the shed. We doused the lamp and, as usual, prepared our shoes. It was pitch dark in the pit, hot, tight. Suddenly I felt something within me that I had never experienced. I tried to calm down, to remain in place, but it was useless. My brain swelled until it seemed ready to pop.

"Light.... Light...."

The lamp was lit. As it burned with a faint yellow flicker, the others looked at me with panic in their eyes. "What happened?" they stammered. I felt a little better with the light on, but still some powerful force was lifting me out of the pit. I felt I must pry open the shelter and run. I moved over to the entrance. "Where are you going?" I heard them ask in terror. I was near the cover. I gave a violent shove and the cover yielded. The realization that, if I wanted, I could open the pit brought relief.

When, toward evening, the shelter was opened, I crawled out immediately and climbed the loft. Dusk, buoyant lilac clouds, April air soaked with pine and sap. Sparrows fluttered under the thatch; hens came up to the loft, clucking sleepily. The last rattle of a peasant cart rolled away, and over the forest a lonesome plane flew, blinking its red and green lights. Then night fell and a pale moon was hoisted into the sky. It floated on reflected puddles of light, then appeared directly over the big opening in the thatch, converting the sty into a silver lake. The manure was gold; the logs ebony. The transparent clouds drifting past the moon were like the spilled hair of insane women. Far away, girls called; someone answered. Herschek was dead and I talked to him, to his bones forsaken on the fields of Shanikow.

Shmyl was getting ready to leave and I slid down from the loft. He was startled and looked at me.

"We are going to Miedzyrzec," I said.

"I am not going to Miedzyrzec. I am going to our shelter."

"Shmyl, I must go away, at least for a while."

"I will come for you." "No, right away, now." "That's impossible."

I looked at his small pony-like figure and felt like hurting him. Shmyl was talking on, swearing he would come soon. I climbed the loft again. The moon was gone. It was very dark in the shed, and in the pine grove nocturnal birds kept up their long, intermittent, hollow crying.

xxviii

It was April, nearly five months since we had come to Koszelowka. On its trails, in the ditches, and under the sycamores bloomed the first daisies, and camomile. The smell of jasmine was in the air. In the calm evenings one could hear the bark open on the trees, gentle sighs pierced by the cry of the wild ducks along the marshes. And across the clear sky drifted inflated white clouds, the majestic sailboats of spring.

There was restlessness on the farm. The cow butted the locked doors, yearning for fresh grass. The cherry tree in the yard unfolded, and we awoke one day to find it all in white bloom, as if stricken with some splendid disease. Bedding and homespun linen dried on the fences. For the first time we got a good look at the farmer's children: three radiant girls with pink cheeks and eyes as blue as bluebells. Their mother bleached the walls of the hut and aired the clothing while Karbicki was out in the field, plowing. Steadfast as an ox, he trudged up and down the black furrows, his huge chest blowing like a bellows, a living part of the soil and spring. On all sides, more farmers worked and sweated and tilled their fields....

On Easter Sunday, Koszelowka was exalted and festive, and over the sundrenched land floated melodies of Polish songs; they came from Koszelowka and Dubicze, and we could even hear the singing in Kornica. Karbicki, dressed in an undersized navy-blue suit, with sleeves that barely reached beyond the elbows, walked around barefoot while visitors in his house drank and feasted on the calf he had slaughtered. We heard the voice of his cousin Antoni and of others as, for hours, the half-drunken singing of *Sto lat, sto lat...* "may we live to be a hundred..." boomed from the houses.

Through Easter and the days that followed, a new spirit prevailed in the farmer's household. Karbicki and spouse began to live as harmoniously as cooing pigeons. Toward us, too, the woman had changed. She would now bring us food and even talk to us. Since the winter had passed without incident, she may have concluded it was not so hopeless after all. Or so we thought before the hints dropped by the farmer soon convinced us that what induced the euphoria in the Karbicki household was not the past but the future. Our original agreement with the farmer was soon to expire, and Karbicki candidly described how he would arrange things after we were gone. He would fill in the pit, buy a horse, a threshing machine, and three new pigs. He even asked us what arrangement we had made to leave the shelter next month.

As May approached, however, the farmer's mentality and vision shifted. The money we had paid him in November had by now become old stuff; what mattered now was his hunger for more. So, when news came of the Germans' surrender in Tunisia and we presented this to him as indisputable proof that the allied conquest of this forsaken piece of desert meant the impending end of the war, Karbicki chose to believe us, and one afternoon, while caressing his pigs and giggling to himself, he agreed to keep us another month. Now the Americans were coming, and all we needed was one more month.

While it was doubtful Karbicki would keep us, we did not think about the problem of paying him, but when he agreed to renew the arrangement, we realized that our money was gone. We did not even have any left for food. Yankel considered sending Wacek to some landlords who owed him money, but it was too risky – for Wacek, and for ourselves, and perhaps even for the landlords. When we could no longer dream up any more nonsense, we asked Motl to come help us decide what to do. It was then that Yankel revealed he had some gold rubles buried in the yard of our house in Losice. Nobody even reacted to this, so far beyond our reach, so irrelevant this buried gold seemed to us; it was probably for similar reasons that Yankel hadn't mentioned it before. However, when the night was ending and everyone had stopped talking, Motl repeated the terrible question: What we were going to do with ourselves after the end of the month? It was then that I said I would go to Losice and attempt to dig out the gold.

Of that moment, I remember only Mother's terror-stricken eyes. With drawn lips, unable to speak, she shook her head convulsively to indicate she would not let me do it. As I bent down to pick up my shoes, Mother jumped. "Nooo...," she screamed. Pressed against the wall, I waited, keeping one shoe in my hand. I tried to calm her. "No, you will not go." She kept repeating in a hoarse voice – "No...." I picked up the other shoe.

The task was simple. The money was hidden underneath the stone steps leading from the building into the yard. We knew that several families as well as a Polish policeman lived there now. Wacek could perhaps guide me to the outskirts of Losice but I would have to enter the town by myself and dig the money out. One difficulty was that, since I did not know exactly where the money was buried, I had to rely on description. The attempt rested on pure desperation, yet it had to be done. I put on my shoes and picked up my jerkin. For a moment, crouching near the cover, I stared into the pit at the sooty flicker of the lamp, Father's bitter eyes over the white jug, the soiled bedding in the corner. My aunt was still explaining that the money was buried under the second stone from the left end of the steps. I hardly listened.

We immediately left on our way. Motl merged rapidly into the night, trying to get away from Karbicki's farm before anyone saw us. I followed on his heels. For the first time in six months, I was out in the open. We were on the trail, and as we passed the farm of Karbicki's nearest neighbor, Rataj, his dogs detected us and began their growling. A milky haze floated low over the fields, and big stars trembled on the clear sky. At first fear gripped me and I felt like running back, but the night – its fog, its sky, its fierce stars that seemed to wonder and disbelieve our existence – soon carried me away. Motl, barefoot, a sack over his shoulder, walked ahead of me, his stick thrust forward. Every once in a while, we stopped to listen for suspicious sounds. But the night was quiet. Only the lapwings cried in the marshes. We passed the little bridge on the brook and the frightened wild ducks, flapping their wings, rose into the air. The windmill of Koszelowka grew and soon towered over us with its huge arrested blades. Past the village, we walked over tilled fields and up gentle hills we advanced, crouching under bushes and hiding under maple trees, deeper and deeper into the night.

On the way we were to visit the farmer who was hiding Yankel's youngest son, Itzek, and pay him for the next month. It was a small white house, not unlike Karbicki's. In the window someone lifted the curtain and, seeing Motl, let us in. I hardly recognized Itzek when he came out from hiding. He had grown tall and bloated, and he could hardly speak. Having forgotten Yiddish and not yet learned Polish, he talked a pidgin that I could barely follow.

The boy had no inkling that we were hiding in Koszelowka, two miles away. To make sure he could not betray us if he were caught, I told him that I was coming from Miedzyrzec and had seen his family there. He did not say much, but only looked at me with big, dark eyes.

"Why don't you talk?" I asked him.

"They will kill you in Miedzyrzec," he said, choking up his funny Yiddish-Polish jargon.

I assured him lie need not worry as we were actually hidden, just as he was. "Good," he said, "for in the ghetto they would kill you."

"What do you want me to tell your father?" I asked him.

"Nothing, except tell him not to be in the ghetto," he answered as we were ready to leave.

We were approaching Dubicze, where Motl's shelter was. At the edge of the village, we crouched and listened. The orchards drenched the night with the smell of cherry blossoms stuck to the trees like white butterflies. With backs bent, on tiptoe, we sneaked across the village to one of the village sheds. Motl pushed open a door and we quickly slid inside.

When I saw Motl's shelter, I realized what ours must look like. I had become accustomed to our tomb, but this pit was new, and as soon as I lowered myself into it, I wanted to run away. It was simply loathsome: the moist, foul walls; the cadaver-like faces of the people; the food they served me on the bench. Everything was the same as in our place: the lamp, the loft, the people, the conversations. But I saw all this anew, and it was horrid. All night I lay awake, loath to touch those sleeping next to me.

The farm girl brought in dinner at noon, and we asked her to tell Wacek we wanted to see him. Later, through the cracks in the loft, I saw her walking in the orchard towards Wacek's house. She moved in boisterous dancing steps, her large feet against the earth. The dog that ran after her jumped against her breasts, and the girl, pulling the kerchief off her head, waved it in the air and ran faster and faster. She stopped at Wacek's window and whispered something inside. Somebody answered, and the girl burst into loud, ringing, happy laughter that made me bite my lips in regret, envy, desire....

Wacek arrived late at night, and I saw again his alert, laughing eyes. He came straight from the field, and he smelled of soil and sweat. Without hesitation, he agreed to lead me to Losice. He could not go that night, he said, because he had to work in the field, but he would go when the work was finished. "I have to go, don't I?" he said, as if his life, too, depended on that money. He sat chatting with us for some time, the only friend we had, the pivot of our wretched existence.

"Don't worry. You, too, will be free," he consoled us, surmising what effect spring was having on us.

On a Monday night, almost a week after my arrival in Motl's shelter, I sat in the pit, hoping Wacek would pick me up for the trip. The march, I figured, should take two nights. Then Shmyl, who was due back from the ghetto in about a week, would come with me on the march to Miedzyrzec, where I wanted to go. The hours dragged on, and still Wacek did not come. We were getting ready for sleep when we heard a rustling upstairs, but instead of Wacek, it was Shmyl who dropped into our midst.

He has returned too soon! flashed through my mind. As we all bent toward him, our shadows on the wall obscured the entire shelter.

"What happened?"

"Can't you see?" he cried.

His lips were black; the shrunken, bloodshot eyes were without pupils. It was the same scalded face he had brought back once before from the Treblinka boxcars.

"They came on Sunday," he rattled, "on Sunday. The whole ghetto was undermined by tunnels and caves where we were all hiding. They came by the hundreds with hand grenades, blood-hounds, and dynamite. And again we marched to the box-cars...." His speech trailed off into a mumble; he keeled over asleep.

He slept uninterruptedly into the following day. We woke him for dinner, but he would not eat anything. Motl kept asking what happened to Manya and Lebel, a relative of the two brothers.

Shmyl said he had seen Lebel in the transport; Manya had probably remained hidden in the ghetto.

"You jumped?" Motl asked him.

"Yes. Our car didn't even have a window. Lebel was with me in the same wagon and also Leyzor with two of his brothers. Somebody had a knife prepared, and we began to drill a hole in the wall. Through the opening we had made, only one at a time could get out, and we would have reached Treblinka before all of us could escape. We pushed out Leyzor's small brother to open the door-latch from the outside. They killed him, but not before he opened the door. I jumped, reached the woods, and waited there. But no one came to join me. They all lay on the tracks. At night I started toward Dubicze."

Wednesday night, Lebel arrived. In the boxcar, Shmyl had told him to contact Wacek if he survived. Wacek brought him to the shelter. Large and bow-legged, he dropped into the opening like a sack. His wild feverish eyes did not see any of us. Shmyl asked him questions, but he did not answer. From the skull down to the chin, a thick crust of congealed blood caked his face, and his left hand had been bared of skin. Hugging his raw, bloody feet with his hands, he kept mumbling: "They are all gone, all...."

I asked him if he knew anything about Manya, who, according to Shmyl, was hidden on Sunday in the ghetto.

"What are you talking about, Sunday? There was a second transport on Monday. They are still clearing the ghetto."

Nearly ten days after my arrival in Motl's shelter, Wacek found time to break away from his spring sowing. We had decided to make the round trip to Losice, about forty kilometers in all, in one night. In order to manage that, we had to start out in daylight.

As I could not start from the village before complete dark, we decided that I would leave for Kornica with Motl the night before and hide in its thickets until Wacek picked us up there.

Everybody was still asleep when Motl and I left the shelter. We cautiously made our way through the village but, once in the open fields, we raced through the quickly fading night. We crossed the Dubicze marshes and waded through the little brook, while, from the woods on the other side, the dawn chorus of birdsong began to wind its crescendo. When the sun rose, we were already deep in the bushes. Motl stretched out and immediately fell asleep. I took off my shirt, found an unshaded spot, and, glory of glories, sunbathed all day.

Toward evening, three coos of a cuckoo resounded from the direction of the Walim road. "It's Wacek," said Motl. I whistled. The cooing was repeated. We approached each other through the thickets until, with a final check of our signals, we met Wacek at the appointed little clearing. I waved to Motl and started off.

Almost immediately, I realized I had overestimated my strength. I forgot that I had lain in a pit for six months and had done no walking. My thighs began to stiffen, and pain spread through all my leg muscles. Fear, too – at times almost panic – began to envelop me upon my realization that I was out alone in a world cleansed of all Jews. Only Wacek's proximity kept me going. I walked into the setting sun, in a dusk filled with a vast anointed peace in which not even the buzz of a fly could be heard. Wacek, moving like a cat, told me to be fast and quiet as we heard the peasants out on picnics. Far away, I could see campfires and loops of dancing girls. The songs drifted over the calm evening, haunting me to tears. I closed my eyes and walked on.

A large and crimson moon was already in the sky when, nestled in the distant valley, I saw the dark outlines of Losice. The

towers of the church rose like masts of a silent ship, and the house roofs shone cold and wet in the eerie moonlight. I told Wacek I would enter the town by myself, and I showed him where to wait for me, but he answered that he would come with me. I looked at him without comment. We agreed that if we were stopped by only one gendarme we would kill him; if by several, we would attempt to escape. Should the escape succeed, we were to meet in the Chotycze woods, some five kilometers from town.

Moving along the ditch of the highway, we crossed the river and reached the first outlying building, where we crouched under a wall and listened. Everything seemed quiet except for the power plant nearby and its condensate bubbling in the drainpipe. I took off my shoes and left them under a barn. Near Miedzyrzec Street, where our house stood, we had to stop to let a patrol of Schupo pass. Then we cut across the street to the house. I pressed the gate, but, finding it locked, I circled the building to approach it from the other side. Once there, we realized we could be seen from the square, so we crawled on our bellies into the yard.

I stopped for a while in the shadow of the archway. There were lights in most windows and I could hear people talk in the apartments. Wacek hid behind the shed while I moved toward the steps. The money was supposedly buried beneath the second stone of the bottom step. When I reached the place, I froze. The steps had been dismantled, and there was no sign of the stones. There was little time for contemplation. Judging approximately where the stone had been, I began a blind and furious digging.

I had a knife, a spoon, and a thick rod, and with these tools I began the search. I had been told the money was buried half a yard deep, but I found no money at that depth. Then the spoon broke. I dug and dug, using the rod, but there was nothing. I had already made a good-sized hole when the rod, too, broke. Throwing it away, I resorted to the knife and my fingers. The knife hit stones, jarred and gnashed. In the stillness of the night, each sound was an explosion. "For heaven's sake be quiet," Wacek's voice implored behind me, "and make it faster. Germans are in the square." Soaked in sweat, I kept digging. But no money showed up in the deep hole in front of me. I was out of breath, my hands were bleeding, and I was losing hope. I was still digging when Wacek came over again: "Have mercy, they will hear you." The money was not there. I stood up.

Wacek said that we had better go back. I stood over the hole, looking at our house with its lighted windows and carefree voices. If the money was still there, I thought, the people would probably continue the search next day and find it. "Let's go," Wacek urged. But, for me, there was no returning. I tried once more. Instead of digging, I began to stab a wide area with the knife. Suddenly, the knife struck something, and after an initial resistance, it sank into a hollow.

"I've got it," I yelled.

"Shhshh," Wacek hissed.

With both hands I dug furiously into the earth, and after a few frenetic moments I pulled out a tin container filled with gold rubles.

Recrossing Miedzyrzec Street, we were soon back at the barn where I had left my shoes. When I tried to put them on, I squealed with pain. My swollen, bleeding feet were not fit for shoes; worse, they were not fit for the return trip. Jumping grotesquely, I began the march of eighteen kilometers back to the Walim bushes. The moon disappeared; the night misted over. Wacek, looking uneasily at the sky, said we had better rush because daybreak was near.

Soon I collapsed and could not get up. I crawled off the road into a ditch and sat. A drilling pain reached from my toes to the chest. My legs were swollen up to the knees; my feet were a mess of dirt and blood. Wacek picked me up, supported me for a while, then let go, urging me to hurry. On tiptoe, hopping like a kangaroo, I followed him, spurred on by the crowing of roosters in the waking villages and the cool breeze coming from the east.

Half the way back, it began to dawn. In the meadows, crickets sang and some farmers were already out in the fields. I managed to pass Wyzyki, but on the other side of the village I fell down again. My legs were crutches over which I had no command. Wacek stood over me, worried. "Go," I told him. "Go on, I will stay here."

"They will kill you. Come on."

I told him I could not make it. "Perhaps I will manage to hide somewhere later,when I have rested. Here is the gold."

Wacek did not take the gold. Instead, he bent down, lifted me onto his back, and marched on, swaying under the load. Kornica came into sight; only two kilometers past the village, we would reach the bushes. I suddenly felt Wacek shudder. Then he dropped me. As I landed on my knees, I spotted four policeman riding toward us. Though they were far away, I recognized their uniforms and saw the sun on their rifles. I shoved the can of rubles into Wacek's pocket. I had often imagined my capture and execution as a horrid moment, but, now, somehow, I was completely indifferent. Wacek whispered in my ear that he would run. "Try, if you can," he said. The suggestion made me laugh, but in that very instant, the police turned off the road and drove into Kornica.

We bypassed the village and headed toward the bushes. Each step on bleeding feet produced fiery rings before my eyes. But the grove was already in sight: another kilometer, half a kilometer, a hundred meters. The sandy trail appeared, then the bushes. As soon as I entered the thicket, I fell to the ground. When I next opened my eyes, I saw Motl over me. He stood there and smiled against the sun.

"I had already given up," he whispered.

xxix

Some days later, on the night of May 13, I left with Shmyl for the environs of Miedzyrzec: I had to find out what had happened to Manya. Also, I had heard rumors about Polish partisans and I wanted to join them. Above all, I had to get away from the shelter.

We walked out into a splendid summer night. On the crest of the hill I stopped and turned around. I stood staring at the shed lying lonely and white in the valley. There, in that pit of agony, were Father's wild eyes and Yankel's insane screams. There Mother lay in the corner, mourning Manya as she had mourned me when, for ten days, I did not return from my Losice trip. As I walked, the pine grove soon erased the sight of Karbicki's farm and the village.

Our first planned stop was at a temporary shelter run by a certain farm woman, Staskowa, where we hoped to meet stragglers from the Miedzyrzec ghetto. We walked the rest of the night, slept in the forest during the day, and arrived at the farm shortly after dark. Staskowa, a thin shrill woman, recognizing Shmyl from previous visits, piped "Oh, are you still alive?" Shmyl asked if any other Jews were in her house. The woman said there were none, but this probably wasn't true; it was only her standard answer.

"They were here after they jumped from the trains," said Staskowa, "but now they have all gone away, some into the woods and some back into Miedzyrzec."

"Back to Miedzyrzec?"

"Yes," she said. "They still left some of you there."

We filled two bottles with water and moved on.

Soon Shmyl lost the way. Trying to guess direction by the stars, we chose one of two possible directions, but it was evidently the wrong one, for we were soon so hopelessly lost we had to stop. We knocked on the door of some house. Nobody answered. Not until the fourth farm did a man dare open a window and tell us how to reach the highway. Fog settled, increasing our difficulties. After a full hour's wandering, we noticed, through the mist, the converging lines of telephone poles leading to Miedzyrzec.

We followed the ditch along the road. About seven kilometers from Miedzyrzec, a shot rang out; more firing came from the direction of the city. We moved cautiously while the firing continued and the moon-soaked woods reverberated with hollow metallic echoes. Suddenly, we heard steps, and several shadows appeared atop the road. Since none but illicit people were out at night, we guessed these were Jews escaping from the ghetto.

A middle-aged man and his boy stood in front of us; holding on to them were two small girls. We had no time to contemplate the pathetic appearance of this little group, and we asked the man whether it was possible to get into the ghetto. At first he did not answer. Then, bending down, he spat into our faces, "Back, get back."

We tried to calm him, saying we had to get there. Turning his head towards the city, the man hissed. "You must? Run! Scram! See the small children? Their mother was just killed. I woke them an hour ago. Run!"

I closed my eyes. The man did not know what he was doing. "Where are you going?" I asked him.

He stopped talking, just then realizing the monstrous weight of the question. He began to spin fantastic schemes of salvage and rescue only to abandon them, knowing he had nowhere to go. With his eyes bulging and his mouth distorted, he implored us to tell him where to go and what to do. There was a magic moon, and the vast night, fields, and woods, but no room for this middle-aged man and his three children. We were getting ready to go when he caught the sleeve of my jacket.

"You are young. You were there. Please, where shall I go? Tell me, for God's sake. To the Bialowieza forest? No, I know! To a farmer. A farmer will take me in. I know! I have cousins in America. They will pay. Where? Tell me where?"

Thus he went on. He was leaving the ghetto for the first time and had no inkling what it meant. He did not know that, although the Polish forests and fields were vast and open, each bush, each inch of earth, each human heart, would be closed to him. He did not know he would envy the dead and pound his breast in guilt and admission that all this suffering was justly inflicted for his crime of remaining alive.

We were leaving him. The man was down on his knees, and as the moon shone coldly on his bald head he whined: "Where shall I go? Where?" The two little girls were sitting in the middle of the highway, their legs curled up, and their father was looking around him with eyes that were already insane. The road curved to the left, and we soon lost them from sight.

A burst of gunfire cracked nearby. The bullets whizzed over the highway and smashed against trees. Over Miedzyrzec rockets hung: one, three, ten. Two flares went up, and we slowed our pace to avoid their light. When it was dark again, we stubbornly pushed on. Then three flares rose and spilled their treacherous light over the highway. Before we ducked, five shots were fired in our direction. The bullets swished past our ears and whammed into the trees and telephone poles. Another flare went up, blinding us. As it faded into darkness, we noticed people in front of us — more Jews escaping from the ghetto.

There were two of them, a father and a son whom Shmyl recognized because they were from Konstantynow.

"Back, get back. Run!" They repeated the words the father of the little girls had said. They did not stop, but kept moving, pulling us along and bending their heads. "They are finishing off the ghetto. Get back!"

We turned, leaving behind us the burning ghetto. The firing subsided. The glare over Miedzyrzec's sky paled; the shouts calmed down. By daylight, we were again on Staskowa's farm.

"Staskowa's ghetto," as we called her farm, was a shelter and hub for many a wandering Jew. It was at least five kilometers to the nearest village of Wazki, and all about the farm was nothing but dense forest. The farm consisted merely of a small house and a barn. Staskowa kept the cow in the barn and the pigs in the house. She was a widow with four small children, the eldest no more than twelve years old. The poor desolate farm was a haven, a royal palace, for all the struggling Jews in the neighborhood. Such hospitality was unprecedented. True, the woman was wretchedly poor and the Jews were a source of income, but this was not the reason for her benevolence. Staskowa simply did not realize the danger. She had no clear idea what awaited her if the Germans discovered what was going on. Her life had always been primitive, and the war had barely touched it. In fact, so isolated was her location that she had never even seen a German. Not knowing the danger involved, she conducted what she thought was a good business.

Everyone who stayed in her house had to pay a fee. The price of water was ten zlotys a bottle. For potatoes, cooked in a large pail, she charged sixty zlotys per spoon supplied, equating spoons with number of mouths feeding. Most of us did not have a grosz, and since penury doesn't impair one's appetite, we resorted to sharing our spoons. For a long time we got away with it, despite the woman's restiveness about declining profits. But one day, when we had bought from her a full pot of potatoes and asked for only two spoons, she found six people eating away at the steaming pot. Staskowa then changed her business methods and charged a flat fee per pot. With all this, one could not deny that the woman had a kind streak, and she did many things for noncommercial reasons.

At evening the atmosphere around the farm verged on enchantment. During the day, we were tense, knowing that any moment the place could be raided. At night, amid these forests, we were the undivided masters. For a short six hours we were almost free men. What a vast, grand feeling! As soon as the sun sank behind the horizon, we filed down from the loft to the farmyard and out into a calm brooding summer evening. From the barn came the smell of hay. Stars lit up the sky, and from behind the forests rose a yellow moon.

Then, from the trails and roads and forests, the survivors emerged, converging on Staskowa's farm like animals drawn to a watering hole. They sat in a circle on the grass. The first question was always what was new in the war. The next priority was where and how to hide, always connected with the listing of names of people killed yesterday and those killed today. Hearing about the Polish underground and their partisan activities, we discussed joining them and looked for means of establishing contact. We mused about the Allies, perhaps a bombing of Auschwitz, perhaps a leaflet from the skies with a warning to the Germans. Then we talked about our own brothers in America and the ghastly silence they managed to maintain – not a single man to contact us, not a single drop of arms, of food, not a word to tell us that at least they weep over their fathers and sisters dying here in heaps, country by country. We thought that perhaps they, too, had died; how else could it be as it was...? But the newspapers told that they were well, quite well, and we continued to wait for guns, food, money, a word, a wink. At this stage, had we been given help, many of us would have survived. Had there been a hint, a promise, even a deception, we would at least have died feeling less than universally and gleefully abandoned. But nothing came, not then, nor later, nor ever. The only voice we heard was of the lapwings and the frogs – and of that permanent sigh hanging over the sky of Miedzyrzec.

At daybreak, only a few of us remained in Staskowa's house. The farm was not a place where people stayed permanently but a transit station where one could camp before moving on to more secure lairs. It was perilous to be there; the village probably knew about the traffic of Jews around the farm, and we expected the Germans sooner or later to raid the place. But at dark the Jews would again come from the forests and we would have another happy evening around the camp fire – while the bull frogs croaked and chanted in the marshes and a large moon hung over the forests like a huge Japanese lantern. Sometimes, from the southern wall of the forest, would come the cry of a speeding train. We looked into that side of the sky, a sky cut with the scars of hissing flares and aglow with a never-ending conflagration, and our lips trembled; Miedzyrzec, Miedzyrzec.... There it was, city of our extinction, the pyre that would not stop smoking....

One day we got news that the bailiff of Wazki had threatened to liquidate Staskowa's nest. We had to think about getting away, but I did not want to return to the shelter without first learning what had happened to Manya. In the afternoon, we met a distant relative of Staskowa's, a small old man with a thick moustache and good, gray eyes. We offered him money to find out whether there were any Jews left in Miedzyrzec.

"No, boys." He shook his head.

We increased the fee, but he laughed bitterly. "So you think it is money. I was in Miedzyrzec on that first Tuesday when they took you out, and from then on I have never been there. I will never go to Miedzyrzec again."

We decided to try ourselves. There were three other boys looking for relatives, and the five of us left for the city as soon as night fell. Our companions knew the road quite well and we moved briskly, avoiding all major roads and particularly the highway. The strip through the forests was the most dangerous spot as the Germans often set ambushes there. But we cleared the woods and crossed into open countryside. We moved cautiously, watching the dark outlines of the military camp to our right and avoiding its searchlight that nervously scanned the fields and woods.

A gray dawn was rising when we saw the ruins of the former ghetto. We stepped over rubble, screeching glass, and discarded packs. Near the wires of the last small ghetto, not certain anyone still lived there, we stopped. Telling the others to wait, I lifted the wire and crawled inside. When I reached the first house, I put my ear to the door and heard people snoring. I nodded my head toward the rest, and they followed me into the ghetto.

The ruins of Miedzyrzec! Only twenty thousand people had lived here, and yet fifty thousand were led to their death over these ruins. For a moment, one felt like smiling, lured by the hush and sway of the fertile steppe of Miedzyrzec. As far as one looked, down its untrodden streets, flush against doors and staircases and windows, grass and giant weeds sprouted. They grew erect and tall as trees until the ghetto was awash, a magnificent green float in the scorched wasteland. Above it, a sky of unbelievable blueness serenely looked down on a beautiful green city of death.

Only two streets were given over to the remaining few, two narrow alleys surrounded by barbed wire. Beyond were the ruins – a vast field of rubble and cinders and trash. The wounds of the fifth slaughter stood out fresh and raw against the mellowed death mask of the four previous slaughters. Feathers from torn bedding still floated in the air; rags and pots and furniture and books and photographs littered the streets. Workers with brooms and pails of water in their hands walked the streets, washing away the blood puddles.

In this tiny corner still lived about a thousand Jews; they passed their time sitting on thresholds and waiting for the next and probably last round. I found Manya among them. She had survived. She told me about the six hundred dead in the ghetto, and she told me how the people in her hiding place had smothered two children to death because they had started to cry. Then she cooked dinner for me and, ordering me to throw away the tattered, filthy clothes I was wearing, she gave me new pants and a new shirt. I ate meat, and for the first time in half a year I was not hungry. And for the first time in half a year I lay in a bed, a genuine bed with white sheets and a pillow under my head. But I did not sleep; through the open window I saw the moon, as large as the one over the bleached Losice ghetto, sailing over the deserted ruins. I sailed along with it.

Several days passed in the ghetto, to which I clung with all my instincts. Shmyl wanted to go back, but I put him off so that I might continue to wander among the ruins and talk to people. Some survivors from the Warsaw uprising told me about German tanks firing into shelters, about soldiers dynamiting each house, about the flame-throwers, the sewers and the poison gas. There was also one boy left from the Miedzyrzec Gymnasium, and we walked together along the barbed wire, smelling the lilac and the linden trees and talking about school. It was Meyer, the tall, lean school clown. He told me about Perelka, who was going to be an actress, whose skull had been cracked by a rifle butt; about Wiernicka, who wrote poetry, good poetry, at the age of twelve, who had been smothered in the train; about Kuba, who was going to be an army officer in Palestine, whose head had been chopped off by hoodlums in the forest; about half-witted Nathan, whom the Germans hanged in the middle of the ghetto. And about Hinda, who died without special distinction.

Before leaving, Manya said some people offered to take her along to a shelter and that she agreed to go with them. I did not tell her I intended to return to the ghetto; instead, I urged her to leave as soon as possible. My leavetaking from Manya was short. I saw her silhouette in the lighted window when I moved down the dark alley of the ghetto. As I crossed the wire, I lost sight of her.

We had a miserable trip. It was pitch dark and it poured all night long. Smiting sheets of water blinded and soaked us. We barely managed to pull our legs out of the mud. The two girls accompanying us to Staskowa's farm gave way. We took over their packs and let them hang on our arms. They fell repeatedly, each time barely managing to get up. We, too, began to sag, and Shmyl proposed that we throw away the books we had taken from the ghetto. I stopped him, and we struggled in the rain and wind and darkness. It was daylight when we arrived at Staskowa's farm.

We lay in the loft almost naked while our clothes dried. It was then I took a look at our two companions. One young, good looking girl, Pesha, came to Lebel, who had been waiting for her at Staskowa's farm and was to take her with him. The other was a young widow, Golda, who claimed she knew a farmer who had promised to help her. Also in the loft were the father and son we had met during our attempted first trip to Miedzyrzec. The father's name was Kielman; he, too, intended to head for Koszelowka, where he knew some farmers. We had brought along food and cigarettes from Miedzyrzec, and we spent all day eating and talking, resting up for the trip.

Toward evening we went down into the house to prepare dinner. The packs were tied and the nine of us – including Leyzor, who had jumped from the train and was waiting for us at Staskowa's – got ready to go. Staskowa even regretted our leaving. Saying good-by to her and to the remaining Jews, we set foot on a calm, warm evening for Koszelowka.

We were again marching through forests and fields – a handful of doomed people fighting death. With us sailed the night's shadows and countless stars. They alone knew our secrets and our roads, and only they did not betray us. We entered groves, emerged from forests, climbed hills, sneaked through villages, and marched on and on and on. Then the crickets began their haunting tzik-trr, tzik-trrr. A single bird twittered in the woods, then a couple, until the whole forest was ablaze with song. Day was coming and we had to disappear. Soon there were the familiar bushes of Kornica. We took off our shirts, lay down in the thicket, and fell asleep.

At dusk, we moved to the other side of the pine grove. I divided the books with Shmyl and reminded him to come for me on his next trip to Miedzyrzec. After waiting for the darkness to thicken, we began to separate. Because none of us was to know where the others went, those who had the furthest to travel were sent out first. Since Golda had said she was going to some village east of Konstantynow, we asked her to start off. She began to mumble incoherently. Her eyes kept getting bigger.

"You have to go first," Lebel said.

"Where?" she managed to say.

We understood immediately; she had no place to go. She broke down, sinking to her knees as she cried that she had not known, that she didn't imagine "it" to look like that, that she was afraid of the night, the dogs growling in the villages, the forests, the loneliness. She began to beg for pity, for someone to take her along.

We repeated to her that all this was of no avail, and that she had better move on. She peered across the night into the valley. "Where will I go? What did I do? Take me back to Miedzyrzec. Take me back to the ghetto."

Nobody was now going to Miedzyrzec, she was told, so her crying was futile. But she did not listen; she only whined:

"Back.... I want to go back."

We lifted her to her feet and asked if she knew any farmers. She said she had a few friends in Staszynow. We gave her directions to that village. She stood at the edge of the woods, crossing her hands at each flash of light in the valley and at each sound of the dogs. "Good-by," she finally whispered. She stepped forward and walked slowly toward the highway with her head dropped and shoulders bent until the blue of the night erased her from sight.

Kielman and his son also hesitated for a while before they collected themselves and walked off towards Wolki. Then Lebel and Leyzor and Pesha left. The barking of the dogs soon indicated that they had just passed Rataj's farm. Then Shmyl went away. I was left alone in the pine grove. I waited until everyone was out of sight and the dogs had calmed down. Then I, too, walked down the narrow trail, heading for the small whitewashed house in the valley.

XXX

> O You Spring, forever remembered in our land,
> You Spring of war, you Spring of plenty ....

The lines Mickiewicz wrote almost a hundred years ago seemed written for the summer that now lingered on the sunsoaked fields of Koszelowka. It was the most fertile summer in memory. The grain fell ahead of harvest and rich bread awaited the peasants. The soil sagged under the rolling sea of wheat, the dunes of clover, and the sumptuous grass that flooded all ridges and groves. Flower beds flamed over the meadows, poppies bronzed in the sun, and we couldn't help but feel it was our blood that had so enriched the soil, our ashes that had fertilized these fields. Wherever a seed sprouted that year, there was our grave; wherever a root sprang, there was our corpse. We returned to life that year all over the vast expanse of Europe, from the Pyrenees to the Volga. Pulverized and incinerated, we pushed through the cracking pores as weeds and saw the sun again.

Then, at its height, the spring turned cold and wet. In June, heavy rains began to fall, and they continued in thick, singing streams. Oblivious to the cold and rain, I sat in the loft watching this demented season. The last extermination of the Miedzyrzec ghetto had taken place on May 26, one week after we left it. I no longer waited for Shmyl, for there was no ghetto to run to. All kinds of mad ideas entered my head. I planned to walk into our house and let the Germans kill me. I intended to go to Staskowa's farm, hoping that there the end would somehow find me. I thought of shooting everyone in his sleep. But nothing happened, and I was in the same sty in the same village of Koszelowka.

Evidently, Karbicki also thought the farce had gone on too long, for he would come in and ask us to go away. He no longer hid his intentions, and he offered no excuses. When composed, he talked to us good-naturedly, trying to convince us that we ought to quit, that it made no sense to go on. We looked at him with our crazed eyes; our lips listlessly repeated his terrible words, and we shook our heads to indicate we fully agreed with him.

"Karbicki," I said, sitting on the manure and not daring to lift my eyes, "there is going to be an invasion. The Americans will come. There will be an invasion in France. They promised."

Karbicki's mouth was agape and his hands shook. "An invasion?" he shouted in rage. "An invasion? This war will never end. Never!"

This war will never end! The words lingered and expanded swelling into a cosmic prophecy, as if they had been uttered not by an almost illiterate peasant but by Moses. We sat on the manure and repeated that sentence to ourselves with trembling lips. What did the peasant say? Never, never.... What were we waiting for?

It was the most agonizing period in the pit, a period of political stagnation and complete stalemate on all fronts, as though there were no war. Morally we were near collapse. The memory of the murder, instead of weakening with time, grew in the vastness of its monstrosity and inflicted injury. To force us out of the shelter, Karbicki again resorted to starvation. He refused to give us bread; all we got was soup once a day. We watched enviously as the pigs smacked away at their full troughs. We were as thin as sticks and moved about the sty like apparitions. When, occasionally, somebody fainted from hunger, we grabbed a cup and stole some milk from the cow, watching with worried eyes the cow's udders lest it be noticed. Outside, the rains kept falling; the fields were soaked; the forest trembled with cold, and the farmer yelled that we go away, that he had enough of us. We promised him more money, but he asked what good the money would be if the Germans killed him. Why should the Germans kill him, we argued. And he answered by asking why the Germans had killed us off.

The rains kept pouring and the papers were blank. The people in the pit stood in the corners like wet scarecrows, not talking to each other. Father's nose was sharp as a beak. Mother looked like Melancholy personified. Yankel grew wild, and smashing his fists against the walls, he screamed: "To Treblinka, all of us. To Treblinka."

Relaxed for a moment, he crawled up to the loft, where he sat motionless, staring with blank eyes at the smoke rising from Karbicki's house and winding his moustache. But soon he had a second fit; he descended in one jump and, running around the sty, yelled at us: "Murderers! What did you want from me? Murderers!"

Father, occasionally losing control, hit his head with his fists, mumbling unintelligible words. The women became even more listless and took to maniacal strolling back and forth. Only Berko remained steadfast as he went on catching flies and executing them with the dull persistence of a robot.

In June our shelter acquired a new tenant. After the event with Manya, Yankel became apprehensive about Rivkah, who was in Losice with the policeman, and we sent Wacek to see how she fared. Instead of news Wacek brought Rivkah with him. She had been rescued just in time. Her hosts were looking for ways of getting rid of her, and the girl told us how one night she overheard the policeman's wife suggest to her husband that he shoot the girl. The policeman refused, but she quarreled and kept insisting, and had we not taken Rivkah off their hands, the woman's nagging might have proved stronger than the husband's scruples.

Other Jews appeared that summer of 1943, mostly escapees from the destroyed Miedzyrzec ghetto. Shymeluk's two girls perished, and according to Shmyl, Manya left for a shelter somewhere near Miedzyrzec. All others jumped from the death trains and came back. The tailor and the shoemaker were again near Dubicze, and Shymeluk returned with a bullet in his leg. In the pine grove, in addition to Shymeluk, there also roamed Kielman and his son, and they were later joined by a young couple. The five of them dug themselves a shelter and together struggled on. In July, Lebel, Leyzor, and six others established themselves in the Dubicze forest. Their first weeks there were harrowing and they almost perished. Then came Wolodia, an escaped Russian prisoner of war who had lived in the woods with a few other prisoners. All his friends were eventually killed, and from November, 1942, he had been living by himself in the Dubicze forest. On one of his nightly trips through the forest he stumbled upon the Jews.

From that day, things took a turn for the better. Wolodia guided the Jews to a safer part of the forest; taught them when and how to cook; how to avoid getting lost in the dark; how to distinguish the steps of humans from those of animals, the glow of phosphorescent wood from that of a flashlight. Under his direction they dug a new pit and disposed of the dirt in a safe and quick manner. Wolodia taught the men how to gather food and where to find water. He imposed a routine and established a code of behavior that became law in the struggle against the forest, the peasants, and the Germans.

That the Jews succeeded in surviving in the forest was also n some measure due to the Polish underground. This organization became progressively more active, and, by the summer of 1943, it had developed into a full-fledged, partisan outfit. We had long heard about their exploits in other parts of the country, and now they increasingly operated in our own neighborhood. Soon almost very young Pole belonged to this *Armia Krajowa*, called, for short, AK, and participated in its work either actively or indirectly. The Armia Krajowa – its name, "Home Army," distinguished it from General Anders's forces fighting with the allies in Italy – was the official fighting force of the Polish government-in-exile sitting in London. Another partisan group, *Armja Ludowa*, the People's Army, as supported by Moscow, but they were of zero consequence; in fact, we never even heard of them until after liberation. For all practical purposes, the AK was the only underground in Poland. Numbering in the hundreds of thousands of men, it had unqualified popular support and was powerful, daring, and effective.

As a result of the AK activities, the Germans, if they could, avoided venturing into the countryside. Gone were the days when few of them would take off into the villages to have extracurricular fun with requisitions and casual killings. The underground is systematically assassinating all their collaborators and spies, except those who also served the underground. They had killed the ARBEITSAMT in Losice as well as the Commandant of the Polish lice. Since all collaborators and German agents were inevitably Jew-baiters, these assassinations often seemed to the peasants an admonition not to harm Jews. This impression was strengthened by illegal pamphlets distributed throughout the country in which official position of the AK was to help the remaining Jews by all possible means. So the underground protected us to some degree, not only from the Germans but also from the Poles. And, indeed, this was the quietest and safest period in our clandestine life. In addition to the two shelters, Motl's and ours, there were Jews in the pine grove and in the Dubicze forest, and a Jewish tailor and shoemaker who had escaped from Miedzyrzec moved about our area – but not a single denunciation occurred.

Our success at survival that summer was also due to the elaborate bond that established itself between the various groups of Jews hiding either on farms or in the forest. A peculiar, unwritten code had gradually developed to which one had to subscribe in order to live. Those of us with money who could afford to hide with farmers had to support other penniless survivors. In this way the four in our family were supported by Yankel; one Goldstein supported four others in Motl's shelter. From our farmer we gathered information for those in the Dubicze forest, and they, in turn, tried to learn whether our peasant was suspected of keeping Jews. Important messages reached all of us within two nights through a relay network led by Wacek. An unusual and unexpected solidarity, often bordering on self-sacrifice, developed among us. We always accepted as axiomatic that, when danger threatened, one would grasp at anything in order to save oneself. But nothing of the sort ever happened. During the winter of 1942, when most of the wandering Jews had to leave Koszelowka, the shoemaker knew about our place, yet he left for the ghetto rather than seek safety with us. Shymeluk, Lebel, and Leyzor did not force themselves on Motl's shelter but went into the forest and all of its perils. People endured danger and some perished, but nearly always they sought to spare others a similar fate.

xxxi

Toward the end of the summer a flood of drunken, near-decisive war news burst upon us. Having blunted the German assault on Kursk in July, the Soviets unexpectedly launched a major summer offensive and drove rapidly west across the northern Ukraine. But the big event was Italy's capitulation. It was September 9, and I lay in the pit, in the stench and the darkness, when Karbicki broke the news to us. I crawled out and, sitting on the manure, I looked into the still blazing summer and whispered to myself, "This is the end." For the first time I felt the actual possibility, the reality of survival. Berko took out a map and blackened all the Balkans and the whole Italian peninsula; this brought the Allied armies right up to the Alps and the shores of the Danube.

In the calm evening that followed, we sat on the manure and talked about the end of the war. The farmer left the door slightly open, and through the crack we could see the grass glistening with dew, the wet furrows of the freshly plowed fields, and the stars over Wolki. In the peasant's house the children sang with sleepy voices, and from Koszelowka came the sound of accordions. The crickets sang louder and louder and the frogs added their longing basso. We were talking about liberation and about leaving the sty.

That evening, with the farmer's rough hand pressed warmly in mine, I spun the threads of a long, long dream. I was raving about the moment when we would leave the shed, move into his house, and look freely into the sun; the moment when we would all sit down at one table and have the feast of liberation we had been planning, when we could announce our common triumph over the Germans and misery and death. Karbicki was silent. He wiped his mouth with the back of his hand and shook his head. While I waited for his bubbling joy, expecting him to share my enthusiasm about this great miraculous moment, Karbicki said in a sullen voice: "...and when this war does end, I don't want... I don't want anyone to know. I don't want you to leave in daylight. Who knows what people might do? I am just a peasant and don't understand things, but there are bad people. You will leave at night. You will go down that trail the same way you had come."

I burst out laughing. I laughed long and heartily. I laughed at the näiveté and ignorance of the peasant. I laughed because I did not understand what the farmer meant and because what I did understand seemed fantastic. But he just looked at me with his white, slit eyes and, shaking his head, cautioned me: "Don't laugh."

One night Wacek came to our shed, the first time he visited us in this place. He woke us all up and shook our hands. He brought us some · bread and meat and, smiling with his good mischievous eyes, told us: "Hold on, hold on." We wanted news from him, but he just patted our backs and asked us to endure a little longer, for freedom was near. How precious was this spark of friendship in the ocean of hate and indifference we had known for four long years. We accepted the meat and the bread and wanted to pay him for it, but Wacek only laughed and said, "You will pay me after the war." Silent and cautious as a cat, he slipped between the beams and thatch and disappeared on the other side. Through the cracks in the wall we saw him sneak across the moon-soaked fields towards Dubicze.

Days of joyous messages! Silent September nights filled with the wildest of dreams! We listened to the cuckoo in the pine grove, to the noise of flirting ducks on the river. Night after night, Karbicki came to the pit bringing messages of victory and hope. He came in his underwear and white flaxen shirt, and he sat with us late into the night, bracing us with his powerful arms and helping us to endure. For liberty was close, so very close. And with us, a whole country and a whole continent and a tortured history waited in awesome anticipation.

First the front cracked and there was heavy fighting. Then the Germans moved to rear positions. Taganrog, Poltawa, and Smolensk had to be evacuated. Another storm and the Soviets were at the shores of the Dniepr. Kiev fell.

Then the last message: The Soviets have crossed the Dniepr and reached the Pripet, a Polish river.

We lay with ears pressed to the ground and waited for the end. Day after day passed. The crowing of the roosters woke us in the morning and the bleating of sheep lulled us to sleep at night. We saw the grain ripen over the fields and we saw it harvested. Only stubble fields remained after the sheaves were collected into the barns. The oats ripened, and under the barn the lupine was out. The sheep coupled in the corners, and last year's young became mothers. Karbicki killed two hogs and bought new ones. The cow calved a second time, and in her belly a new calf was swelling. All the cherries were gone from the tree in the yard, and the little girls brought us berries and mushrooms from the woods. The small chicks grew up, little ducks were hatched, and in the village the women were getting ready for potato digging. Smoke trailed from the early fires started by the shepherds, announcing a new season – and we waited.

Days and weeks and months flowed in a patient, slow, steady stream. Life in the shed did not change; we endured the same starvation, the heat, and the flies. Even the farmer began to have pity on us; when he walked out of the stinking, fly-ridden, hot sty into the open air and sunshine, he groaned as if he felt our agony. He wanted to save us; we were no longer just money. With closed eyes we lay on the manure and endured a long, never ending punishment. Only Berko held up, catching flies and killing them with his razor blade.

The hopeful signs and messages hung on for a while. The Soviet armies were supposedly already in Poland; hundreds of thousands of planes were devastating Germany; the Allies were marching on Berlin through the Danube, the Alps, and the Channel. The euphoria climbed to a zenith, then froze. A sudden silence descended, irrevocable and deep as the calm of a dying man. We had our ears trained and we heard this silence coming. It spread wider and wider, muffling the song of summer and blackening the sky. We looked at each other with terrified eyes and asked whether there was something to be heard. But no one had heard anything. Our panic rose and we crossed our arms in lament. Karbicki did not come to the shed any more. When, eventually, the papers came, they told us that, instead of the reaching the Alps and the Danube, the Allies were exactly where they had been before Italy's capitulation. There was nothing left for us to do but bury our faces in the manure and live with it.

xxxii

Bare stretches of land, the hurried bloom of late summer flowers, the drawn-out blare of the cattle – all intimated the arrival of autumn. It was the season of potato digging, and long lines of peasant women dotted the fields plucking at the furrows in quick jerky motions. All sheaves disappeared from the stubble fields, and only the flax, white and clean, dried in the faded October sun. The farmer removed the manure and bedded the shed with fresh straw. He fixed the holes in the thatch, drawing a tent of darkness over us. We lost the blue patches of sky overhead and the resinous air that had drifted in from the pine grove. At my insistence Karbicki left one tear in the roof, our peephole into the outside world.

The first anniversary of the slaughter of Losice passed, followed by the anniversaries of the first and second slaughters of Miedzyrzec. Almost half a year elapsed without news from Manya, although Shmyl assured us she had left for a shelter with some other people. Several times we had police in the sty, and we heard them walk over our heads. Leyzor visited us on his way to Losice, where he was going to contact his brother and bring him to the forest, and again on his way back, when he told us his brother was dead. Time, the colorless, endless quantity of life, flowed on and on and on.

The night of October 22, I went to Losice a second time to get more money. After Italy capitulated we had spent our money freely, certain that freedom was around the corner. But liberation had not come. Instead of surrendering to the Allies, Italy surrendered to the Germans, and we were again penniless. Yankel then revealed that another portion of gold was buried in the yard of our house. Again there were Mother's panicky eyes, Father's groans, and the same gloomy waiting for Karbicki to open the shed. And then, once more, I was on my way to Losice.

I was not alone. I took Leyzor along because he had a pistol, a small shiny Browning he had managed to purchase. Everything went as it had the first time until, about five kilometers from town, we were detected and a troop of Schupo surrounded us. Managing somehow to sneak into a grove, we lay in the undergrowth as our tense eyes fixed on the silhouettes of the Germans between the trees and the occasional gleam of their lowered rifles. They did not find us and drove off toward Losice. We followed in their tracks, entered the yard of our house, and very quickly located the money. When dawn began to break, we were back in the Kornica bushes.

After turning the money over to my family, I ran away from their agony and delirium for life in the forest; I preferred it to the pit. I walked out with Leyzor into a clear starry night, its air crisp with the first slight cold, the green grass sprinkled with hoar frost. Overhead, the moon shone fantastically in floating rivers of green and silver light. We skirted Koszelowka in a wide circle, and once we passed Dubicze, the forest emerged like a black forbidding wall. As we entered it, its darkness thickened and expanded until it surrounded us on all sides, the treetops hushing and whispering in a muffled, mysterious roar that made our loneliness as vast as the forest itself.

We walked for almost an hour, sneaking from thicket to thicket, cutting across trails in pitch darkness. I stayed close to Leyzor, who plodded, stolidly as a moose, on and on. Then I stopped: I smelled smoke. I told Leyzor about it, but he just motioned me on. As we pushed our way through the thick undergrowth, the scent of smoke became sharper. Finally I smelled cooked food, and in a moment we were at the dugout.

I lowered myself into the pit, and there David and Dora, the couple from Sarnaki, received me with a freshly cooked supper. The fire on the stove was expiring, and thick billows of vapor rose from the cave, cooling the interior. Leyzor, who had remained upstairs, came down, and Dora gave him his soup. He ate, crouched in the corner, smacking his lips and ignoring the others. David ate little but talked on, all of it amounting to one thing only: How much longer? Although full of skepticism myself, I avoided instilling it in others, and so I told David about the Pripet and Cassino, about those victories that had happened, and about those that were bound to happen. "Pripet," groaned David, "how long the same Pripet and Pripet?" The fire on the stove went out. Dora washed the dishes and stacked them overhead. Leyzor tipped his pot and finished off the remaining food. We did not have much time for conversation. Day was breaking, and for the people in the forest that meant sleep and silence. When Leyzor and David went up, I heard them mask the entrance to the shelter, taking everything down and covering the area with fresh leaves and grass. We put out the lamp. For a while, the open entrance was pale with the graying dawn; then the two men slid down and closed the cover. The shelter was now totally black. Outside, the first birds greeted the rising day. We stretched out on the bunk and the hush and murmur of the forest lulled us all to sleep.

The forest in which the bunkers were dug extended from the village of Walim to the Bug. David had set his pit not far from the only road that cut across the forest; he thought that this would be the least suspicious spot. Both David's and Lebel's shelters were skillfully constructed. Without tools or nails, the people concocted holes that were functional and expertly concealed. When Lebel took me to his dugout the next day, he stopped within several feet of the entrance and challenged me to find it. I could not. Then he bent down and lifted a slice of undergrowth, and there was the bunker. Five people occupied Lebel's shelter: Lebel, Pesha and her mother, a boy from Lodz named Yotek, and Wolodia, who was away when I arrived. My visit brought forth protests because we had come during the day, a violation of forest rules. We soon went to sleep, but every once in a while somebody would awake to listen carefully to the voices of the forest, alert for any suspicious sound, any foreign rustle. To me the speech of the forest was inarticulate and alarming; I seemed to hear running, firing, whispering, calling. But the veterans knew exactly what these sounds were, and they could tell whether the dogs were barking in the village or the woods, when it was the deer walking to the pond and when it was the Germans combing the woods, when the branches were broken by humans and when by wild boar.

Our best time in the forest was in the evening. The night still belonged to us. It was our kingdom. As soon as dusk settled over the forest – and this, too, we could tell by the sounds outside – we opened the cover of the pit, and although we would not go out yet, we crouched on the bunk and watched evening descend between the tall, ancient trees. The birds were asleep; the knocking of the woodchoppers had died out. There was no one in the forest but ourselves. Then, in the depth and darkness of the night, we even had happy moments. We crawled outside into an air smelling of sap and berries and stood in the open under the stars gleaming down on us through the treetops. Everyone was assigned a job. To do some physical work was heaven. While the women prepared supper, the men went to get water and wood. Our backs loaded with dry branches, we returned to the shelter, threw the wood inside, and started a fire under the stove. For hours then, we squatted on the bunk and watched while the flames danced and flickered on the bare walls. Unforgettable were the moments when we lingered outside, listening to the hush of the forest – our dark impenetrable home – and watched the steam rise from the stove and the glare of the fire that reached outside and lit up the powerful tree trunks, telling the primeval Polish forest a tale of men cheating death.

I was soon forced to acquaint myself with the demands and rules of forest life. They were hard rules. I had come to the forest in "good times," after the shelters had already been dug through backbreaking toil, after Wolodia had already transferred all his graduate knowledge of forest life to the newcomers, and after the AK had killed the forester, a German stoolpigeon who had been on our heels. I came at a time when the people had already supplied themselves with tin cans and had carved some wooden spoons and managed to stop the seepage of water into the pit. But it was also a time when whatever little money they had was gone, and there was none left for buying food.

We began to steal food from the farmers. We did not particularly cherish the idea, not because we had scruples but because it was dangerous. To steal, the people had to go out into the villages and farms, and each theft alerted and angered the farmers. Potatoes were easily gotten, for at this harvest time they were stacked in the open fields. Even so, the job entailed much care and work. We could not take the potatoes from the fields adjoining the forest because the farmers would have guessed where the thieves had come from. We could not raid the same place too many times because we did not want to infuriate the farmer or harm him excessively. After each expedition we had to make our return in a roundabout way so that the tracks we left would deceive the farmers. There were nights of long, aching marches with heavy sacks on our shoulders, fighting the darkness and the dogs and the exhaustion. For three nights, we dug a new pit, lugging the dirt for miles to dump it into a pond. In that hole we stored the potatoes for the coming winter.

At the beginning, Wacek used to bring us bread, but the frequent baking soon aroused the suspicions of his neighbors, so we had to steal it instead. We needed other foods, too: kasha, barley, oats, fats. We organized what Wolodia termed a *dielo:* in Russian, a cross between a work of art and a physical exploit. Before a dielo was undertaken we collected information and details and established a course of action. Then three or four of us would go out to the assigned place, usually far away, and enter the shed while one of us, flattened against the wall, stood guard outside.

After the first clumsy attempts, we learned the trade. We could fell a pig or a sheep with one blow, then slaughter and disembowel it. The rest was sliced into several parts and put into sacks. The most difficult job was with sheep. While pigs were usually quiet, sheep always started a melée. We then discovered that if we directed the beam of our flashlight into their eyes, they would stop and submit meekly.

There were cases, however, when, coming to an assigned place, we found the shed locked and could not get inside. Then we had to employ the help of the farmer himself. We knocked at the farmer's door and asked for food; in most cases the farmer did not refuse it. We would caution him not to reveal that we had been there, threatening to burn down his farm if he did, and then disperse in various directions to cover our tracks. Hours later, we would reassemble in a previously designated spot and continue back to the forest. Whenever possible, we raided the places of known anti-Semites and collaborators.

So we lived, removed from all civilization and the eyes of all men. Foxes and wild goats roamed around our dugout, farmers cut trees nearby, people traveled back and forth along the road – all unaware of the life going on in the depths of the forest. Still, anyone with sharp eyes would have noticed something suspicious around the two bunkers. He would have detected that too many branches were broken; that, in addition to the trail the animals took to the pond, there was another, not cut by animal hooves. These were still minor worries in comparison with what was coming. The murmur of the forest was changing into a deep roar, and the flood of rainbows on the foliage augured winter, and snow – mortal enemies before whom there seemed to be no escape. We dreaded the thought of it. We closed our eyes to it, lit the fire under the stove, and, bathing our faces in the warm glow, sang all the songs we knew to the Polish forest.

On one of these nights, as we slouched on the bunk singing, Wolodia appeared. It was the first time I met him. He slid down and crouched on the bunker steps with his head retracted between his shoulders. Jumping onto the bunk, he embraced his knees with his arms and looked at me with a half mocking smile. At first I thought he was laughing at me and at our efforts to survive. But soon I learned that his smile was without mockery or malice.

He shook my hand warmly. "I heard that there was a visitor in the shelter, so I came," he said, his Polish softened by a Russian accent. He took off the jerkin, showing a strong, muscular body under the unbuttoned homespun shirt, and gripped the can of hot, steaming soup that Pesha handed him. The fire on the stove began to subside, the glow on the walls became ruddy, and everybody was full and relaxed and safe for the few remaining nightly hours. While the forest above murmured and roared, Wolodia, flooded by my questions, began to tell his story.

It was a detail taken out of the holocaust of the Soviet prisoners of war, four million of whom the Germans systematically starved, hanged, machine-gunned, and poisoned. Wolodia, nineteen, from Borodino, managed to be at the front only a few days before the *Panzers* mauled his unit. Captured, Wolodia traveled west for two long weeks, crossed the Bug, and landed in Suchozebry, near Siedlce, the huge POW camp in our region. Through deliberate starvation and mass shootings, the Russians were rapidly being annihilated. Men fought violently over the skimpy food rations and were eventually driven to eat one another. After a few weeks half of the prisoners were dead. Then the survivors staged their famous breakout. In bright daylight tens of thousands of half starved men began to walk towards the barbed wire. Heedless of the rifles and machine guns that opened fire, they threw their blankets, their coats, and then their own bodies on the tall fences, crushing them with their weight. Most of them remained dead on the barbed wire, but some survived, and these headed for the woods.

Wolodia was one of the escapees, and for awhile he begged, stole, worked for some farmers, slept in the open, lived off the country. When the Germans imposed the death sentence for helping the Soviet prisoners, Wolodia had just contracted typhus. The farmer for whom he had been working told him to leave. Clad in rags, ravaged by fever, he crawled unnoticed into a barn and lay in the loft for three days, eating nothing but the snow that had accumulated on the thatch. After being discovered, he spent the whole night in the open, where he nearly froze to death. For two more days he struggled onward on feet crippled by frostbite, but then he had had enough. He crawled into some stall, fastened a rope to the beam, and tied it around his neck. However, when he pushed himself away from the wall, the rope broke. The thump of his falling body alerted the farmer, who ran in and chased him.

The typhus abated just as the weather relented, and he and six other Russian prisoners grouped together. Over the next half year, they maintained themselves in the same forest in which we were living. But one fall dusk, as they were sitting around a small fire baking potatoes, the green uniforms of the Schupo appeared all around them. Three of the Russians were killed instantly, two threw themselves against the Germans and were shot in the back, and a sixth escaped.

The seventh was Wolodia. He bolted to the end of the grove and was about to jump the trail when he noticed two Germans. He backed up, but there were others. He charged straight ahead and fell. When he tried to get up, he couldn't. He remained motionless. The Germans approached, kicked him several times, and walked away.

Wolodia lay in the forest with a bullet hole in the liver. The pain slowly mounted until he could stand it no longer. He dragged himself to Walim and into the first farmhouse. He had luck: he fell into unusual hands. The farmer not only called a doctor but even kept him in a barn for three weeks until he recovered. Wolodia, now alone, then returned into the woods. He slept in trees, drank from the pond with the animals, and stole food from the village. In this way he lived a whole year. In September he met the Jews. From then on, his fate was connected with theirs.

On the night I was on my way back to our own shelter, Wolodia, too, was leaving. I waited for him outside the bunker, watching the glow of the fire on the tree trunks and listening to the roar of the forest. I heard Wolodia bid good-by to those inside, and he came up, the familiar fatalistic smile on his face. I asked him why he left the bunker so often and roamed the forest. He answered that he did not feel safe staying in one place. "I run so that I myself won't know where I am." At the edge of the thicket, we shook hands and Wolodia turned off to the right. His silhouette floated away without making any sound. I took off my shoes and, keeping to the dark side of the trail, headed back to the farm.

xxxiii

We were going through a particularly severe period of starvation in our shelter. This time, it was not all the farmer's doing. Even with good intentions he could not provide enough food for us. He barely had enough grain for his own needs, and to have bought supplies would have aroused suspicion. An unexpected visit by Leyzor brought us a solution. One morning I woke up to find Leyzor stretched out alongside me on the loft where I usually slept: he had crawled in so skillfully that I had not even heard him. Jokingly, he remarked, "This stealth is due to our experience with the diela." When I mentioned our food situation, he said he had often bought food from Rataj and suggested I go with him. Once Rataj got to know me, I could make these trips by myself.

We left the shed late at night with the first snow falling – a wet November snow. After fending off Rataj's dogs with sticks, Leyzor knocked on the window while I hid around the corner. The shutter cautiously parted. Recognizing Leyzor, the farmer opened the door, but when I tried to follow, the door slammed shut. It took a while before Leyzor convinced the farmer I was "one of ours." We entered the vestibule where, in the dim light of a kerosene lamp, I saw Hipolit Rataj, the owner of the farm, still edgy and suspicious of my presence.

Leyzor dealt with the farmer over the victuals and the prices while I gaped at the spaciousness and warmth of the house. A cicada sounded a melancholy tune, just as in my grandfather's house. The stove, already heating for the winter, blended its glow with the snores of the sleeping farmers, the smell of freshly baked bread, and the gleam of white pillows in the bedroom. With blinking eyes I looked at the laundry neatly arranged in the drawers, at the crucifix on the wall, and at Hipolit's young, blonde wife sleeping in the open bedroom, her hair spread over the pillow, her arms bare and full. My knees yielded. I sat and stared at this sudden reenactment of normal life. Outside, the dogs kept barking and the snow fell and melted on the window panes.

The bags were filled with foodstuffs and Hipolit asked what else we wanted. I begged him to pacify the dogs outside, but he said that they would go on yelping so long as strangers were in the house. Responding to Rataj's dogs, all those in Koszelowka began barking, and I could also hear Antoni's dog near our farm. I paid and told the farmer that, from now on, I would be coming to buy food. Since we were people without names, my password was to be "the dark one." Hipolit again admonished us, should we be caught, not to reveal where we had gotten the food. Then, wishing us luck, he let us out. For a moment I stopped on this border of life and hell. Hipolit put down a dish with food to distract the dogs and told us to move on quickly. We started, not toward Karbicki's farm but in the opposite direction, so that Hipolit would not know where we were heading. The dogs left their meal and sped after us, howling at the top of their lungs. All the dogs in the village joined them. The November snow fell wet and soft and steady.

I crawled into the pit, where the people surrounded me with questions about the trip. My first and only word was *snow*. In our underground life, many sounds and gestures outgrew their meaning and became symbols; the word *snow* was one of them. Perhaps this was because of its association with Soviet offensives, or perhaps because snow attested a change of season, the passage of time. For us to whom a new sheep in the shed, an additional potato, or a new telephone pole on the highway was news, the first snowfall portended great, awesome changes.

The trip to Rataj ended a starvation that had lasted since the middle of last winter. Karbicki could now cook hot meals twice a day for us, and this relieved him from baking bread. Whenever the food supply was depleted, I went out to fetch new provisions. Though dangerous and painful, going out was a great event in the grisly monotony of our underground life. Aside from their practical aspect, these trips were an important boost to our morale. I brought back a little fresh air, a few snowflakes from the night skies – and it was not only I who enjoyed these snatches of liberty, for they were shared by the others in the pit.

When the moonless nights came around, I once again went to Rataj. Making the trip late, I learned, was more dangerous than in the early evening. The barking of the dogs late at night immediately signaled an illegal person roaming about, whereas in the early evening it might mean nothing more than a passing villager. So, the next time, I left the shelter at nightfall. The lights in Karbicki's house were on and I saw his wife silhouetted against the window, heard the children playing in the kitchen. Karbicki was not at home; evidently he had gone to the village, listening to "politics." I sneaked along the barn and diagonally across the fields and made my way towards Rataj's farm. I felt uneasy. Late at night, when all was dark and silent, I felt safer. Everything in that black, extinguished world the hopelessness, the loneliness, the regret – was familiar: they had become a part of us, and so they did not scare us. But now the lit windows, the voices behind the walls, the presence of people around me threw me off balance. I kept looking back, dogged by a feeling of somebody trailing me, of the lights in the windows poking fingers at me and asking where I had suddenly come from. I walked through the swampy fields, sinking to my ankles in mud and water, and when Rataj's two dogs opened up with their frantic hoarse barking, I stopped and almost ran back. I controlled myself, however, and entered the farmyard.

Leaning against the wall, I first listened for the sound of strangers inside, then knocked on the shutter. The same white, clean, warm rooms enveloped me. A sparkling fire roared in the stove. Hipolit's young wife sat at the spinning wheel, and next to her an adolescent who kept laughing, flashing her white teeth. They received me warmly, gave me a chair, and asked whether, having come from so far, I was tired. They of course had no notion that I came from the neighboring farm and that I had been looking at their place for the past twelve months. Hipolit's old mother began to pity me. She handed me a glass of hot milk and white rolls, and I had to eat despite my claim that I was not hungry. I listened to the crackling of the fire under the stove, and through the rainbow colors of the milk vapor I watched the smiling face of the girl, the blond hair of Hipolit's wife, the crucifix on the wall, the loaf of fresh bread on the carved table, the crib in the corner. I wanted to stay, to lose myself in this dry warmth and peace. But, outside, the dogs did not cease barking, and soon the bags I had brought were filled with flour and kasha. As I paid Hipolit for the food, he repeated his plea not to betray him. "We are not afraid of the Polish police, for they would kill only you. But the Germans..., the Germans...." I nodded that I understood. I would do my duty.

The familiar stretch of land. Muddy flat fields, huddling farms, the blinking lights of Wolki, and the pine grove where I always imagined our grave would be dug. I walked, strangely apathetic, bitter only at the thought of having to leave that warm house where there was a fire on the stove and the blond hair of the young woman. I walked, sinking into the mud. I stopped to look at the red roof in Koszelowka where Manya had worked the winter before. "Where is she?" I asked myself. Everybody told us she was in a shelter, but there was no sign of life from her.

Suddenly I saw human figures approaching. It was too late to hide, and an escape in this mud was impossible. When they came nearer, they shuffled sideways, trying to avoid me. As soon as the group was behind me, I swung around. The others, too, had swung around, as if we were all afraid of being shot in the back. I recognized them as the Jews from the pine grove. Kielman, once broad and husky, had become a shriveled old man, half his former self. Kielman's son, his scrofula spilled all over his face and neck, kept smiling at me with an idiotic expression. The other two, a young couple, did not speak.

"What is new?" begged Kielman. He seized the lapels of my jerkin, imploring me to tell him how much longer this hell was going to last.

"O, for sure, not much longer." I mumbled.

"That is what we had been telling each other for years."

I was getting ready to leave when I realized that, instead of five, there were only four of them. I asked for Shymeluk – the original "inhabitant" of the pine grove. I did not get an answer. When I asked again, Kielman, raising the collar of his coat and starting on his way, said, "Shymeluk is dead."

Next day we learned that Shymeluk had been shot in Wolki. It was not the Germans who killed him. Shymeluk had gone to Wolki for food one night and did not return to the shelter. At first the farmers denied he had even been in the village, but eventually we learned he had been killed by the "the boys." Shymeluk was in a farmer's house when the AK arrived, and they took him with them. Although there was no direct proof that they had killed him, the fact remained that Shymeluk never returned.

The farmers' reaction whenever we talked to them about the AK was strange and disturbing. Karbicki, Motl's acquaintances, friends of Lebel, and Wacek himself did not have the Germans in mind when they continually cautioned us against roaming at night. Whom did they caution us against? We knew some local members of the AK, and although these people insisted that the Polish underground was out to help us, they advised us to be careful and to avoid them. We did not believe our ears, and these friends of ours refused to elaborate. Eager to join the AK, we had come to these

people for contacts, but they advised us against it, offering conflicting reasons. We did not understand at all.

Wacek was the first openly to express the view that we were
being threatened by the Polish underground. It was an unbelievable
piece of news. Nevertheless, Wacek insisted they were after our
lives. Ignoring our reasoning, he advised that, with regard to our
safety, we look upon them as we looked upon the Germans.
Karbicki eventually began to say the same thing. Others concurred.

We were furious. Only the thrilling, exalting vision of armed
resistance to the Germans had sustained us in that period. What
else did we have if not that atavistic satisfaction that someone was
repaying with blood the monstrous injury inflicted upon this land.
How beautiful were those nights when, hearing scattered firing or
seeing an occasional conflagration, we knew it was the work of the
partisans, and we blessed their deeds and hoped to join them. Were
these people, too, bent on our destruction?

xxxiv

Low over the fields, snowy vortices milled and shifted,
wrapping the pine grove in white mist. Neither Koszelowka nor
Wolki was visible along the highway: only the telephone poles,
floating, like a caravan of gallows, above the snow. The wind
howled wolfishly around the corners of the shed, and large whirling
flakes drifted in through the torn roof. Pressed against the cracks
in the walls, we watched the passage of a second winter in our
entombment.

It was our fourteenth month in the pit. Occasionally police
raids broke the tedium, and we heard them walk around the shed,
rattling their guns. Once, spilled kerosene caused a fire in the

shelter, burning off my eyelashes and brows. Days and nights followed in endless replication: the same faded gray dawns, the seeping manure, Father's beaked nose, Yankel's screams, long evenings with the dim kerosene lamp – and another day. Then, at the beginning of January, something happened.

The flutter of hens leaving the loft awakened us, and Yankel, as usual, was the first to climb into the shed. We were about to follow him when he jumped back into the pit. We automatically called out to him to close the cover, an old rule in the shelter, but Yankel did not listen. When I tried to close the cover, he said it was not necessary. We asked him what he had seen that made him run back. Choking tears, Yankel whispered: "Polish partisans!"

We stared at him in disbelief. He must have had a vision. "On all neighboring farms and near our own shed, there are partisan troops," he babbled. "Polish uniforms, eagles on their caps...."

We were so stirred we shivered, and for a while we did not move. "Why do you sit here?" I finally called and sprang into the shed.

The first man I saw was a sentry wearing a four-cornered Polish army cap. With a sheepskin thrown over his shoulders he stood in the yard and scanned the highway through binoculars. Through the half frozen windows of Karbicki's house, I saw men washing and shaving. The kitchen was busy. Fat billows of smoke poured from the chimney. On Antoni's farm, groups of men were walking briskly to and fro. New partisans arrived in batches, submachine guns slung over their shoulders, grenades dangling from their belts. Later, when the ice thawed on Karbicki's windows, I saw rifles stacked against the wall and a machine gun in the corner. Mesmerized, I kept looking at these four-cornered hats and at the machine gun. Tears welled in my throat....

I looked about me. All eight of us stood glued to the walls, drinking in the scene. We rubbed our eyes to assure ourselves it was all real, for there was to the event much more than merely the stirring sight of partisans. On that day we had a right to live, for Koszelowka was governed by the AK. I kept murmuring to myself that I must go out, show myself, follow them. Only the walls of the shed separated me from them....

At that moment, those around me, the women first, began to leave the shed and lower themselves back into the pit. When I asked why they did that, they said they did not know, but they advised me, too, to come down into the pit. Why? They shook their heads. I thought with terror of what events had done to us. We were unable even to face freedom. Then, even while I argued with them, I, too, returned to the shelter.

At ten o'clock Karbicki brought us breakfast. He left the door of the shelter wide open and greeted us with his jerky, free laugh. "Polish troops, AK boys," he whispered. There was pride in his words about the presence of partisans on his farm, and a sense of victory that we had lived to see this moment. His narrow, white eyes gleamed, and one felt he would gladly have shown us to the partisans to prove his bravery and his defiance of the Germans. But before leaving, Karbicki cautioned us not to talk loudly, and he very carefully closed the cover of the shelter.

And so we stayed inside. Karbicki came again later with more details about "the boys." He said that the AK had brought carts full of arms and ammunition and that they occupied the entire stretch from Wolki to Walim. Karbicki marveled at their new weapons and told us that they had a mobile office and a radio transmitter with them, and that they behaved very correctly. They ate with the farmers and gave the children sweets. Among the partisans were many boys from the neighboring villages whom Karbicki knew personally.

At noontime, angry with myself, I once again went up into the shed. Nothing was to be seen outside; even the sentry was gone. Dry, fluffy snow continued to fall. Dinner time came and passed with no sight of the farmer – always a sign of trouble. Then, toward evening, Karbicki came running to us, groaning: "They caught some of your people in the pine grove...." He threw a load of manure on the cover, stamped it with his boots and quickly left the shed.

On the day the partisans arrived, Irka, the young woman from the pine grove, was in Rataj's house. She was a dressmaker and the farmers occasionally kept her for a day or two to sew clothes for them. She was at the sewing machine in the basement when the partisans arrived. After an intensive interrogation they found out she was one of a group of four Jews hiding in the woods. But Irka, sensing danger, refused to divulge where the others were. She was assured by the AK that no harm would be done to the Jews, that, indeed, they were out to help them; they even offered to go to the woods without weapons and showed her printed pamphlets in which the AK called for helping Jews. But Irka's distrust only intensified with their insistence, and she steadfastly refused to say where her husband and the two others were hidden.

Unable to persuade Irka of their good intentions, the AK resorted to violence, beating her with sticks. Now convinced they were out to kill them, Irka maintained stubborn silence. The "boys" then began to torture her with hot irons. Seeing this, Rataj's old mother broke down and shouted that the Jews were in the pine grove.

That same day, other AK troops were stationed in Dubicze. A group of them came to Wacek and asked him to inform the Jews he knew that the AK was ready to take the men into their ranks;

the women and children would be set up among farmers. Wacek retorted that he did not know any Jews. When he later heard of the incident on Rataj's farm, Wacek alerted the Jews in the Dubicze forest. Lebel immediately went over to one of his friends, an officer in the local AK to ask for intervention, but the man answered that he could do nothing.

"You can't save a woman from the hands of your own men?" Lebel cried. "Don't ask too many questions," came the threatening answer. Lebel rushed back to the forest. That night, no fires were lit and no one dared leave the shelters.

The Jews found in the pine grove that day were not harmed. A crowd of peasants had followed the AK as they marched off with Irka to the pine grove; and so, in public, not only did the AK refrain from harming the Jews, but a speech was even delivered encouraging them in their fight. The same night, however, the four Jews in the pine grove, not convinced by the speech, abandoned their dugout and, with the help of Motl and Wacek, escaped to the Dubicze forest.

They had barely left when a troop of partisans returned and, without even looking, tossed a bundle of hand grenades into the shelter, blasting it to bits. *

---

*The Armia Krajowa's policy of killing Jewish survivors started in late summer of 1943. This policy endured throughout the German occupation and continued with increased violence after the Jews had emerged into the open with the entry of the Red Army. It culminated with a full-fledged pogrom in the town of Kielce, where forty survivors were massacred and many more wounded. After my return to Losice, there was twice an attempt to kill me — in one case, the grenade tossed at me going off a fraction of a second too late. Eventually we had to abandon Losice when, in the neighboring town of Mordy, all its thirteen survivors were massacred in their sleep by a troop of AK men. The order by AK Commander-in-Chief General Bór-Komorowski to exterminate the Jewish survivors is photographically reproduced below. The story of the attempt on my life and of other killings of Jews in our area by the AK is told in A Choice of Masks, (Prentice-Hall, Englewood Cliffs, N.J., 1970).

Above: Karbicki and two of his children in front of the sty where the pit was dug. *Below:* In the distance, the pine grove that was the center of our landscape.

Nr 482

GEN. KOMOROWSKI DO N.W.: MELDUNEK PÓŁROCZNY
O SPRAWACH AK I POŁOŻENIU W KRAJU

Dnia 31 sierpnia 1943 r.   O.VI L. dz. 3214/tjn/43
Poczta Ławiny ¹   Dnia 24 kwietnia 1944 r.

MELDUNEK ORGANIZACYJNY Nr 220
za czas od 1. III. 43 do 31. VIII. 43

Naczelny Wódz
Przedstawiam meldunek organizacyjny Nr 220 za czas od
1. III. 43 do 31. VIII. 43 w ślad za meld. org. nr 190 ¹.

4. Bandytyzm. Silnie uzbrojone bandy grasują nieustannie w miastach i po wsiach napadając na dwory, banki, firmy handlowe i przemysłowe, domy i mieszkania, większe gospodarstwa chłopskie. Napady rabunkowe połączone często z morderstwami, dokonywane przez ukrywające się w lesie oddziały partyzantów sowieckich wzgl. przez zwykłe bandy rabunkowe.

Te ostatnie rekrutują się z przeróżnego elementu zbrodniczego i wywrotowego. W napadach biorą udział mężczyźni i kobiety, szczególnie Żydówki. Niecna ta akcja zdemoralizowanych jednostek przyczynia się w znacznym stopniu do zupełnego wyniszczenia wielu obywateli, znękanych już i tak czteroletnim zmaganiem się z wrogiem.

Okupant nie przeciwdziała zasadniczo temu stanowi rzeczy, wzywane niekiedy w poważniejszych wypadkach na pomoc niemieckie organa bezpieczeństwa odmawiają pomocy, unikając z reguły interwencji i nie walcząc z bandytami, często wręcz przeciwnie, większa akcja bandytyzmu wywołuje represje w stosunku do niewinnej ludności polskiej. Aby dać pewną pomoc i osłonę bezbronnej ludności wydałem, w porozumieniu z Gł. Del. Rządu, komendantom ·Okręgów i Obwodów instrukcję. dotyczącą bezpieczeństwa terenowego, w której nakazałem kmdtom Okr. i Obw., w razie potrzeby, występować zbrojnie przeciwko elementom plądrującym, bądź wywrotowo-bandyckim. Położyłem nacisk na konieczność likwidacji przywódców band i na usiłowanie zniszczenia całych band. Poleciłem komendantom terenowym zapewnienie sobie współudziału miejscowej ludności i agend Del. Rządu w zorganizowaniu samoobrony i służby alarmowej.

The order from General Bór-Komorowski directing his troops to kill the Jews hiding in the countryside, whom he labels "bandits." From *Armja Krajowa w Dokumentach, 1939-45*, Volume III (London, 1976), p. 92.

Left: Photograph I had taken in August, 1944, a few days after liberation, in anticipation of someday being able to publish my story.

Below: Treblinka after the war. The stone on the left marks the death of Losice's 7,000 Jews.

On my way to the Puradt trial: the opening shot of a 1984 documentary based on the present account.

Upper right: The planner: Ludwig Fischer, Governor of the Warsaw region. Tried in Poland, he was hanged in 1947. *Above:* The executioner: Puradt, in uniform during his Losice days, and during his trial, seated at the left of his lawyer. Tried in West Germany — in 1980 — he was acquitted.

XXXV

After the spring day Shmyl had brought the news of Herschek's death, I could not endure the shelter for any length of time;
the trips to Miedzyrzec and Losice were all a sort of escape. When
Miedzyrzec was gone I began to commute between the farm and
the forest. Depending on the season and on what kind of dangers
we faced — for there were always new ones — either one or the
other place was more unendurable. That winter, surely, life in the
forest was at its grimmest. I had gone there again soon after the
incident with the AK and found the two shelters almost on the
point of dissolution.

Although the winter had turned wet and rainy, there was still
snow in the forest. Paradoxically, this simplified our routine. We
now "lived" even during the daylight. Because of our movements,
the snow around the shelter was trampled, and much of it had
thawed. There was no point in staying underground during the day,
for, had anyone come, it would have been obvious that "illegals"
lived nearby. So we moved about freely, taking care only not to
venture deep into and outside the forest. Instead of bringing
satisfaction, this tramping on the surface made us jumpy, for it
increased our danger enormously. Aside from meeting peasants, we
were haunted by the fear of an encounter with the AK, which was
particularly likely in the forest. As we had anticipated, the winter
brought unrelieved starvation. We ate moldy bread, rotten potatoes
and raw peas, and since going to the pond would have left tracks
in the forest, we melted snow for drinking water. Another problem
was the discovery that David's wife was pregnant; none of us was
capable of imagining how this disaster would be resolved. So we sat
under the open sky, watching the rain or the sunshine on top of
the snowcaps and listening to the woodpeckers signal each other
across the primeval forest, our ears achingly alert for the sounds of

the steps that were one day bound to stumble across one or the other of the exposed shelters.

Unable to bear the tension, I went back to the farm to find these same problems in a different edition. Our shelter, too, was deteriorating, showing the traces of wear and time. The walls were receding, and we feared the beams would give way. Under the foundation a hole appeared through which, like a dead dull eye, peeped a beam of daylight. Water leaked in as the rains fell in steady, unrelenting streams.

That winter I started to read the Psalms, instigated by Father's promises that I would become religious under their influence. I envied all believers and I thought it would be a sort of salvation if I joined them. I could then transfer all responsibility to the Almighty and our ordeal would become just compounded interest for a future payoff. But the Psalms' anthropomorphic God, instead of awakening religious feeling, left a distaste in me. No, He did not descend into the pit.

Our money was again being depleted, and we did not want to make the same mistake as last time under the illusion that the war would shortly end. We still had money for several months but we no longer thought about the war in terms of months. And we knew there would be no new source of funds. We decided again to lower Karbicki's pay. We had already once reduced his rent to half what he had been paid, and we now decided to cut it again. That way, we figured, we would have enough left to last through the coming summer. We told Karbicki about it openly, for we no longer dealt with him in the old way. The farmer's attitude toward us had changed. He sincerely wanted to pull us through the war. When we told him about our situation, he listened quietly and walked out of the shed without comment.

Just at that time the Soviet southern offensive started in the Ukraine. The attack soon reached its full momentum and the Soviet armies surged forward. Later, the offensive spread to the middle sector, and after capturing Sarny, the first Polish town, the Soviets neared Kowel, only one hundred and twenty kilometers from us. The war ceased to be an abstraction, something that existed only on the map. We could expect "it" in our territory any time now; it had come to our front door. Yet, when the date for extending our stay came around, Karbicki refused our terms.

We prepared to leave the shelter. A mild evening lingered over the wet country, an evening that already carried the promise of spring. A warm breeze sifted in from the west and sheaves of light from a clearing sky revealed the first splashes of blue. Both Karbicki and we felt rather sad. Even this pit of agony stirred parting regrets. Unbelievably, fifteen months of living here had created ties difficult to sever. We did not tell Karbicki we were moving into the forest but claimed that now, with the Russians entering Rumania and Kowel, farmers simply begged us to come to them. Karbicki groaned, "But I can't keep you for nothing."

The plan was to move three of the men that night, to be followed the next night by Yankel and the women. When we were leaving, Karbicki turned his head away. I thought he would yield and tell us to stay, but he kept the door open until we had filed into the farmyard.

For Father, it was the first time out in more than fifteen months. At the sight of the starlit sky and the moist spring air, he broke down and tears rolled down his sunken cheeks. We had to support him, for he could hardly walk. "You are young," he thought out loud as he dragged himself forward. "You are fighting for a whole life. What do I fight for? A few more years?" But we did not pay him much attention; we were too preoccupied scanning the darkness and keeping our ears alert for any suspicious sounds or shadows. For the first time, we avoided the trail to Koszelowka and instead cut across the marshy meadows. Our pants were soaked and we were losing our way when, finally, we saw the knoll near Dubicze and the grove at the top of it. We decided someone would take Father and Berko to the forest while I remained with Motl to return the next night for those still in Karbicki's shelter.

It was no simple matter, this transfer of ours. Ignoring the initial difficulties of digging holes and building the shelters in the forest, I did not quite see how we could survive. Of our eight people, only Berko and I and perhaps Yankel had the physical strength to carry out the necessary chores. None of the others could have managed to walk ten or twenty miles every few nights lugging the heavy loads. In other shelters, most of the individuals were young and rugged, but in our group we had children and aged people. We had the additional danger of the AK, and with the war approaching our territories, there loomed the unspoken but inevitable threat of discovery by German armies preparing to defend these forests. Bitter thoughts and regret sucked at our hearts as we realized we had struggled and fought and suffered only to perish as our ordeal neared an end.

In Wacek's home Motl and I took a brief nap on the straw in the corner of the alcove. When the roosters crowed their second round, we rose and, under cover of a dense morning mist, moved back to our shelter. The previous day, Karbicki had gone on a trip to Biala and brought back newspapers. We read them with glee. They were full of Soviet victories. Bessarabia and Bukovina were captured, Tarnopol and Kowel were surrounded, and the Soviets were nearing Zloczow. It was not unlikely that we would soon see signs of the approaching front: troops on the highway, planes in the sky, the roar of artillery.

They came that afternoon. A delicate vibration disturbed the air, drifting from afar like a deep murmur, like the breath of an approaching storm. We stayed upstairs, looking at each other, listening to the heaving, afraid to speak lest we stop it all with one word. Karbicki was out in the yard, pricking his ears. His mouth was wide open and his eyes shifted from the eastern horizon to the shed and back. Finally he could not hold out any longer and came in. The women sat on the straw in the corner, packing their bundles. The farmer looked at them and tried to say something, but finding no words, he spat loudly and left, slamming the door.

A few hours later, a convoy of military vehicles appeared on the highway. All the farmers stopped their work to watch the Germans. On that very day, it so happened, the first group of Soviet partisans crossed the Bug to launch diversionary operations, and the troops on the highway were moving up against them. At the time we did not know any of this, and the sight of German columns moving westward, combined with the distant heave of artillery, added up to a heavenly story. Karbicki, who had been standing in the yard watching the German columns, suddenly rushed into the shed, flailing his arms.

"So, I kept you through the worst times, and now you are going to somebody else? Now? Oh no! Bring them back. Back," he shouted, as if afraid that it might be too late and that someone else might already have deprived him of the privilege of keeping us. We shook his hand and he pressed us to his huge chest, happy with the artillery roar outside, and with us. He agreed to take as much money as we could afford, voicing his belief that, after the war, the American Jews would repay him for it.

We now had to bring Father and Berko back from the forest, but the moon was out, forcing us to wait until it got darker. So, on our way, we stopped at Wacek's house. There we found the shoemaker Abram and the tailor Pinia, and later Enoch and Shmyl came from their shelter. We sat, a handful of Jews, nestling our bones on a pile of straw in the corner of the alcove. This simple hut was an oasis to which we came from the scattered haunts where, crippled and exhausted and shamed, we carried on our lonely struggle. These were unforgettable moments spent under the roof of Wacek's hut. Unforgettable the oak table and the carved simple bench where we put down our sacks and our sticks. Unforgettable also the milk jug and the cup, always waiting for the thirsty ghosts who converged from all roads. Who among us did not know the bread kept for us in the corner of the alcove, and the dry straw on which we collapsed at the end of our endurance? The only man who would tell what we went through, we knew, was Wacek. Had we asked for a stone on our grave, we knew that he would place it. No, he did not do any of these things, for soon after liberation, the AK murdered Wacek for saving our lives.

We lay on the straw, talking in whispers and falling into sleep. I watched the greenish night outside the window and the moon over the horizon. Nearby rose the dark wall of the forest; hearing the dogs baying on the Walim and Dubicze farms, we knew that the Jews from the woods were either going for food or water or coming to the village. Behind the forests, flares hung in the sky. I recalled the night I went to Miedzyrzec: the firing over the highway, the trembling flares, the sky lit up over the burning ghetto, and the incessant lament.

When the moon set and got dark, Shmyl went to the forest for Father and Berko. Motl and I were to take two loads of bread from Wacek and carry them to our shelter. When Shmyl left, Motl moved closer to me and stared into the misty night. I thought he was seeing his wife and five children floating there under the milky sky in cloudlets of fine ashes. But Motl's thoughts were evidently of a more practical nature. Before leaving he said that, since we were short of money, we should stop at the house with the red roof and take back the few things Manya had left there.

"I will not take them," I said. "Let Manya do it herself."

"We should take the things back," he repeated.

"We will wait for her."

Motl, who was looking down all this time, raised his eyes and looked at me. I wanted to stop what he was going to say, but I knew it was pointless. Lowering his eyes again and hiding his head, Motl said, "Manya has been taken to Auschwitz."

xxxvi

Spring was borne in on the bubbling of water and the flapping of wings, on winds and streams and clouds and seeds. Spring fluttered in the white bedding aired on the fences, the clay pots dried in the farmyards, the clank of plows, and the calls of peasant women. Karbicki went into the barn, looked around at the empty bays, shook the plows, lifted the flails, stamped his feet on the earthen floor, and, shielding his eyes with his powerful hand, looked long and carefully into the bright sun.

He was soon out in the field, plowing. Flocks of birds trailed behind him, picking at the uncovered earthworms. He walked the furrows, large and strong, confident of this earth and sure of its harvests, regardless of regimes, invasions, partisans. Not far from him plowed Wacek's eighty-year-old father, and a short distance away Rataj led his horses. Everywhere, peasants worked and tilled their soil.

Then the manure was taken out of the stalls, the potato dugouts were opened, the houses were aired and the barns cleaned. Scarecrows rose over the seeded gardens, long lines of cattle moved into the pastures, young chicks filled the yards, and the cherry blossoms erupted again in white and pink umbrellas. Nights, Karbicki now slept with his wife in the barn. When Easter came, the Karbicki girls painted eggs and decorated the doorsill with flower garlands.

And we stayed in our sty. The Soviet offensive stopped a few days after it had reached its peak, and the fronts froze again. The Russians were now only about a hundred kilometers away and there was no point in reading the papers; if anything important were to happen, we would be the first to hear and see it. But the highway was empty, the skies remained clear, and Wolki slept in the shade of its trees. The only thing new was a muffled grumbling from the southeast, when the shed would start to tremble and the cattle would prick their ears and cluster fearfully in the corners. The farmers sitting in front of the houses would get up and turn their heads, and the carts on the roads would stop, afraid to move on. After a while, the distant thunder would cease and calm would return to the sunny, somnolent landscape.

In this uneasy calm we heard more and more of the AK. They were in all villages and woods, and almost all Polish youth joined. Fighting them required the deployment of regular army troops and heavy weapons, so the Germans avoided them, thereby allowing the partisans to become the real masters of the Polish hinterland. The AK were so sure of themselves their armed troops moved about the country in bright daylight. The Poles could almost consider themselves free men. Had it not been for their murderous deeds, we, too, could have lived on the surface. But some members of the underground whom we knew personally now openly admitted to killing Jews, and they told us that the organization had instructions to liquidate us. When Karbicki talked of fear in those days, he was no longer talking about the Germans or the police. "For God's sake, watch out for them," he said, hesitating to utter their name. The peasant was ashamed for his compatriots, and he covered his eyes when he cautioned us against them.

Although it was now very dangerous to move about, the spring was too rapturous for me to remain in the pit, and I took off with Shmyl for the forest. We walked the Koszelowka trail past the village and its windmill, along the Dubicze marshes, and then up the wooded hill — the vast stretch of land over which we had dragged our wretched lives now for a year and a half. We needed food for the forest, and along the way we opened a dugout with potatoes. We worked as quietly as possible, watching out for the AK; we knew that they were in the neighborhood. Occasionally shots were fired and, flattened against the warm earth, we scanned the darkness for approaching shadows. We heard the stamp of feet and saw the silhouettes of commando parties moving down the country road. Then a machine gun spattered on the other side of the grove. We crawled up the trees and hid among the branches. We heard them walk across the woods toward the farms, and we knew we had better clear out. We got going across the plowed fields, bent low under the heavy potato sacks and alert to any sound or rustle.

When we reached Lebel's shelter, we found only Pesha's mother. We asked where the others were, and she said they were in David's place; his wife was delivering her baby. After an hour's wandering in the dark, we finally saw the light of David's dugout.

Everyone was sitting outside the pit, glum and silent. I wanted to go down into the shelter, but Lebel stopped me. I asked how the new mother was.

"Oh, she is all right," he said.

"What did you do with the baby?" I asked.

Just then I heard some commotion in the bushes: a man was weeping. I looked at Lebel.

"What else could be done?" he said.

"Who is doing it?"

"What do you mean, 'Who?' " Lebel was irritated. "Would you do it?"

I sat down alongside the others. David came over to us several times, begging that someone else take over. But nobody moved. After a while we heard him run into the shelter and slam the cover. Somebody dug a hole and buried the infant. Later we tried to go down into the shelter, but David shrieked in a wild voice to stay out. We backed away, lay down outside, and then forgot everything: the Germans, the AK, the war.

After we learned that the AK was murdering us, we had to change our way of life in the forest. We dug two new pits, one for Lebel in a wooded area where there were no berries and mushrooms and thus, we hoped, no pickers – and the other for David near the old grave of Wolodia's five companions. That grave had collapsed and the bodies of the Russians had come to the surface again. Animals had torn the bodies apart; two skulls lay at the edge of the collapsed hole. In one of the skulls stuck two golden teeth by which Wolodia recognized Grisha, his closest friend. The cave-in had torn the roots from under one of the trees which then bent over the hole as if in mourning. We dug David's shelter in this particular spot, hoping that most farmers in their superstition would avoid wandering around the grave of killed people. The young couple from the pine grove joined David while Kielman and his son dug a third pit for themselves.

In the forest there were two new men from Biala. At the beginning of spring we learned of a handful of Jewish workers, still miraculously alive, slaving for the Gestapo in Biala; we brought two of them to the forest. We no longer stayed in the shelters all day. As soon as morning came, we dispersed into the forest. In twos and threes we hid in the thickest bushes we could find, and we stayed there, afraid to stick our noses out. Gone were the nights when we sat near the fires and sang to the Polish forests of our agony and hope. The nights did not belong to us any more, and they were becoming as dangerous as the days. We still sang, but we would suddenly stop and listen in fright lest they be standing above, waiting for us with tommy guns in their hands. We ran out, looked into the dark, listened to the cry of the birds, and sat down, asking ourselves what irony had given birth to this new terror. And we went to sleep with a feeling that this new death, death with the White Eagle on its cap, was standing among the trees mocking us: our eating, our sleeping, our ridiculous hope, and our silly stubborn will to live when the whole world had decided against it. We fell asleep near the bones of the Russians – dry and luminous calcium – and Grisha's gold tooth, still stuck in his perforated skull. We almost slept with them, all huddling together under the tree bent in mourning over the collapsed grave.

One evening when I came back with water from the pond, I found everyone outside the dugouts, gathered around two peasants who had stumbled on our group. We asked the Poles what they were doing in the woods, and they said that they had come looking for some trees to chop down. It seemed true, although we could not be sure of it. We told them who we were, the dangers that

threatened us, and that their own compatriots were after our lives.
We knew this meant nothing to the indifferent peasants, so Leyzor,
pulling out his pistol, told them that the moment they dropped so
much as a word about us to anybody, we would come and kill them
and burn down their farms. We asked them to hand over their
documents and wrote down their names and addresses. Then we let
them go.

Two days later I heard a suspicious rustle in my sleep. Lying
still, I opened my eyes and saw a shadow sneak through the trees.
I gave an alerting whistle and Wolodia started out into the thicket.
In a few minutes he came back, pushing a shabbily dressed
individual. The stranger smiled and tried to back away, but, feeling
Wolodia behind him, he stepped forward. "Good morning," he said
with overzealous goodwill.

Shmyl whispered to me that we were in trouble. The man,
Pytka, was a local thug. We knew from Wacek that this Pytka had
been telling the farmers that there were Jews in the forest. Shmyl
asked what he was doing. Pytka explained that he had come to
gather mushrooms. When we asked to see the basket for the
mushrooms, he stammered that he had left it in another part of the
forest. "Show us," we demanded, but he hedged, unsure he could
find it.

"Don't be afraid." Pytka shifted conversation to the level of
familiarity. "I wouldn't do anything to wrong you. I have to hide
too, like you."

"What did you come here for?" Shmyl insisted. "Don't be
afraid." "We know that, but why did you come to this wilderness?"

Having no answer, Pytka began to tell stories about how he
cheated the Germans, how he helped the "boys," how much he
sympathized with us. Were we not in the same boat? Yet we were

convinced that he had come with a definite purpose and that it spelled danger.

Before we could decide what to do with him, Pytka jumped to his feet and backed away. We could have shot him, but we were afraid to alert the AK, and besides, we were not completely sure of his purpose. Pytka stalked off as we stood and watched, torn by a grim premonition that he was carrying our lives away with him.

One other seemingly innocent event occurred. Due to the danger of the AK, we usually stayed in the thickets during the day, weaving baskets and snoozing. With evening, Kielman left to collect firewood for his shelter. I rose as well, to fetch water from the pond, but before I left, Kielman came back and told us someone had felled two young trees over his shelter. At first it seemed insignificant, but the more we thought about it, the more disturbing it became. Why had we not heard the trees being cut? And why chop down two healthy saplings when good dry wood lay around? And if they were already cut, why would the farmers leave them?

The mood in the forest turned grim. The air was laden with hope but also with foreboding. Leyzor reminded me that all he wanted was to live, just to live. Yes, that was all Herschek had wanted, all Motl and Hinda had wanted, all the millions had wanted. He pointed his stubby finger toward the eastern sky, and I, raising my head, heard the grumbling of the front.

"Now listen there," I said.

From the forest trails came the thumping of feet and the clatter of horses' hooves. Far along the forest we heard the creak of cart wheels and singing:

> Oto dzis dzien krwi i chwaly
> Trabo Polska wrogom grzmij...,

This is the day of blood and glory
Polish trumpet blast your enemies...,

At the end of the week, Wacek came to us with a warning
that the AK was about to bivouac on the Dubicze side of the forest;
he cautioned us to be on guard. All those hidden in the villages
stopped coming to the forest. Eventually, I, too, decided to return
to the farm. On the last night, while countless stars and glowworms
flamed through the trees, I said good-by to the people in the forest:
to Wolodia with his pale smile, to Kielman's scrofulous son, to the
young boy from Biala, and to Leyzor, big and slow as an ox. I promised to bring kerosene and salt the next time I came. But when
Leyzor said, "O, you will not come here any more," I did not
contradict him. As I walked down the thicket, I saw them huddled
against the faint light of the dugout until the darkness closed on
them, leaving me alone with the hushed threat of the forest. By-
passing all trails, I made my way through its densest sections. Just
as I reached the wood's edge, I heard the stamping of feet and the
snorting of horses from the main road. The AK was riding into the
forest.

xxxvii

On June 22, some two weeks after the allied invasion of
France, the Russians opened a powerful new offensive in the East.

One quiet afternoon, a long line of carts appeared on the
highway. Karbicki, who had been in Biala on the previous day, told
us that there was quite a commotion in the city, that people were
closing their businesses and leaving town, and that there were many
Ukrainian refugees. When we saw the carts on the highway, we
thought they were Ukrainians escaping from the advancing Soviet

armies. We saw Karbicki stroll into the yard. After a moment's hesitation, he dashed into the shed, his face flushed with triumph.

"The Germans, the Schwabs.... They are running."

In our hearts a bitter, hateful happiness exploded, releasing feelings so deep and vast that tears welled in our eyes. These were Germans, and they were retreating! There, on this dusty highway on which our eyes had lingered for twenty months, the defeated German army now stumbled. The carts rattled on, the horses barely moving while their rider's heads slumped as if they were all asleep. A thick cloud of dust marked the route of their retreat. On the farms and in the villages the peasants were out watching in awe. While the older people were quiet, Karbicki's children danced about the house, chirping: *Szwabi uciekaja* – the Schwabs are turning tail.

The Wehrmacht continued to fall back all of the next day. We woke at early dawn and stood glued to the walls of the shed. Our bodies did not then register anything: neither flies, nor manure, nor stench. For there, near Wolki, our dreams walked in glory over a goldtrodden, sundrenched boulevard. The front thundered that day without interruption, joined later by a near and vicious crack of flak. We heard the drone of aircraft engines and, in their wake, a rolling wave of explosions. Soviet planes were bombing Biala.

The roar and crack of the front grew with the days. The air was hot, tense, restless. Along with other farmers, Karbicki moved into the field to collect the harvest. While the scythers toiled and sweated, the planes roared above and fires on the horizon blew their hot breath and we all knew liberation was coming with quick, crashing steps.

The last troops of the AK left our territory to concentrate in specially assigned locations where they were to hold out until the front passed through. Around July 10, the troops stationed in Dubicze received the order to move towards Warsaw.

It was some three weeks before liberation. Those in the forest were clinging desperately to life, watching, as we did, the vision of coming freedom unfold. One late afternoon, after hiding in the thickets all day, they were returning to the dugouts to get ready for the night. There were at the time three shelters in the forest. Lebel with his group headed for his dugout, and David with his wife to theirs. Leyzor, who was living with David at that time, went that evening to Kielman's place to help him collect firewood. The softness of the dusk was blanketing the declining day. For the people in the forest, it was time for their one cooked meal, a reprieve from the daylight tension. Suddenly a volley from an automatic gun shattered the evening. Everyone ducked into the nearest bushes. Nothing more was heard, and as night fell, an overwhelming, deafening silence settled over the forest.

Leyzor, who, after helping Kielman, was supposed to return to his shelter, did not return. Kielman, who was to visit Lebel that night, did not appear. As the hours went by and they did not show up, the men from the remaining two shelters got together and stealthily moved toward Kielman's place, some half a mile away. As they approached, no light showed from the dugout, no voice was heard. Nearby they found two blood-soaked hats. Sprawled on the bottom of the uncovered pit they saw Leyzor, Kielman, and Kielman's son. They had been shot to death and thrown into the hole, where they lay face up, looking through the open cover into the July sky lit with the glow from flares and fires, a sky illuminated with all the colors of approaching liberation.

They were gone. Five years of wrestling with ghettos, burning ditches, and gas chambers had terminated in a flash. They had survived the monstrous Germans, only to be killed by their neighbors who kept printing pamphlets of how they helped the Jews. Crawling through an interminable landscape of blood and darkness, they had just managed to glimpse the flame of reprieve and the "boys" blinded them forever. There lay Leyzor, a man who twice escaped the ovens of Treblinka, who on my last visit to the forest, had formulated his great demand on society: I just want to live. That was too much to want, and so they took it away from him – they, victims of the same heinous invader.

After the killing of these three men, panic took hold of the rest; everyone tried to save himself in any way he could. Wolodia moved to Walim, to the same farmer who had saved him before. Lebel found a place in the village and took Pesha and her mother along. The shoemaker Abram and the two boys from Biala also found a place on a farm. Those remaining split into pairs, and dug themselves vertical holes just large enough to accommodate two people in standing positions. They collected food and water to last for a few weeks, thus avoiding all necessity for moving about. No more fires were lit in the forest, and there was no more cooking. At night the people opened the covers to admit a little fresh air and listen to the roar of the approaching front. Their senses filled, they again closed the covers and returned to their hibernation.

One week later, the AK murdered three more of our men. The shoemaker and the two boys who had escaped the Biala Gestapo were killed on the farm where they had moved after Leyzor's death. The farmer's daughter had told her boy friend they were hiding Jews. Like most young men, the boy belonged to the AK. On a night frenzied by bursting flares and roaring horizons, they came to the farm, and while the three Jews lined up against a barn watched the flaming sky, the AK executed them.

Murderers of shadows, men who threw grenades into graves
and killed cadavers, like others before and alongside them they
even knew a God to pray and sing to. It was a powerful song they
sang as they walked away from the cooling corpses of the Jews:

> In smoke of fires, in mists of my brother's blood,
> To you, O Lord, I raise my voice:
> We are innocent!
> Punish the hand but not the blind sword....

But, like the others before and alongside them, they were the hand
and they the sword.

xxxviii

Motl paid one last visit to our shelter to warn us that the AK
knew more Jews were hidden in the two villages and that they were
tracking us down. Some of the AK troops, having failed to retreat
westward, made it their task to liquidate us. Motl added that his
group no longer stayed in the shelter at night but lay hidden in the
fields. He advised us to do the same.

"What are you talking about!" I laughed at his desperation.
"Troops will flood the country any day."

"I know," he said.

We heeded Motl's warning but could do little more than keep
watch each night and alert those in the pit if the partisans came
to get us. Ridiculous as it seemed, we felt that no perverts could
take our lives after we had lasted so long, that, even if they came,
we would run toward this burning sky and no bullet would be
powerful enough to kill us.

On one of those nights, Father and I were on watch, scanning
the country for shadows. In front of us unfolded the spectacle of
the approaching front. Thunder rolled in a rising growl, subsided,
rose again. Artillery cracked and detonations ripped the night,
followed by gigantic splashes of fire. Woods, farms, villages – all

sank into the earth as if afraid for their existence. A sea of blinding
fire rolled over the night; the flood spread far and wide until it
reached our farmyard and poured inside the dark sty. The Germans
were destroying industrial and military objectives, and all the
surrounding cities were burning. There was not enough strength in
us to absorb what we saw. I sat down on the manure pile and
listened to the roar of the distant battle. My head sank, and I fell
asleep.

When I awoke, Father still stood staring through the slots of
the wall. He was weeping.

"Go to sleep," I told him. "Day is near."

"No, no," he mumbled, "let me look." The bombing
continued. From the highway came the incessant clang of retreating
troops.

At noon of July 26, a violent firing broke out to the east: the
earth shuddered as if its intestines were being torn out. The tanks
and vehicles on the highway stopped. The battle seemed to be near
the Bug. Farmers ran out of their houses and began to prepare for
the advancing front. They pulled farm machinery from the buildings
into the open fields; they drove the cattle into the woods and the
pigs into the bushes. Karbicki dragged out all his meager possessions
and packed them into two large chests. In the afternoon, as the
firing increased, he dug a hole in the wheat field and buried all his
belongings.

A few hours later, a column of staff cars branched off the
highway into Wolki. Two cars roared in our direction: one stopped
at Rataj's farm; the other, with eight soldiers in helmets who
cradled submachine guns on their knees, continued toward our
farm. We scrambled into the pit. We heard the screech of brakes
and the gibberish of the soldiers outside the shed. Then the car
rolled on to Antoni's farm. Soon the farmer's wife ran into the
shed, groaning, "O Jesus, what will happen now?" German troops
were to arrive tomorrow, she told us. Crying, she ran back out into

the yard where, near the barn, Karbicki sat with a lowered head and mumbled to himself in despair.

The farmer came to us late at night in the middle of our debate over what to do. We had to reach a decision before daybreak. When I proposed moving to the pine grove, the farmer shook his head, "No, no.... You will perish there. Let's stick it out together. Stay here. I will think of something." He could do very little, but he was now ready to do more than we asked of him. Patting Berko's head, he insisted that we stay. "You will see. You will survive here."

The perils of our staying in the shelter with German troops bivouacking on the farm were too frightful to contemplate. The soldiers were likely to be everywhere. We would not be able to go upstairs even to urinate. The farmer would be unable to bring us food or water. The slightest noise would alert the soldiers' attention. More literally than ever, we would be buried alive. It seemed hopeless. But, as was the case from the very beginning of our ordeal, the hopeless was what we had to face and overcome. And so we reconstructed the shelter that night in an attempt to remain in it, despite the presence of troops on the farm. We dismantled the bunk and gave the farmer all our bedding and most of our clothes. Karbicki helped, and by midnight the shelter was completely bare. We covered the bottom of the evacuated pit with straw and took in as much bread and other food as the farmer had. We also took in several pails of water. Exhausted, we lay down and watched the eastern glow dim and redden on the rim of the dugout. Soon an early summer dawn broke through the flames and then we heard the roar of troops riding toward our farm.

We stayed underground all morning, but by noon my curiosity got the better of me and I crawled out. It was an impeccable summer day and the brilliant sunshine made me close my eyes. When I opened them and looked toward the pine grove, I saw a battery of flak on the hill. Near them the Germans had dug trenches and posted machine guns. On the trail leading from Rataj's farm, soldiers were stringing field communications. But no one was in our yard. The chickens clucked sleepily in the shade, and geese waddled around the barn. The farmers all sat on the thresholds of their houses and did not go to work. They waited. We, too, waited.

That night we all slept peacefully. With the Wehrmacht around we did not have to keep watch against the AK; ghoulishly, it was the Germans who probably saved us from the Polish patriots. Having just awakened, I lay watching the sun slide over the straw toward the pit when I heard oncoming airplanes. The drone grew rapidly and rolled over the shed with a deafening thunder of low-flying engines. In a flash I was upstairs. At the very moment I pressed against the wall to look out, I heard the whine of falling bombs and a string of explosions cracking over Wolki. Flying at treetop level, the planes vanished on the other side of the village.

The troops disregarded the raid and kept pouring over the highway. The first planes were barely gone when we heard again the whining pull of engines. On the hill under the pine grove the barrels of the guns revolved nervously in a wide arc. We could not see the planes, for they were above our heads. But then their drone dispersed and they dove, one after the other, glistening like lenses in the sun. Falling and rising over the forest, they dropped bombs in oblique strings while the muzzles of the machine guns mounted in their wings boiled with puddles of fire. Walim and all the villages along the Bug were bombed and long streamers of fires and belching smoke shot out against the sky. The planes coming back from their low passes roared over Koszelowka and over our farm, shaking the buildings, pulling the air, singing in the July sunshine.

After the raid the country was full of galloping troops. Infantry, poised eastward, lurked in the ditches, and staff cars rode over the plowed fields, coughing and backfiring and stopping here and there. When two cars drove into the farm, we all jumped into the shelter.

We did not stay there long, for the planes were soon back. This time they picked as their target the segment of highway passing through Wolki, directly in front of us. We were barely out of the pit when we heard them dive over our heads. On the highway the vehicles stood abandoned with doors left open, the soldiers running into the fields in every possible direction. With the very first stick of bombs that hit the ground, billows of smoke shot up over Wolki, followed by flames. We were close enough to the burning houses to feel the hot breeze pulsating against our faces. Smoke drifted into the shed, and the flocks of cinders that sailed in our direction settled over roofs and haystacks. At any minute, we expected to become a part of the conflagration, but we could do nothing and had to stay inside.

Before the next air-raid started, we managed to get Karbicki into the shed and begged him to do something, but he grinned his crooked smile and pointed happily to the destruction on the highway. He could rejoice, we told him, but we were going to burn to death in the shed. We asked him to dig a slit trench for us in the wheat field across the shed: if the farm caught fire, we could perhaps dash into it unseen by anyone. The farmer said there was no need for all these preparations – the Russians would soon be here. I told him he was crazy, but he only grinned again: he, the strategist, was assuring us that it would soon be over.

"We will go away," I threatened.

"All right," he answered, and walked out to begin digging a hole large enough for eight people to stand in. Other farmers, too, were digging trenches, so he did not arouse suspicion. His work was repeatedly interrupted by bombing, yet he completed the job in about three hours. In case of fire, we hoped to be able to sneak into the trench during the chaos of the raid and stay there till dark.

The heaviest air raid came that evening. Planes appeared so suddenly we did not even have time to crawl out of the pit. The attack was also a surprise for the troops who were still moving when the first bombs hit. Almost touching the tops of the vehicles, the planes flew low, tipping forward like scorpions with uplifted tails. One after the other, like matches lit in succession, the vehicles caught fire. Soon the planes were lost in smoke and only their flaming muzzles flickered in the haze. All around us the villages were on fire.

Whatever all this meant to the various human beings involved – to the Russian pilots likely to be shot out of the sky, to the farmers whose houses were going up in smoke, to the AK to whom the liberators had become a new enemy, to the Germans who, in their death throes, did not even have the right to groan – to us, this landscape torn asunder by fire and destruction was the peak of triumph. Never afterwards, not even at the actual moment of liberation, was the brief moment of elation so sharp and poignant; it was the only moment when I could tell myself it was worthwhile to have lived to see this moment of German defeat.

The raids ended and calm descended over the countryside. The clatter of retreating troops on the highway resumed, strangely muffled, as if even to retreat, to give up, was too much of an effort. Night fell, a night lit by the glare of near and distant fires. Wolki was still burning. So was Kornica. Long lines of refugee peasants with sacks on their backs were leaving the burning villages, driving the cattle with them. Others were busy throwing furniture and clothing out of the buildings that had caught fire during the evening raid.

Exhausted, we sighed our relief when night came. Not having eaten all day, we consumed with a hearty appetite the bread and milk Karbicki had brought us. Refugees milled in the yard; mothers nursed their children; cows slouched near the barn. Some women wept, relating how their homes had burned down, and Karbicki's wife handed them food and straw to rest on. As we were too excited to sleep, we wandered about the shed. The night deepened, the fires in Wolki expired, the sky darkened. By midnight, the stars reappeared. We stood about, expecting, waiting....

Then came the day of July 30, 1944, a bright Sunday. In the morning German troops were still retreating along the highway. As the hours went by, the troops began to thin out, and we felt they would soon be gone. There were no Russian planes that day. A vast silence lingered over the landscape, its depth growing by the hour. Some smoke still trailed from the charred remains of Wolki, but no other fires were visible. The horizon once more burst into a brief vicious cracking; it was not the familiar roar of artillery but a rattling noise, similar to that of a washing board − the sound of mortars and machine guns. Soon thereafter all movement of troops on the highway ceased. The road on which the German columns had been retreating for weeks was now deserted.

Around ten o'clock, squads of German infantry appeared on the trail leading from Rataj's farm. They moved slowly, apathetically, as if without aim. The first soldier to enter our yard asked Karbicki's wife for a piece of bread. When I saw this German soldier, I knew it was the end: drained, unkempt, he could barely drag his feet. It seemed he would gladly have thrown away the submachine gun that hung loosely on his belly. His plea for bread and his meek, almost servile "Thanks" were such far cries from the shrill robots we had once known that my eyes popped in disbelief. "It is the end," I whispered to myself. More soldiers entered the yard, and we went down into the shelter.

I sat on the floor of the vacated pit with my head on my knees, listening to the deep calm that grew outside the walls. For a moment I had a spasm of panic lest it all be another joke cruelly played on us by events. But then I recalled a similar frozen calm five years before, when, amidst the rattle of a single machine gun, the Germans arrived; that sultry stricken day of September 12, 1939 when nested in its valley Losice still looked like a white butterfly, the day I still had a home, relatives, a people.... A similar calm, reversing the course of history, was now creeping closer, growing by the minute, accelerating, but for us it had come too late, too late....

I shook my head, crawled into the shed, and looked out. Karbicki's home stood empty. No farmers were to be seen in the fields. In the yard, German soldiers slouched with their backs against the barn, their eyes closed, heads drooping. Some of them had thrown away their helmets and rifles as if they considered them useless. Hens walked among them, clucking sleepily and pecking on their sleeves. The soldiers did not react. On the highway, not a rat was visible. It was very, very still.

About three o'clock, a sharp whistle cut the air. The explosion that followed burst somewhere behind the barn. Our senses pricked up like the needles of a porcupine. There were no planes in the air – where, then, did the shooting come from? More shells exploded in the stubble field. We closed the cover of the shelter, sat on the straw, and watched a narrow beam of light come through the hole where the soil had washed away. The firing continued and moved closer. Some commotion developed around us. We heard the stamp of boots, shouts and commands in German. Shadows dashed by, and then, through the eroded hole, we saw a pair of boots. We remained absolutely still, holding our breaths.

There was a distant call: *"Hans.... Zurück.... Hierher, hierher...."*

The voice trailed off, ceased. From the other side, another voice called: *"Hier F-2. Herüber, herüber."*

The boots in the opening disappeared. New steps approached. A German belt fell on the grass, its buckle – with the motto *Gott mit uns* – shining straight into the pit. Then the buttocks of a soldier appeared and we heard him defecate overhead. Over the clover field the same distant call continued:

"Hans, zurück, zurück."

Someone still commanded in a feeble, receding voice:

"Leutnant Hermann, Stellung besetzen.... Stellung besetzen."

The soldier's belt and buttocks were still staring at us when somebody in the pit inadvertently knocked two pots together. A treacherous screech cut the deadly silence and we froze in terror. The buttocks disappeared, a hand quickly grabbed the belt, and the

clover rustled beneath the feet of the scampering soldier. Again
there was light in the shelter.

Once more we heard German voices. Some lost soldier was
wandering over the fields. *"Hermann, Hermann, wohin? Wohiii...."*

There was no answer.

A break came in the firing and I crawled into the shed. I
looked out over the country. It was numb and still, the same
country we had seen two years ago when we arrived here: the pine
grove on the hill and Koszelowka with its windmill, the bushes
which had hidden us faithfully so many times, the fields and forests
over which we had wandered like scarecrows, and the expanse of
sky we had prayed to and cursed in the alternating flow of hope
and despair. In its calm, exhausted expanse, there was not a bird,
not an insect, to disturb the gravity of the moment.

At nightfall everyone emerged from the pit. Eight emaciated,
rag-clad figures leaned against the walls, watched and waited.
Sporadic firing continued. But now, whenever a shot cracked, we
saw its muzzle flash. It came from the highway east of Wolki.

The door of the shed opened from the outside, but no one
entered, even though the door remained ajar. We did not see
Karbicki, but we saw his hand, his big peasant hand stretched out
towards Wolki. And we heard him say, "Russian tanks...."

For a while the huts and trees of Wolki masked the oncoming
Russians, but then a box-like shadow appeared on our side of the
village. While the warm July night brought the smell of sap from
the pine grove, a bulky tank approached our farm, its caterpillars
squashing the soft soil. Then it stopped and its gun slowly turned
toward us. For a while it was very still. Then a flare rose into the
sky and its trembling magnesium light fell on our faces and into the
pit.

Huddled together on the manure, we all looked through the
open door at the glare of that light and waited for the tears of joy.

They did not come.

Epilogue

About thirty Jews returned to Losice after it was liberated, thirty out of seven thousand. We arrived soon after the Russians had taken the town, and amid the stares of unbelieving Poles headed toward our house. It was occupied by a Polish family. As we stood on the sidewalk not quite knowing where to go next, Mother suddenly said to no one in particular, "Manya isn't here." Only then did I realize that I had never told my parents the truth about Manya. Somehow they had expected her to be waiting for us, if we ever returned. In fact, as I would later learn, Manya was still alive in the Auschwitz camp as we stood in front of our occupied house, but in January 1945, when the Russians stormed into western Poland and approached Auschwitz, the Germans gassed all the Jews they had used as slave labor, among them my sister.

The two brothers, Motl and Shmyl, returned to their home in Konstantynow, where they found ten other survivors. Neither they nor we were particularly eager to return to our home towns, which to us were nothing but gravepits. But there was little choice. The Russian armies were halted at the Vistula, so the front was only eighty miles to the west of us, and the Soviet border was ten miles to the east. We were held in a narrow strip of land, waiting for the end of the war, which was not to come until May 1945. Eventually Motl and Shmyl made their way to Israel, where they learned that the war had dealt them a final blow. Their families wiped out, Motl and Shmyl had taken consolation from their brother Asher's departure before the war to live on a kibbutz in Palestine, and they talked of joining him. However, Asher had volunteered for the Jewish Brigade and fallen on the Italian front in 1944. Both brothers married, had children, and lived out their lives in Israel.

Wolodia had to suffer the Calvary of the Russian POWs in that, after the ordeal under the Germans had ended, he still could not go home. Aware of the fate of war prisoners repatriated to the Soviet Union – the Gulag, or worse – Wolodia stayed away from the Red Army when it arrived in our area. Instead he had to cease being what he was and he became a Pole, with a new name and an invented biography. Wolodia married a Polish girl and settled in Miedzyrzec, where he opened a bakery, baking good Polish, Jewish, and Russian bread. To this day his family knows nothing of his fate, and presumes him dead. Our lives in Losice through the fall and winter of 1944-5 continued to be menaced by the Polish Underground, whose acts grew more lunatic the more desperate their political future became. They continued to hunt us down, and several times they came close to killing me. We armed ourselves with Russian weapons and fought them off. But they were a powerful organization, and we were bound to lose in the end. Wacek, who had given so much of himself during our struggle, was killed by them shortly after liberation. Eventually, in March 1945, on Passover eve, the AK succeeded in murdering all thirteen survivors in the neighboring town of Mordy. Following this event all thirty of us abandoned Losice and headed for the DP camps of postwar Europe. There we sat and waited to discover a country, a people, a home to go to.

After a three-year wait in a DP camp in Germany, Yankel and his family ended up in the USA, where his two sons became pharmacists and Rivkah a high-school teacher. My parents died a natural death, Father reaching the age of eighty-one, and Mother, ninety-four. Belcia married a camp survivor she had met in Italy; he later became an inventor and manufacturer of dental products, had two daughters, and lives comfortably in a Manhattan brownstone. She and I continued to send money and packages to Karbicki, who, upon the war's end, acquired two more acres of land, finished the barn, dug himself a well, and purchased a horse. In typical manner, with each package he received, he would write back that what we sent him was OK, but what he really needed was this, and this, and this. When we sent him this, this, and this, a reply would come that this was OK, but.... He died in the late sixties, still relatively young, of causes and in circumstances that his morose wife would not elaborate on. Nor did I ever discover what happened to Staskowa, for with the final destruction of the Miedzyrzec ghetto, my wanderings there ceased.

After we moved to Lodz, then the country's *de facto* capital, I finished both Gymnasium and Lyceum in an intensive four-month stint. With diploma and war diary in my rucksack, I left Poland, never to return. I headed as far south on the continent as I could, ending up at the tip of Apulia in Italy. There I tried for two years to reach the Jewish state then in the making. At one point I had already boarded an illegal boat for Palestine, but the British fleet stopped us. Other attempts also failed. Having had six years of my life wasted during the war, then two more years in a DP camp, it looked as if the wastage would become permanent. Unable to go to Israel I went to the USA where, for forty years, a professional career provided me, my wife, and my two children all possible daily comforts. The nights, of course, were and remain quite different.

* * *

NEARLY half a century has passed since the Germans exterminated Europe's Jews. One of the unique characteristics of that Act is that each additional piece of evidence that accumulates with the passage of time only magnifies the enormity of the event. Thus, contrary to time's normal tendency to heal and redress, the deed perpetrated by the Germans becomes ever more monstrous. The more it is argued that enough is enough, the more ghoulish the shadow becomes. This also holds true for the survivors. The more they assure themselves they have started a new life, the more they return to the flames and ditches of 1942. Although it has been many years since I began waking in the middle of the night and whispering to myself that, no, this could not possibly have happened, the frequency of such awakenings has increased, and the disbelief has grown into an independent persecution. The uniqueness of our extermination has thus produced a response new to human nature. This persistence of the trauma seems due to two elementary realities: any horror ever rumored to have happened to the Jews of Europe has turned out to more true than the rumors: and, except for one or two cases, whatever solace or mitigating gesture ever rumored to have taken place has turned out to have been not only false, but worse.

When talk shifts to what the rest of humanity did while the Germans were gassing millions of Jews, a basic difficulty arises. It is impossible to talk about the Lithuanians, the Ukrainians, the Croats, and the Poles, or about the acts of commission and omission on the part of the Catholic church, the Mufti of Palestine, the Red Cross, or the Jewish organizations in America without seemingly committing a very grave offense. The danger consists in giving the impression that these people and institutions are being lumped together with the Germans and Austrians who conceived and committed the Act itself. One must therefore state and restate the obvious: the Germans were the killers, and they put themselves beyond the pale of humanity. That fact has to be proclaimed as though it were an incantation. Then time must be allowed to pass before starting with the "other" topic: what did the Lithuanians, the Ukrainians, the Croats, the Vatican, the Red Cross, and Rabbi Wise do as the Germans went on with the killings. On these questions quite a bit of evidence has accumulated since the first publication of *The House of Ashes* twenty-five years ago. And the record is such that, had a fiction been commissioned to blacken the face and conscience of western civilization, it could not come close to what, in fact, happened.

Two facets of the world's attitude to the German genocide were touched upon in this book. One pertained to the murder of Jewish survivors by the Armia Krajowa, the London-based Polish underground. I dealt with this in some detail, not because it was worse than what the Lithuanians or the Croats perpetrated but because it affected our group in the most direct way. At the time, survivors returning from the wastes and forests of the Polish countryside could do no more than tell what they knew to be facts. But responsible people would not take our word for it; they told us to leave history to the historians. To the question as to who these authorities might be – Soviet historians, German historians, Arab historians, historians who will go by Red Cross documents describing Theresienstadt as a typical Nazi concentration camp – we received a dismissive wave of the intellectual pen. The Poles, both historians and non-historians, at first said the story was a libel. When too much evidence had accumulated to permit saying simply the story was false, the apologetics shifted to a version maintaining that the murders had been perpetrated by individuals, by right-wing splinter groups, even by the Communists.[1] When this, too, proved untenable, other explanations abounded. Eventually, making my way through a pile of the AK's wartime documents in 1979, I came across the very order in which the AK Commander-in-Chief, General Bór-Komorowski, instructed his troops to kill off the Jews hiding in the villages and forests.[2] A copy of that order also reached the Polish Government-in-Exile sitting in London. The AK, in publishing their wartime documents, of course weeded out a number of compromising records, but this one evidently survived through oversight. Until that confirmation, one could still harbor the illusion that, perhaps, the killing was indeed done by individual troops, or in moments of aberration, or because of some other unsystematic spasm. But no! The history of our extermination would not permit any consolation, any glimmer of comfort.

Next, the American Jews. Since they are as human as the Poles, their story runs a parallel course. But if their crime is one of omission instead of commission, it is in fact graver, for whereas to the Poles we were despised aliens, to the American Jews we were their own people, if not their own families. In passing, *The House of Ashes* mentions our astonishment during the war at the lack of any piece of bread, gun, money, contact, or as little as a word of recognition from our brothers across the Atlantic. At the worst, we thought they had tried and failed. But the truth was that they had never tried, and never even thought of trying. When, in the years after my arrival in the United States, I said to a friend that

[1] See: *New York Times Sunday Book Review*, October 25, 1964.

[2] See p. 239.

American Jews had done nothing to help, the man was so offended he stopped talking to me. When the accusations persisted, there came, as from the Poles, a hierarchy of explanations. The most vociferous was the claim that they did not know what was happening. But its life was short. Many emissaries, including SS men, had brought out the news about the extermination of the Jews while it was taking place. Perhaps the most telling of these witnesses was one Jan Karski, an erstwhile diplomat and member of the Polish Underground.[3] In October 1942, he had deliberately smuggled himself into the Belzec camp to be able to testify later that he had seen with his own eyes the ongoing exterminations. Soon thereafter he left on a clandestine mission for the West. In England he saw and talked to Eden, Labour leader Greenwood, H.G. Wells, Arthur Koestler, and the editors of all major newspapers; in the USA, in 1943, he saw and talked to Roosevelt, Cordell Hull, Archbishop Spellman, Rabbi Stephen Wise, Felix Frankfurter, Walter Lippmann, the New York Times, the Herald Tribune, and so on, and so on; in 1944 he published his book, Story of a Secret State, which became a best seller; he gave two hundred speeches, travelled, talked, and implored. His failure was total.

That nothing was done was finally conceded in March 1984. A committee of twenty-five American Jews, including eight rabbis, under the chairmanship of Arthur Goldberg, had the job of establishing the facts. It was a case of a jury trying itself. Yet, after two and a half years of wrangling with the language of the report, even this assembly was forced to conclude that nothing had been done to help Europe's Jews. Of course they found reasons for this oversight. As reported in the New York Times, the reasons for the

[3]Congressional Record, December 15, 1981.

failure to help were that the American Jews were "disunited, financially limited, and ... afraid of stirring up anti-semitism."

In the end the discussion turns on itself, raising the question of why one goes on stirring up and probing the ashes. This is particularly puzzling because, whereas in most other human domains, knowledge helps to explain and understand, here the exact opposite occurs. The reason for this morbid sifting through the charnel houses of our extinction lies then in another truth about the holocaust: it is impossible to talk about it and it is impossible to abandon it.

Other Books by Oscar Pinkus:

Friends and Lovers (novel), 1963

A Choice of Masks (autobiography), 1970

Embers (poems), 1979

The Son of Zelman (novel), 1982